CHARLES RANDALL

INTERNATIONAL

BOOKS BY CHARLES RANDALL

Window Fashions

The Encyclopedia of Window Fashions

The Encyclopedia of Window & Bed Coverings

Charles Randall's Designer Sketchfile

The Window Decorating Book

Dream Windows

Dream Walls

DESIGNER
WINDOW
FASHIONS

CHARLES RANDALL

DESIGNER
WINDOW
FASHIONS

CHARLES RANDALL

CHARLES RANDALL
INTERNATIONAL

*For my wife, Patricia,
my inspiration for creating this book*

Published in the United States by:
Charles Randall International
Las Vegas, Nevada, USA

www.CharlesRandall.com

The publisher has made every effort to ensure that all suggestions given in this book are accurate and safe but cannot accept liability for any resulting injury, damage, or loss to either person or property, whether direct or consequential and however arising. Variations in color may occur during the printing process. The publisher will be grateful for any information that will assist in keeping future editions up to date.

Editor-in-Chief: Charles Randall

Book Designer: Diego Carlos Linares, Argentina

ISBN: 978-1-890379-44-5 (Hardcover edition)
ISBN: 978-1-890379-45-2 (PDF)

Names: Randall, Charles T., author.
Title: Designer window fashions / Charles Randall.
Description: Las Vegas, Nevada, USA : Charles Randall International, 2020.
   | Includes bibliographical references.
Identifiers: LCCN 2020007237 (print) | LCCN 2020007238 (ebook) | ISBN
   9781890379445 (hardcover edition) | ISBN 9781890379452 (pdf)
Subjects: LCSH: Windows in interior decoration. | Window shades. | Blinds.
   | Bedding.
Classification: LCC NK2115.5.D73 R353 2020 (print) | LCC NK2115.5.D73
   (ebook) | DDC 747/.3--dc23
LC record available at https://lccn.loc.gov/2020007237
LC ebook record available at https://lccn.loc.gov/2020007238

Contents

Introduction

What a fantastic journey the last thirty-five years has been! When I wrote the original *Encyclopedia of Window Fashions* in 1986, I certainly did not expect that book to sell more than one million copies. Nor did I expect it to become the world's best-selling window decorating book.

The goal of this new book is to help home decorating enthusiasts gain the knowledge to select the best window treatments for their windows. And, to help window decorating professionals provide all the information necessary for their clients to make the best possible decisions for their window covering needs.

Is one picture worth a thousand words? Graphics have always stimulated the creation and communication of ideas. The uniqueness—and success—of *Designer Window Fashions* lies in combining the presentation of 2,000 illustrations and photos with a genuinely encyclopedic display of window and bed covering knowledge. *Designer Window Fashions* is the best organized, most effective design aid available for choosing and designing window treatments.

If your profession is interior design, this new edition belongs in your library, on your worktable, and with you in the field. Visual definitions of window treatments are immediately useful communication tools. When accompanied by specific yardage requirements, by glossary-supplied performance summaries of fabric properties and appearance and by alternative approaches to creating the desired effect, you have all the information necessary to work with your clients. Whether a budget is lavish or modest, this new publication offers the optimum number of choices in an individual design situation. *Designer Window Fashions* is sure to become an indispensable resource tool in your work.

The black line illustrations next to many of the photographs are there to spark your imagination by showing variations in the window covering treatments. They also show additional design elements you may not have thought about in your initial design concept: tiebacks, jabots, rosettes, trims, banding, top treatments, and hardware, for example.

Charles Randall

DecoratingDen.com

What Works Best

A Treatment for Every Window

What works best? Here are some recommendations:

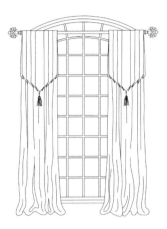

Flip topper panels over wood rod. *Custom rendering by DreamDraper® design software, www.dreamdraper.com © 2009 Evan Marsh Designs, Inc.*

Arch (Palladian): Horizontal blinds; pleated & cellular shades; shutters; top treatments (such as cornices or scarves); some fabric treatments such as arched draperies.

Bow & bay windows: Just about any window treatment will now work in bay windows.

Corner window: Blinds; curtains & draperies; shades; shutters and top treatments.

Double-hung: Blinds (horizontal, vertical); curtains & draperies; shades (pleated, cellular, Roman, roller); shutters; top treatments (all kinds).

Fixed pane: Blinds (horizontal, vertical); curtains & draperies; shades (pleated, cellular, Roman, roller); shutters; top treatments (all kinds).

French doors: Blinds; some fabric treatments such as hourglass; all types of shades; some small top treatments, such as small cornices; shutters with door handle cut-outs.

In-Swinging casement: Blinds; pleated & cellular shades; shutters.

Picture windows: All categories; a great palette for window decorating!

Ranch (strip) windows: Blinds; some fabric treatments; all categories of shades.

Skylights: Motorized pleated, cellular & solar/screen shades.

Sliding glass doors: Vertical blinds; pleated & cellular shades, if motorized, bi-pass shutters.

Left: Goblet pleated drapery panel with gold banding trim works beautifully with the gold fabric cornice box. The clear acrylic decorative rod with golden hardware set against the black wall is delightful. *Decorating Den Interiors, Abby Connell, Cincinnati, OH., www.decoratingden.com*

This designer creation consists of an arched cornice under arched inverted box pleated drapery panels. The nail heads securing the panels and wrought iron grill adds extra interest. *Decorating Den Interiors, Nola Shivers and Linda Tully, Nixa, MO., photographer Jeremy McGraw, www.decoratingden.com*

IMPORTANT QUESTIONS

While a basic window treatment will cover your bare window, it will not necessarily address other requirements you may have. Window treatments are not just about beauty but also privacy, sun protection, sound absorption, and more. Take some time to ponder the points listed below. When you sit down with a window treatment professional, he or she will ask your opinion on these topics. The better prepared you are to answer them, the more satisfied you will be with the result.

Existing Treatments

- What don't you like about your existing window coverings?
- Where is your window located?
- What is currently on the window? Is it easily removed? Do you wish to retain it in some capacity?
- Is the window non-traditional in shape? Do you have mismatched windows in the same room?

General Questions

- Have you given any thought to your budget? Do a little research online and check "The Facts" boxes located in each chapter. Costs for treatments can vary considerably.
- Is this a window that will open frequently?
- Consider sound. If the room is noisy, would you like fabric at the window to help absorb the sound?
- Who lives in your home? Children, pets, adults, elderly? How might your window treatment affect those who dwell in your home?
- Are you interested in motorizing your window treatments? Consider motorization for any application, but particularly for hard to reach areas or treatments, you may have difficulty operating. See page 17 for options.
- Would you consider employing the services of an interior or window treatment designer?

Qualities Needed

- How long do you expect to keep this treatment?
- Does it need to be moisture resistant?
- What types of safety issues might you have; are small children or pets in your home?
- How important is energy conservation?

Time Frame/Installation

- How quickly do you hope to have your window treatment installed?
- Is this something you want to install on your own, or do you plan to hire someone?

Design Thoughts

- If you are completely redesigning your room, what is your design style? Do you prefer a soft, romantic look or a warm, traditional appearance? (Don't worry if you don't know — as you page through this book, you may discover a style that's just right for you.)
- Is this window something you wish to emphasize — or de-emphasize?
- Do you want to be able to maintain view (i.e., ensure privacy but still be able to enjoy sunlight)?
- Are there any architectural hindrances, such as window cranks, radiators, unsightly moldings, or light switches?

Finishes, Colors & Patterns

- Consider texture. How does a heavy velvet drapery compare to a sleek horizontal blind or a lacelike roller shade? Different textures make different statements.
- Patterns can add interest and depth to a poorly designed room or make it appear smaller and wider. How do you feel about decorative fabric patterns? Stripes? Checks? Florals? Small details?
- Color can tie together disparate elements in the room through a unifying tone or soften harsh lines. What kinds of colors do you like best? How will they fulfill the needs of your design scheme?

Maintenance/Protection

- What type of stain, soil, or odor protection concerns you?

This eye pleasing design consists of pole swags (more examples pages 148 & 149), and stacked cascades. What's interesting about these kinds of treatments is that they consist of multiple parts, yet look like one continuous piece of fabric.
Interiors by Decorating Den, Barbara Hayman, Pottstown, PA., www.decoratingden.com

How to Select Window Treatments

Perhaps the two most important considerations to keep in mind when deciding on a window treatment are function and style. Knowing what you need the window treatment to do, and what kind of feeling you want it to invoke, will allow you more focus when making your purchase.

Function

First, decide what role you want your window treatment to play: purely aesthetic or a more practical purpose such as creating privacy or blocking out the sunlight? Do you want to draw attention to a fabulous view, or hide the spectacle of the unsightly home across the street? Create a list of the most important features your window treatment should have. These desired features will influence which types of window treatments may be appropriate. If you have small children or pets, you do not want window coverings with dangling cords or expensive silks that can become easily damaged. If you care more about the ornamental value of your window treatment, a drapery made of silk fabrics that puddle on the floor may be perfect for you. For privacy, Roman shades or wooden shutters paired with draperies are both excellent solutions.

Style

Once the more practical aspects of window dressings are solved, you can begin the fun part: using your creativity to beautify your home. Although you needn't stick with a theme when decorating, your new window treatment should complement the existing features of your home. Think about the mood you are trying to evoke. If you want your bedroom to appear sumptuous and exude warmth, use lots of luxurious textiles, layered in rich tones. If you want your office to appear chic and modern, go with simple lines and minimal detail. Window treatments can disguise flaws in a room or highlight features. If your living room has only a tiny window, you can make it appear larger by hanging your draperies higher and wider than the window. If a room is lacking texture or warmth, you can introduce these elements by choosing opulent fabrics or vivid hues. If you want to display a stunning ocean view, keep the window treatment simple yet elegant to draw the eye to the outside. And, make sure the window covering stacks back from the window to expose the view.

Most importantly, stay true to your style while being realistic about how your window treatment will perform inside your home.

Common mistakes to avoid

I don't recommend installing non-motorized or horizontal blinds or shades with cords over sliding glass doors or French doors. Because of the height of these windows, the strings become too long once the blinds are pulled up. Some shades and blinds (woven woods and wood blinds, for example), will stack so thickly at the top of the windows that you may have to bend down while passing through the doors. Exception: Mount treatment high enough to clear the window when raised. To do this, check the manufacturers' "stack-back charts." You will still have very long cords when raised; therefore, it still may be a bad idea altogether. Of course, the best option is motorized blinds to eliminate the cords, but most motors are slow, and you will have to wait quite a while for the blind to rise and lower. For most design choices, verticals or draperies are a much better idea for sliding glass doors. Never use a fabric tape measurer or attempt to "eyeball" a window's size. Always use a steel tape measurer to take measurements. Don't forget to consider whether your window treatment will be visible from another room, or from outside the house, and account for those issues when choosing colors, textures, and shapes. Curb appeal is important.

Don't try to do it all yourself. Custom window treatments are just that—custom, if you make a mistake, you cannot return the product. I highly recommend consulting a window decorating or interior design professional--see page 15.

Feeling good about utilizing the design services of a professional begins with your own involvement. This breakfast nook offers a variety of patterns pulled together to a cohesive whole using orange, white, and black as the major design colors.
S.A. Maxwell and Company, Chicago, IL.

HIRING AN INTERIOR DESIGNER

Get over your fears

IT IS A COMMON FEAR. Hiring an interior designer releases the design of your personal space into a stranger's hands. You no longer have control! They will enter your residence like a crazed designer, throwing their hands up in the air about your current style. Then start submitting bills that would gag a gazillionaire. First, you don't want to live through the embarrassment of showing your current interior space to a professional. Second, you don't want to pay for something you don't like but were too intimidated to say so.

It's time to get over your fears and accept that you not only need a designer's opinion; you will probably save money, too. They won't measure three times for 12 windows worth of blinds, place the order, then when it comes to installation — discover the measurements are all wrong. So, how do you reconcile yourself with hiring an interior designer and feel good about the process? It's called teamwork. Designers cannot read your mind — they need your help. Here's how you can make it easier on yourself and get what you want:

- Pick up a few design magazines. Clip out the rooms that appeal to you. Soon you will find there is a common thread running through the photos you have selected. Perhaps you'll find that all the rooms have a blue/green coloration. Maybe you're discove-

can produce when your designer asks you, "What are you thinking about for this room?"

- Interview prospective designers and review their portfolios. You may find that some designers specialize in an area of design that doesn't interest you. Another may not be a good personality match, while another may be the perfect match.

- Discuss your lifestyle, and don't hold back. If you have pets, children, if you smoke — all this will be taken into consideration. Be sure to complete the "Important Questions" on page 11 of this book and share it with your designer.

- Talk about fees upfront. Despite that this project is personal, you are conducting business. There is a variety of ways designers charge: by the hour, by a percentage of the project fee, and some with a flat fee. Then, get it in writing. Sign a contract that clarifies everything: time frames, cost overruns, designer's appearances on the job site, and how often you would like them to update you on the progress.

- Finally, talk about your needs. Don't say 'yes' to something unless you are certain it is what you want. Most designers will respect that greatly.

IT IS TIME TO ACCEPT THAT YOU NEED — AND WILL COME TO VALUE — THE OPINION OF A QUALIFIED PROFESSIONAL

ring that the photos you pull are all sparsely decorated rooms. Now, put these photos into a file you

Despite that, this is a creative profession; a designer is in business to serve your needs, not their own. Your happiness is their triumph.

When a window treatment is very tall, as the Roman shades are in the above photo, or when one has to reach or climb over furniture (see Roman shades on pages 248 & 249, for example), consider the ease of motorization to make your life easier. Also, note that cords become very long when pulling up shades on tall/high windows. Even with rope cleats at the sides of the window would still make for a lot of work wrapping the rope around the cleats. Motorization solves these issues perfectly. And please don't forget—cords are always a strangulation hazard for children and pets.
Private Residence, Bel Air, California. Photography by Charles Randall.

MOTORIZATION IS NOW AFFORDABLE!

Battery operated or hard-wired? How to decide

One item not discussed in this book, except for this page, is the topic of motorization.

It is a common occurrence to be able to push a button and change a television channel or open a garage door. But have you considered the possibilities of motorizing your window treatments? There are several kinds of motorization; which type is best for you depends on the window treatment(s) you are interested in motorizing and your budget. There are three types of possible applications: battery operated, low voltage, and hard-wired.

Battery Operated

Although inexpensive to install, battery-operated systems require more regular maintenance than low voltage or hard-wired. Batteries need to be changed occasionally. Consider that in areas where you may need to use a motor control most (such as a skylight system), you will need a high ladder to change the battery. If you are planning to motorize more than one treatment within a room, the good news is battery-operated systems now offer "group" control options. If you have an easy-to-access, lightweight treatment (like a pleated shade), the battery system is a good, affordable choice.

Low Voltage

Low voltage is easier to install than a hard-wired system. A plug-in style that can easily operate a group of window treatments with the push of a button. Ideal for "smaller" treatments (such as a group of blinds or shades), it is smaller and quieter than a hard-wired system. The down-side to this type of electrical product is that it is reliant upon its voltage and longer wire lengths don't always deliver with optimum efficiency.

Hard-Wired

With the greatest capacity for lifting, drawing, and tilting, a hard-wired treatment is the most hardworking of the motorized systems. Hard-wired is the system you will need, for example, to draw heavily lined and inter-

CONSIDER THAT YOU CAN ALSO ENSURE YOUR PRIVACY WITH MOTORIZATION: NO MORE STANDING IN A DARK WINDOW AT NIGHT CLOSING YOUR BLINDS.

lined heavy draperies. Hard-wired motors make it easy to accomplish. The downside to hard wiring is that it is best mapped out and installed in pre-construction, rather than afterward. Home automation is not a new concept, but the industry is fast-growing and ever-changing, offering new possibilities and levels of convenience. From shades that will lower at dusk to those that open and close while you are away on vacation, to the ease of covering a skylight with the touch of a button, motorization makes life better. Ask your designer about all the new exciting possibilities.

Designing on a photo provides the most realistic portrayal of a proposed treatment, complete with any color or fabric pattern. Skewing capabilities permit the treatment to be constructed from any angle.

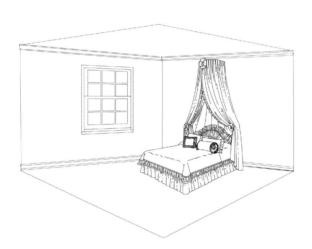

The design and graphics capabilities of the DreamDraper® software enable you to create colorful perspective renderings of a total room setting, including window treatments, bedding and furniture.

Alternative room arrangements, window treatments, furniture, wall colors and flooring are easily shown. Furniture and accessories imported from vendor websites complete the picture.

PROFESSIONAL WINDOW DECORATING SOFTWARE

The key to helping your clients visualize their dream window treatment

Computer rendering of window treatment styles is rapidly becoming the norm in interior design. Pioneered by the DreamDraper® design program (www.dreamdraper.com), this approach allows a designer to take an uploaded photo or architectural rendering and showcase window treatment styles, fabrics, patterns, and colors. It's not magic, but it may certainly seem that way. This visual communication tool will help prevent costly mistakes and take the guesswork and uncertainty out of what may otherwise be an agonizing choice over what is most appropriate for a window. The DreamDraper® program offers the opportunity to personalize window treatments with embellishments,

> IT'S NOT MAGIC, BUT IT MAY CERTAINLY SEEM THAT WAY. VISUAL COMMUNICATIONS SOFTWARE WILL PREVENT COSTLY MISTAKES.

specialty hardware — and layer the computer-designed treatment behind existing furniture in your photo. The client can see exactly how the treatment will appear before placing the order. Add in wall color or paper if you like, too! No more using a paper grid and counting boxes, this program can do it all to scale. An extensive library of beautifully illustrated window treatment styles from swags to goblet pleats to blinds to shades, decorative hardware, embellishments, and even furniture and accessories are available for you or the interior design professional. Detailed drawings are available in many different design styles, be it modern, traditional, contemporary, Art Deco, and more.

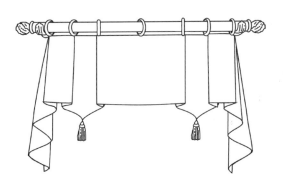 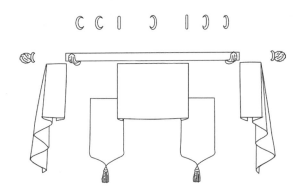

Break-apart® designs and thousands of design elements available within the DreamDraper program allow for unlimited creativity. All can be resized, modified, mixed and matched, and shown in any color or fabric.

DRAPERIES & CURTAINS

Curtains and draperies have enjoyed their decades of excess and floundered over times of pared-down minimalism. Consider all the wonderful uses for fabrics at the window: an interlined silk pinch pleat panel hanging stately in a period-style home, a simple sheer brushing lazily against a window frame, a dainty gingham checked café curtain decorating a kitchen. Fabric at the window softens edges, emphasizes (or de-emphasizes) architectural qualities and shortcomings, and provides a needed barrier between the outside elements and the inner harmony of the home.

My dream window treatments are honeycomb shades or shutters as the first line of defense against heat and noise. Then subtle sheers to soften the glare when the shades or louvers are opened and finally custom draperies with lining and a fabulous top treatment.

Those are my dream window treatments—what are yours?

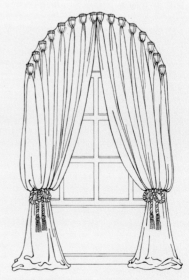

Arched goblet pleated draperies with rope ties

Left: Goblet pleated arched drapery panels hung on standard drapery pins and a metal slotted track onto poured concrete moldings. Italian Stringing used to hold the draperies back. The lined and interlined frontal silk fabric supplied by Plumridge Silks. Look closely, and you will see the clever use of top-down-bottom-up honeycomb shades used for heat reduction and privacy when needed. *Jamie Gibbs and Associates, www.jamiegibbsassociates.com*

DonnaElle.com

History in the Making

It wasn't until the second half of the 17th century that draperies truly began to decorate homes. Shutters were the window treatment of choice for centuries. There are many reasons why fabric at the window was missing, among them was lack of industrial output, lack of fibers to work with, and distance from the Far East. A move to luxurious comfort did not occur until well into the 17th century, most unmistakably at French King Louis XIV's Palace of Versailles, for example.

Spinning wheels, the Industrial Revolution, increased trade routes, and human ingenuity helped the drapery industry flourish. Soon, cornices, pelmets, and passementerie (decorative trim) followed. Bed coverings became lavish. Sashes pulled draperies to the side during the day, portieres (draperies for doorways) kept drafts at a minimum. Festoons, which could be pulled up the window to create a swag effect, were followed by graceful reefed curtains. Cotton and silk fabrics replaced velvet, wool, and tapestry. Layers cropped up: a window treatment of the Victorian era, for instance, might consist of four to five layers.

Draperies began to occupy a pared-down role in the mid to late 20th century, especially with the development of a variety of shades and blinds. While homes of the 1960s witnessed the heyday of pinch pleat draperies, the 1970s were all about horizontal and vertical blinds.

The call for fabric treatments has not slowed.

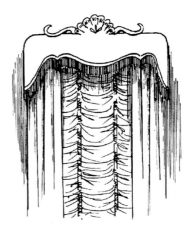

Above: Austrian shades were a popular treatment for well-to-do households in the Rococo and Louis XV period of 1730-1760.

Left: Tiebacks with trim over timeless Austrian shade. *Donna Elle, Interiors by Elle www.donnaelle.com, photograph courtesy of Jeff Allen*

Today's Curtains & Draperies

Today, as windows swoop to the ceiling — and even into the ceilings of many a home — fabric at the windows is an important statement. Indeed, some designers begin with the window treatment color palette before making decisions about anything else in a room. Decisions about draperies in the home fall into distinct categories: privacy (which also includes protection), physical and visual touch; light control; sound control; and color. Put these categories in order of preference; it will make a difference. For example, if you wish for privacy at night but have your heart set on a sheer to only diffuse light during the day, you may need to add another treatment, such as a cellular shade, to take care of both needs.

Do not discount the emotion that fabric can bring to your home. The mood of an interior can be affected by the colors you choose; sunny versus somber, heavy fabrics versus light fabrics, casual versus elegant, or romantic versus businesslike. You will see examples as you page through this book. Examine the rooms. Find one similar in shape and scale to your own. Then, visualize how the treatments and fabrics will change the look of your space.

Peach draperies swag elegantly with opulent puddling onto the terra-cotta tiles below. Creative use of bullion fringe under the cornice box helps to hide the mounting hardware. Notice, too, behind the drapery panel lies a translucent sheer to pull across the window opening when the sun is intense. *Beth Hodges Soft Furnishings, www.bethhodges.com*

DraperyAvenue.com

Multilayered traditional drapery that includes silks, velvets, and trims come together in this harmonious design created by artisan talent. Custom draperies can evoke lavishness and sophistication. *Designed and made by Custom Drapery Workroom, Inc., www.draperyavenue.com.*

The Facts: **Draperies & Curtains**

Advantages: Can camouflage bad woodwork and other architectural flaws; sound absorbent; can insulate, such as masking cold air leaks in windows. Also effective in blocking the sun's damaging rays; can be a room's focal point; if lined well, can offer privacy; softens the look of hard window treatments when used in combination; mount a drapery rod at ceiling level to enhance the height of a room; colored and patterned fabric can provide visual interest.

Disadvantages: Can be affected by moisture; color can fade when exposed to direct sunlight; improper dying can cause color transfer; can harbor dust and other allergic airborne entities. In general, sun and air pollution will work against fabrics, although some are more resistant than others. Drapery linings will offer good protection and lengthen the life of your drapery.

Cost: Inexpensive drapery panels can be acquired for as little as $20 at a local discount store—but if your goal is something more unique and perfectly suited for your environment, you should consider that cost may increase quite a bit. Quality, design, fiber type, linings,

interlinings, embellishments and more will all factor into the price. Curtains and draperies are works of art, hand and machine sewn by talented workrooms.

Lifespan: Many variables will affect your draperies including sunlight, dust, humidity and smoke fumes to name a few. On average, however, unlined draperies will last about four years; lined about six.

Most Appropriate Locations: Bedrooms, living rooms, dens, although fabric at the window has been long accepted in any location.

Care & Cleaning: Cleaning draperies on ones own can be tricky. Vacuuming with a soft brush is acceptable. Taking a drapery down to hang on an outside clothesline is fine (as long as you know how to rehang it properly) but depending upon whether your drapery is lined and/or whether it has decorative embellishments make cleaning draperies primarily a job for experts. Consult with your local dry cleaner, or employ an onsite drapery cleaner for best results.

This unique window treatment consists of twenty-foot long drapery panels in a medium weight polyester viscose in shades of charcoal gray, and the use of angled stationary panels allows for more light and less coverage of the background window and walls. Custom board mounted spindles were used to mount the medallions — the result: dramatic window coverings that complement the windows and architecture rather than distract from it. *Decorating Den Interiors, Peggy Herrick, Missouri City, TX., www.decoratingden.com*

Good to Know: Fabrics

There are many fabrics today. In general, crisp fabrics lend themselves better to tailored treatments such as cornice boxes, pleated valances, draperies, and Roman shades, while soft, pliable fabrics are good for swags and cascades, Empire, and Kingston valances. Pliable fabrics also work well with balloon and cloud shades, London shades, and relaxed Roman shades.

Brocade: Rich and heavy, this multi-colored jacquard (see definition) fabric is typically used in upholstery but occasionally in draperies. Sometimes incorporates metallic threads as part of its all-over raised patterns or floral designs. Traditionally created from a background of cotton with rayon/silk patterns.

Burlap: Loosely constructed, this plain-weave jute fabric is most often seen as housing for sacks of coffee beans or as backing on some types of flooring products. However, in recent years, this rough, coarse fabric has made its way into trendy interiors, reinvented as casual draperies — also, Jute.

Burnout: A technique used on many kinds of fabric but in general is a chemical solution applied to destroy a portion of the fabric while leaving other areas intact. An example would be burning a floral pattern out of the pile in a velvet piece while leaving the backing fabric intact. Burnout sheers are extremely popular, as they allow light to filter through at various intensities.

Calico: This term is used primarily for simple curtains; this cotton fabric boasts small floral patterns (typically) on a contrasting background. An inexpensive fabric, calico is thin and not particularly colorfast, but crisp when ironed.

Canvas: A sturdy, plain weave cloth, this cotton or cotton/polyester cloth offers a stiff and tailored, yet casual look. Best for stationary drapery panels. Consider duck or sailcloth (lighter weight canvas) if you require a little bit of draping.

Chintz: This cotton cloth offers bright colors, patterns, and floral motifs. Consider having this fabric lined if used in a window that receives direct sunlight, as the fabric will weaken, fade, and possibly rot over time. Sometimes chintz is finished with a slight glaze to offer a polished look, although it will wash or wear off with repeated handling. It was prevalent in the 18th century, though it is still used frequently today due to its lower cost and bright patterns for curtains or draperies.

Damask: A finer, thinner fabric than brocade, it nonetheless mixes shiny and dull threads to create beautiful patterns of high luster. Crafted of silk, cotton, rayon, or linen. Its patterns are usually reversible, an example being two-color damask in which the colors reverse depending upon the side viewed. For draperies.

Dotted Swiss: A delicate, lightweight cotton fabric best suited for curtains. Small raised dots printed on either side of the fabric are the identifying detail. Most often, they are woven into the fabric but, sometimes applied to the surface (not as lovely).

Crisscrossed rod pocket panels swag gracefully across the arched window, enhancing but not hiding it.

Dramatic crisscrossed sheer panels from the ceiling all the way to the floor unite the top window with the rest of the room. Shorter angled panels on medallions continue the imaginary line created by the crisscrossed panels, unifying the design. *Susan Keefe, C.I.D.*

Gingham: Usually seen in a plaid or checked pattern, gingham is a plain weave cotton fabric used most often for café curtains and very light draperies. Typically, white with one color accent.

Jacquard: Refers to a type of weave more so than a fabric. The Jacquard loom was invented in France, 1804 by Joseph Jacquard. Brocade, damask, and tapestry are some of the fabrics manufactured with a jacquard attachment, which permits separate control of each of the yarns processed.

Lace: A light, openwork cotton fabric typically used for sheers or curtains, its delicate mesh background consists of openwork designs. On window treatments, it is best to choose a synthetic lace so it will hold its shape when hanging.

Linen: This fiber is more robust and glossier than cotton, linen fibers obtained from the interior of the woody stem of the flax plant. It is strong but not pliable. It will wrinkle readily and is somewhat stiff. However, its sturdy and textured beauty can make for a more earthy style at the window in curtain or drapery form. Excellent sun resistance.

Matelassé: French meaning "padded" or "quilted," this medium to heavy double cloth fabric comes from silk, cotton, rayon, or wool. For draperies.

Moiré: French meaning "watered," this silk, rayon, cotton, or acetate fabric has a distinctive wavy pattern on the surface that reflects light in the same way that light reflects off the water.

Muslin: For casual curtains and draperies, cotton muslin can be fine to coarsely woven. Typically used as liner fabric but has been the primary material. Coloration is neutral.

Nylon: Perfect for sheers, nylon is durable, washable, and inexpensive.

Organza (Organdy): This lightweight, crisp, sheer cotton fabric has starch added that will wash out. Will wrinkle quickly if crumpled or not finished with a wrinkle-resistant finish. It can take a variety of finishes and embellishments, including bleaching, dyeing, frosting, flocking, and more, for curtains and draperies.

Satin: With a matte back and a lustrous front, satin is available in many colors, weights, and degrees of stiffness.

Traditionally for evening and wedding garments, as well as high-end bedding, it is sometimes used at the window. Expensive and slippery but used occasionally for drapery.

Silk: Silk is a natural filament, a product the silkworm creates when constructing its cocoon. There are many kinds of silk: tussah (wild silk, which is shorter and wider), shantung (raw and irregular), and dupioni (uneven and irregular threads), to name a few. Shiny and luxurious, it is a beautiful choice for drapery panels but will be affected by sun and water. Expensive, it is best to line and interline this fabric when used at the window, to protect it and lengthen its life.

Taffeta: A crisp fabric known best for its wonderful "rustle" sound, taffeta is a lustrous plain weave fabric usually made from synthetic fibers but sometimes made from silk. Best used for draperies, it has a crisp hand and a lot of bulk.

Tapestry: Heavy and deliciously dense, the tapestry is often hand-woven and features elaborate motifs such as pictorials, floral, and historical scenes. While rarely used for curtains, tapestries are frequently used as wall hangings and occasionally fitted with rod pockets to hang in front of a window. Today, the tapestry is more frequently constructed on a jacquard loom.

Toile: French for fabric or cloth, toile is best known as toile de Jouy, a finely printed design resembling a pen and ink drawing. Found primarily on cotton fabric, toile de Jouy depicts romantic, idyllic scenes of pastoral countrysides, florals, and historical motifs. For curtains and draperies.

Velvet: Plain and figured velvets are beautiful and soft, and best employed as drapery fabric. A medium weight cut-pile fabric typically constructed of silk, rayon, cotton, or synthetics, its high luster, and smooth-hand create beautiful, graceful folds. Crease-resistant and inexpensive.

Voile: A lightweight, thin, semitransparent fabric of cotton, wool, or silk. Voile is plain and loosely woven. Perfect for curtains or sheers, it gathers and drapes well.

DecoratingDen.com

These window coverings are a good example of a designer thinking outside of the box. The wrought iron grilles covering the arched windows make a bold statement. The grilles harmonize perfectly with the double floor-length draperies on decorative rods. Look closely, and you will see the wrought-iron grille vent on the left wall. *Decorating Den Interiors, Bohnne Jones and Chantae Thompson, Nashville, TN., www.decoratingden.com*

Curtains vs. Draperies

These two terms are not interchangeable, at least not on American soil. Consider that curtains are a less formal choice than draperies — they are typically less heavy, lighter, shorter, and more fanciful. Draperies utilize heavier fabrics, usually lined to protect their beautiful colors and patterns from the sun's damaging rays. While both curtains and draperies may employ the use of decorative trims and tassels, a curtain typically uses smaller bands, braids, and trims. Drapery fabrics can handle heavy trims, tassels, and tiebacks easily.

Bolstering Your Fabric

There are many ways to keep your fabrics looking their best at the window. Always have your treatments lined, unless you specifically want the light to filter through. The lining gives draperies bulk, protection, and stability. Some unlined draperies can look like "ready-made" draperies, so use caution when deciding if they should be lined or unlined.

Here are the options:

Interfacing: Fabrics used to offer support and give shape to the primary fabric. Some are designed and stitched to the primary fabric; others fused through heat.

Interlining: An insulation of sorts to pad, stiffen, and protect the decorative fabric, as well as provide added insulation between the outside and the inside of the home. Interlining is sewn to the backside of the decorative room facing fabric and then covered with the lining, which typically faces the street side of the window. Interlining is not seen but provides a great deal of protection and strength to a drapery.

Lining: A layer attached to the backside of the decorative room facing fabric or interlining to protect drapery fabric from sunrays and potential water damage from leaky windows. Adds bulk to a drapery.

Designed for the affluent Greco family in their estate home in Wayne, Illinois.

Designed and made by Custom Drapery Workroom, Inc., www.draperyavenue.com

DraperyAvenue.com

Curtain & Drapery Styles

A short tutorial

Arch-top: A treatment for the specialty shaped arch top window. A special frame is sometimes constructed with small hooks or pegs to shadow the curved area of the window. Loops are attached to this simple curved top treatment and hooked into place. It is a stationary treatment with the sides pulled out of the way.

Bishop sleeve: Tieback drapery panels bloused vertically at least once, and most resemble the puffy sleeve of a fancy garment.

Café curtain: Often designed as a two-tier treatment, café curtains are set at a variety of heights for maximum privacy and light control, although usually at the top of a window, and then again midway. Most café curtains can traverse if necessary.

Curtain: A simple treatment, typically unlined, usually stationary or possibly hand-drawn. Usually hung on a simple rod.

Drapery: A heavier treatment, often lined, and usually able to open and close, or stationary, which means it flanks either side of a window, rather than hanging in front of it.

Festoon: Folded drapery fabric that hangs in a graceful curve from the top of the window, usually drawn upon cords. The term festoon can also refer to a ribbon-tied garland balanced between two points (such as either side of a window), which drapes down in the center.

Flip topper: Typically, a flat, contrast lined fabric panel that flips over a rod and sometimes adorned with trim or beads to draw attention to its unique style. Flip toppers may also be cinched or triangulated in some way for added emphasis.

French pleat: A three-fold pleat found at the top of a drapery. Also known as a pinch pleat.

Goblet pleat: Like a pinch pleat, only the top of the pleat resembles the shape of a goblet. Sometimes the goblet is filled with batting to provide bulk or contrasting fabric for emphasis.

Hourglass: A permanently installed treatment that is attached at the top and bottom of a glass door or window, and then pinched in the middle to create the hourglass shape. It provides some privacy but is mostly for decoration.

Inverted pleat: A reverse box pleat, also known as a kick pleat, which conceals the extra fabric in the back. The pleat meets in the middle, rather than is folded back at the sides.

Italian stringing: A historical way of drawing fabric in which diagonally strung cords attached to the back of the drape —about one-third of the way down — are manipulated to draw the drapery open and closed. For this to work, the top of the drapery must be stationary.

Knife pleat: Evenly spaced, tight, crisp, narrow pleats that run the length of the top of a drapery.

Pinch pleat: see French pleat

Portiere: A drapery treatment that hangs in either a doorway or room entrance. Usually stationary, its main function is to soften and beautify an area. When operational, it can serve as a sound barrier between two rooms and alleviate drafts.

Rod pocket: This drapery style is a hollow tube-like sleeve located at the top of a drapery (and sometimes top/bottom of a curtain) that will accommodate a rod. The rod is attached to the wall or ceiling, and the drapery, suspending from it, and able to traverse back and forth, with some difficulty. Not recommended for traversing draperies.

Sheer: A light, see-through or opaque fabric, never lined and often used for beauty and some sun/glare control, usually used in conjunction with draperies or modern shade treatment, such as cellular shades or blinds.

Stationary draperies: Usually hangs to either side of the window and acts as a decoration. Not meant to provide protection from the sun or offer privacy.

Tab: A series of tabs at the top of the drapery, either a closed loop or a tie, which a rod either slides through or is tied to it.

Tent fold: A drapery that constructed to resemble an old-fashioned pup tent opening. The middle edge of the treatment is pulled back and secured, overlapping the rest of the drapery, rather than pulling it all back. Will conceal much of the window, even when open.

DecoratingDen.com

These dramatic window treatments were created to complement the prominent arched windows. Soft chenille in turquoise damask was an inspired choice. Silver medallions were inserted into self-covered miniature cornices and placed at the drop point of the swags. The side window was treated in a similar design to harmonize the design. *Decorating Den Interiors, Barbara Elliott and Jennifer Ward Woods, Stone Mountain, GA., www.decoratingden.com*

DecoratingDen.com

These lovely silk window coverings had to complement, but not distract, from the unique and astonishing focal point of the room: the fireplace. The fireplace is covered in a beautiful Art Deco "relief" pattern with gold leaf. A couple of sitting areas for guests surround the fireplace.
Grand Great Room. *Decorating Den Interiors, Lynne Lawson, Laura Outland, Columbia, MD., www.decoratingden.com*

Austrian shade is ballgown beautiful when paired with dramatic fuchsia
side panel paired with an Inverted box-pleated drapery.

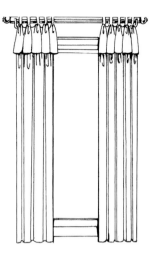

Flounce tab top draperies

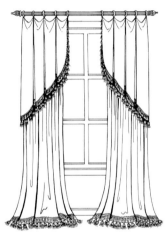

Cuffed asymmetrical panels over pleated
puddled draperies.

French (pinch pleated), color-blocked
panels glide easily back and forth on
modern ring and rod hardware.

DecoratingDen.com

Pleated draperies and a cellular shade combine for a rich, compelling treatment. Look closely to see buttons on the pleats. *Decorating Den Interiors, Patty Hughes, Clarence, NY., www.decoratingden.com Photography: Dennis Stierer*

DraperyAvenue.com

Custom made red drapery panels paired with black wrought iron drapery rods in bay windows. Luxurious fullness and an elegant traditional style for a home in Hinsdale, Illinois. *Designed and made by Custom Drapery Workroom, Inc., www.draperyavenue.com*

Gathered tab top draperies with large flags and tassels.

Bow-tied Bishop sleeve draperies gathered on decorative rod.

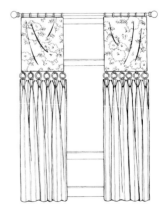

Stationary pleated draperies connected with rings under flat flag panels. Beautiful when done properly.

Gathered and puddled stationary drapery panels with swag flags. *Design by Susan Gailani, ASID Allied, Gailani Designs Inc., www.gailanidesigns.com*

A combination of fabrics adds depth and bulk to this simple charming design.
Seabrook Wallpaper, www.seabrookwallpaper.com

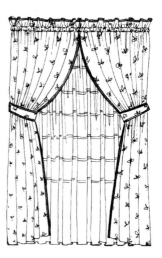

Rod pocket draperies with banding and high tiebacks.

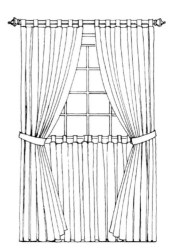

Tab draperies over matching cafe curtain.

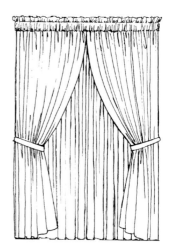

Rod pocket draperies over sheers.

Tone-on-tone white rod pocket draperies and sheers are gorgeously sophisticated, coupling with lush shabby chic furniture.
Photo courtesy of David Duncan Livingston, www.davidduncanlivingston.com

Above and below: Custom made drapery with unique tiebacks created for a custom home builder. Tailored in exquisite style for an aesthetic living space. *Designed and made by Custom Drapery Workroom, Inc., www.draperyavenue.com*

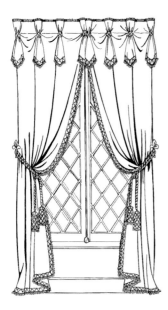

Fringe-edged goblet pleated drapery panels with jabot accents are contained by fleur-de-lis tieback holders and tassel ties.

This asymmetrical treatment is a beauty with goblet pleats and bullion fringe. Note that the right-hand panel has top and middle tassel tiebacks, which balance and enhance its beauty.

Custom designed flags atop dramatic two-story draperies. Add shutters for privacy and light control, and you have a perfect designer window treatment.
Cynthia Porche Interiors, www.cynthiaporcheinteriors.com

DraperyAvenue.com

Left: French pleated draperies in striped gold and red fabric under a decorative real wood rod with rings. Add color-blocked swags with coordinating buttons, trim and tiebacks for a stunning custom window treatment.
Designed and made by Custom Drapery Workroom, Inc., www.draperyavenue.com

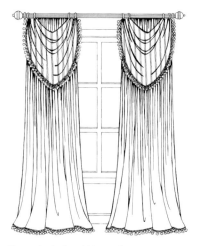

Open pleated and trimmed swags are pole-mounted on rings. Fringe added to the puddled hem of the pencil pleated drapery add a touch of drama.

Triple blouson tops on the drapery panels draw the eye with their unique beauty.

Feeling good about utilizing the design services of a professional begins with your own involvement. This sitting area offers a variety of patterns pulled together to a cohesive whole through the use of red and gold tones. *Decorating Den Interiors, www.decoratingden.com*

Clever use of vertical and horizontal rod pocket draperies with coordinating fabric for the Roman shades shows off a stunning display of creativity.
Decorating Den Interiors, www.decoratingden.com

Arched Bishop sleeve panels with rosettes and rope tassels.

Close up of drapery jewelry opposite page

GailaniDesigns.com

Two-layer treatment with sheers over solid silk lined and interlined draperies add opulence and drapeability. Sheer swags hung from custom-designed hardware on both the top and side crowns. Crystal drapery jewelry (see close-up opposite page) used to coordinate with crystal chandelier.
Susan Gailani, ASID Allied, Gailani Designs Inc., www.gailanidesigns.com

This creative designer window treatment consists of ceiling-to-floor inverted box pleated drapery panels adorned with geometric banding. Wood holdbacks work nicely to anchor the panels. It was a touch of genius to tilt the left and right panels to accommodate the decorative wood paneling on the ceiling. Look closely to see the tone on tone buttons just below the top banding. *Decorating Den Interiors, Barbara Tabak, Harrisburg, PA., www.decoratingden.com.*

Lush and luxuriant, rich royal blue panels hang heavy, pulled back pup tent style. This color, this style — is exceptionally rich and affluent in tone.
ADO USA

SmithandNoble.com

Ring top panels frame the indoors (and out of doors) to perfection with fluid grace. A quick flip of the panel over the decorative holdback will allow the panels to traverse easily by hand, providing nighttime privacy. *Smith + Noble, www.smithandnoble.com*

Right: This vertically striped silk goblet drapery panel is held back with a rope and a tassel tieback. Real wood decorative rod in an antique gold finish complements the wood paneling rather than blending in with it.
Designed and made by Custom Workroom Inc., www.draperyavenue.com

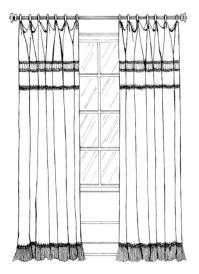

Flat-panel/Athena style draperies with applique and bullion fringe hems hang gracefully on a decorative rod.

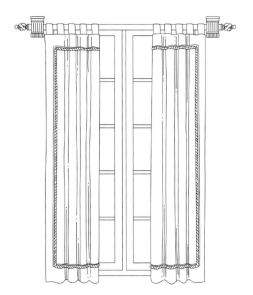

Tab top panels with contrasting banding.
Custom rendering by DreamDraper® design software, www.dreamdraper.com
© 2009 Evan Marsh Designs, Inc

DecoratingDen.com

CasaFiora.com

Above: This ceiling height drapery treatment in striped silk pulls in tones from throughout the room décor. The real wood antique gold rod and matching rings work perfectly.

Left: A "flip topper" is a simple to construct window treatment, created by flipping the top of a long drapery panel over a rod to display the contrasting lining. The cinched band makes a great focal point.

Puddled top flip panels with a legacy valance.
Custom rendering by DreamDraper® design software, www.dreamdraper.com © 2009 Evan Marsh Designs, Inc.

DecoratingDen.com

Unabashedly eye-catching, arched Bishop sleeve drapery panels with rich coloration, coupled with over-scale tassels, are entirely sophisticated.
Decorating Den Interiors, ww.decoratingden.com

Left: Note how neatly the box pleated drapery lines up with the tabs. Attention to detail is always a feature of excellent interior design work.

Below: Print draperies in kelly green, charcoal, and cream colors flank the window. Kelly-green colored tabs contrast with the black iron rod. The inside wood trim on the window was painted a glossy black to create a depth to the window. The window treatment created a focal point for this dramatic dining room. *Decorating Den Interiors, Lois Pade, Kenosha, WI., www.decoratingden.com*

DecoratingDen.com

DavidDuncanLivingston.com

The cool elegance of multiple complementary earth tones has been placed at ceiling height to add dramatic impact. Removable tiebacks allow drapes to fall easily into privacy mode, and despite their sophisticated styling, these draperies are a cinch to pull back into submission, come daylight.
Photograph courtesy of David Duncan Livingston, www.davidduncanlivingston.com

DecoratingDen.com

Tall, color-blocked, linen drapes dress these two-story living room windows in transitional style. Neutral bands accented with grey and blue bring a human scale, while motorized blackout shades combine with the drapes to provide control of light and glare.
Decorating Den Interiors, Rebecca Lane, Olath, KN., www.decoratingden.com Photographer: Jeremy McGraw

Goblet pleated cream-colored draperies were used to create drama but maintain a soft, pleasant appearance. Decorative tape banding in gray and cream highlights the vertical edges of the panels. Chrome metal rods with elbows were selected to accommodate the bay window angles. Chrome rings, crystal accents, and finials complete this inspiring design.
Decorating Den Interiors, Barbara Elliott and Jennifer Ward Woods, Stone Mountain, GA., www.decoratingden.com

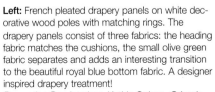

Above: Stationary side panels consist of textured velvet fabric and sheer sparkling fabric. Matching velvet upholstered medallions adorned with antique crystals inspired by the side lamp. *Design by Susan Gailani, ASID Allied, Gailani Designs Inc., www.gailanidesigns.com*

Left: French pleated drapery panels on white decorative wood poles with matching rings. The drapery panels consist of three fabrics: the heading fabric matches the cushions, the small olive green fabric separates and adds an interesting transition to the beautiful royal blue bottom fabric. A designer inspired drapery treatment! *Decorating Den Interiors, Kathie Golson, Orlando, FL., www.decoratingden.com*

Arched pleated and trimmed draperies on curved wrought iron rods with matching tableaux grille in the top window.
Designer: Gillian Wendel Workroom: Bonnie Sides, Photo: Brandy Stoesz

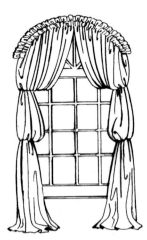

Arched rod pocket draperies with double Bishop sleeves.

Instead of hiding the shape of this grand window, a drapery treatment was chosen to accent its graceful arch. Tassel detailing is an inspired choice.

Intriguing drapery hardware provides the focal point for this arch top window; drapeable fabric provides a soft accent.

Pleated and puddled drapery panels attached to a curved decorative rod.
Le Fer Forge Drapery Hardware, www.leferforge.com

Self-lined, flat sheer blue panels were tied onto a custom iron "birds on branch" rod with ties threaded through buttonholes in the panels, allowing for a small droop between ties. Pulled back gently with iron bird tiebacks.

Designer, Susan Keefe, CID

Arched goblet pleat with medallion holdbacks.

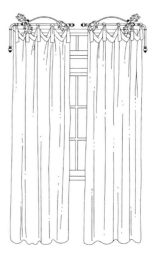

Tie top on swing arm rods.

Both illustrations: Custom rendering by DreamDraper® design software, www.dreamdraper.com
© 2009 Evan Marsh Designs, Inc.

Wide width embroidered sheer fabric was used "up the roll" to create maximum fullness - shirred at the top, overlapped and stapled onto a large wood rod.
Designer, Susan Keefe, CID

Ring top draperies with simple braid tiebacks.

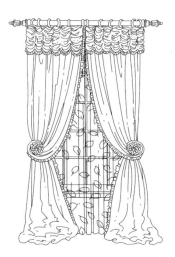

Sheer undertreatments are enhanced with puddled ring top drapery panels and gathered valance.

Both illustrations: Custom rendering by DreamDraper® design software, www.dreamdraper.com © 2009 Evan Marsh Designs, Inc.

CynthiaPorcheInteriors.com

DraperyAvenue.com

Above: Color-blocked silk draperies match perfectly with vine inspired wall sconces and custom wrought iron railing. *Designed and made by Custom Drapery Workroom Inc., Drapery Avenue,www.draperyavenue.com*

Left: Flat-panel draperies attached with wrought iron medallions gracefully swag across this magnificent window. This treatment matches perfectly with the inviting room décor; a delight to behold. *Cynthia Porche Interiors, www.cynthiaporcheinteriors.com*

Stationary panels with banded, ruffled top make an elegant statement. *Custom rendering by DreamDraper® design software, www.dreamdraper.com© 2009 Evan Marsh Designs, Inc.*

Puddled draperies with swag embellishment are hung slightly lower to expose decorative glass. *Custom rendering by DreamDraper® design software, www.dreamdraper.com © 2009 Evan Marsh Designs*

DecoratingDen.com

The high ceiling and Palladian windows made this formal living room a design challenge. The inspired solution was to bring down the ceiling visually to create a more intimate space, accomplished by using a dark navy horizontal fabric band placed at the bottom of the draperies to draw the eyes downward. The medallion holdbacks tie in with the Venetian style windows. The colors of the room, in addition to the ceiling treatment, enhance the room's grandeur while, at the same time, help to lower the height without adding too much vertical weight. *Decorating Den Interiors, Mimi Wilson, Bristow, VA., www.decoratingden.com*

DecoratingDen.com

A decorative window grille in white works well with the arched window. One drapery panel tied back allows for a better view of the arched window. A rich deep blue fabric accent on the leading edge of the drapery focuses the eye on the center of the window. Crystal finials and the lucite rod is a splurge of elegance. This one-panel approach is less crowding and heightens the room. *Decorating Den Interiors, Gretchen Curk, Cincinnati, OH., www.decoratingden.com*

JCandlerDesign.com

These grand windows are flanked by trimmed and lined draperies on 3" real wood poles with matching rings. Private residence, Bel Air, California, *Jeanne Candler Design, www.jcandlerdesign.com, Photo: Charles Randall*

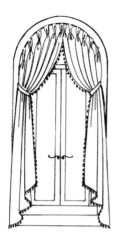

Arched rod pocket draperies with ruffle banding and high ties.

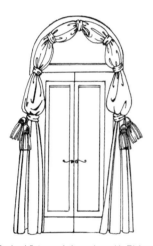

Arched flat panel draperies with Bishop sleeves and large tassels.

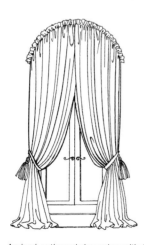

Arched gathered draperies with tie-backs and large tassels.

These delightful arched windows are embraced with matching custom curved drapery hardware. *Le Fer Forge Drapery Hardware www.leferforge.com*

DonnaElle.com

These pages show good examples of what American's refer to as "Curtains."

Notice that they are less formal and usually made of transparently sheer fabrics such as voile or batiste, but not always, see photo to the right. This curtain is made of a lightweight print. The small size of the treatment and the placement—usually in a small kitchen, bathroom, or laundry window—is what signifies it as a curtain rather than a drapery.

Left: *Donna Elle, Interiors by Donna Elle, www.donnaelle.com, photography by Jeff Allen*

Right: Pretty pleated and scalloped heading ring top cafe curtains add softness to horizontal blinds. Lining provides extra protection from the sun.
Donna Elle, www.donnaelle.com, photo courtesy of Jeff Allen

Castec.com

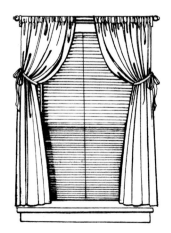

Rod pocket sheer curtains with tiebacks over miniblind.

DonnaElle.com

Pleated draperies

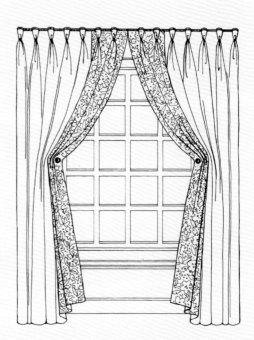

A small window is made to look larger by placing drapery panels higher and wider than the window.

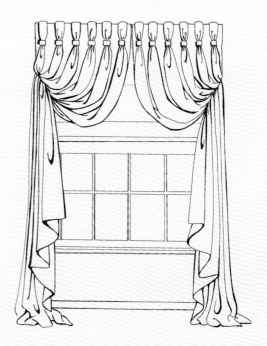

Goblet-pleated Italian strung drapery panels cascade to the floor. A flat-panel Roman shade underneath provides privacy and sun control.

Pleated draperies

Arched goblet-pleated draperies with jabot accent are pulled back with Italian stringing. Note the pretty braid and fringe trim.

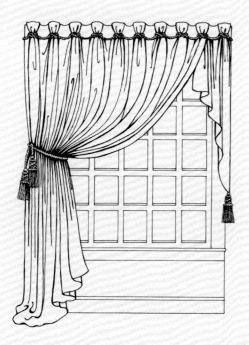 

A goblet-pleated drapery treatment is enhanced with a small cascade on the right-hand side. Tassels and interesting details.

Pleated draperies

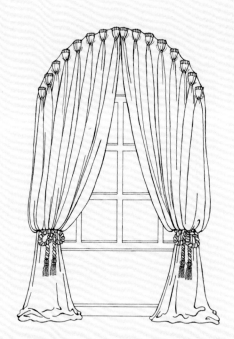

Arched goblet-pleated draperies with bishop sleeves and rope ties create a visually dramatic window treatment.

Pencil-pleated draperies are enhanced with intricate trim and are held back from the window with Italian stringing to reveal the sheer undertreatment with bottom banding.

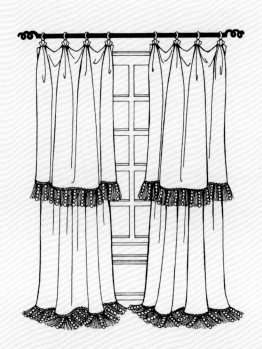 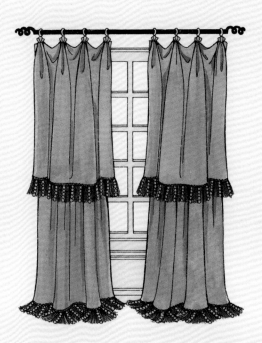

Slouched pleated ring top drapery panels are doubled up to draw the eye to the center of the treatment, showcasing intricate fringe and bead trim.

Slouched inverted box pleated & cuffed panels provide an unusual look. The longer far edges of the cuffs pull the eye down and focus it on the puddled fabric and trim puddling on the floor.

Rod pocket draperies

Double Bishop sleeve rod pocket panels on a decorative rod.
Simple treatments can be elegant!

Flounced rod pocket panels with coordinating banding on the leading edge and hemline "kissing the floor"
style puddling.

Specialty swinging hardware allows for easy access to French doors. Coordinating fabric adds a nice touch. Hidden wands can be used to pull back the panels.

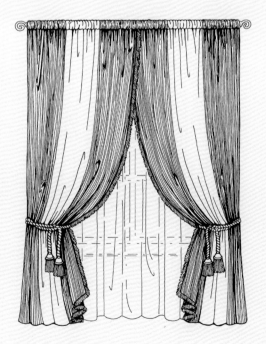 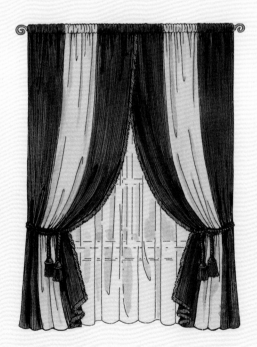

Color-blocked rod pocket drapery panels with a sheer panel underneath are lush and eye-catching.

Rod pocket draperies

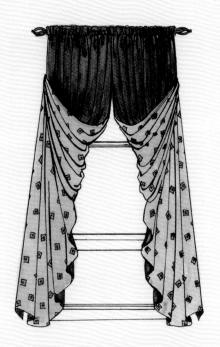
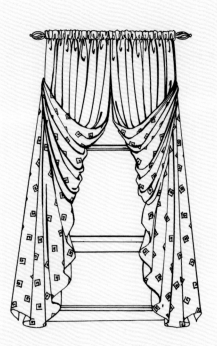

Rod pocket panels with coordinating lining with high ties on a decorative wooden rod.

Arched rod pocket Bishop sleeve drapery.

Rod pocket draperies

Double rod pocket side panels. The outer panel is on a wood rod, whereas the back panel is on a hidden 1" metal rod. Medallion hold back finishes the treatment.

Simple and cost-effective rod pocket treatment with 2" stand-up ruffle sleeve and medallion holdbacks.

Flat-panel draperies (unpleated)

Instead of hiding the shape of this grand window, a drapery treatment was chosen to accent its graceful arch. Tassel detailing is an inspired choice.

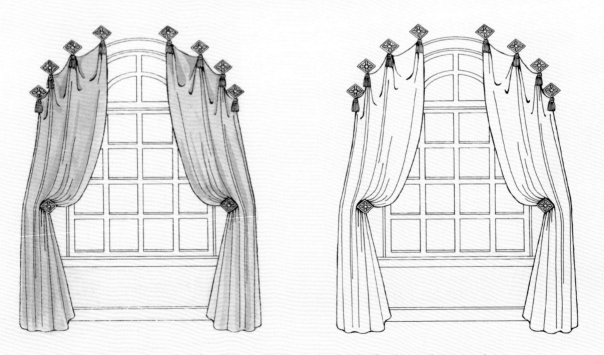

Intriguing drapery hardware provides the focal point for this arch top window.

Flat-panel draperies (unpleated)

Arched Bishop sleeve panels with rosettes and rope tassels.

Crisscrossed flat-panel drapery on a decorative rod, completed with tassel tiebacks.

Flat-panel draperies (unpleated)

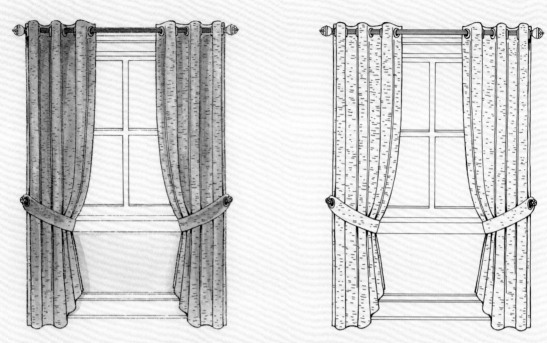

Grommet topped drapery panels held back with coordinating fabric tiebacks.

Single-tone panels are set off by complementary decorative hardware.

Flat-panel draperies (unpleated)

Stationary drapery panels soften the window frame, whereas the striped Roman shade provides privacy and sun control.

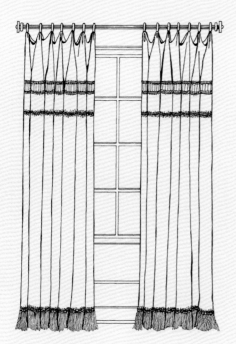 

Ring top draperies with multiple horizontal banding finished with bullion fringe.

Specialty heading draperies

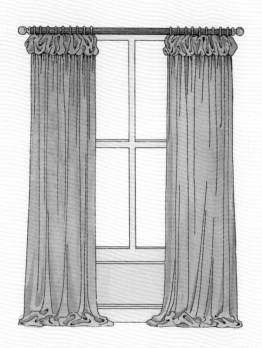

Puddled blouson drapery panels hung with rings offer casual elegance.

Triple blouson tops on the drapery panels draw the eye with their unique beauty.

Specialty heading draperies

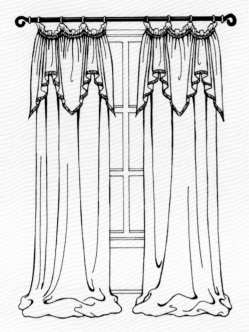

Multi-arched flounced gathered and puddled panels on shepherd's crook decorative
wrought iron rod.

Stationary tab top panels with gathered knots hang on a decorative rod over a trimmed roller shade.

Drapery Yardage Specifications and Technical Information

What is it about fabric at the window that makes such a compelling statement? Of course, it can soften the architecture of a room, but it also has the unique ability to accentuate it. Fabric can hide flaws around a window area, trap drafts, shield a room's furnishings from the sun, and provide a needed focal point.

It can help to muffle sound, manage to pull all the disparate elements of a room together, provide balance, and best of all: bestow beauty.

Curtains are mostly just unlined versions of draperies, a simple single or double layer of fabric that is hemmed and hung from a rod at the top of a window frame. Not all curtains are short, but the most recognizable of curtains are those that do not extend to the floor.

Curtains are lighter and airier than draperies. Most often used in kitchens, bathrooms, and children's bedrooms, where fun cotton patterns incorporating various related motifs are standard. So, by nature, they are always a less formal style of window enhancement.

Draperies are the grand older sister to curtains, all dressed up and ready for a night at the opera. They are for formal areas, areas in need of lush accents, and employ complicated stitching and multiple layers.

Draperies are the kind of window treatment that you invest in and expect to keep on the windows for multiple years. While some drapery fabrics are lightweight, such as silks and sheers, most are heavier materials such as velvets, jacquards, satins, and damasks.

And, if made of a lighter material, you will more than likely see that the fabric has been lined at least once, if not twice or even three times. You will find more information on these types of linings on page 30.

What follows are specifications for a series of popular curtain and drapery styles, as well as information on a variety of other related topics. Of course, I am only scratching the surface of these remarkable treatments. You will see many others throughout the pages of this book.

Uniquely knotted tab top drapery panels with coordinating tiebacks. This is obviously a stationary treatment.

Custom drapery information

Standard custom quality features

- Double wrapped headings.
- 4" or 5" permanent buckram headings unless "slouched" (without buckram).
- Pleating is custom tacked with extra thread.
- All seams serged and overlocked.
- All draperies perfectly matched & sized on a table.
- Blind stitching bottom and side hems. Chain weights might be necessary to prevent billowing in lightweight fabrics.
- Double wrapped 4" or 5" bottom hems and 5" double side hems.
- All draperies weighted at corners and seams.
- Multiple width draperies constructed to hide seams behind pleats.

Drapery terminology

- "Single width" is generally one strip of material pleated to a finished dimension across the top, usually between 16" and 24". For example, using a 48" wide material, a width that finishes to 24" is considered double fullness, or 2 to 1; a 16" finished width is considered triple fullness, or 3 to 1. Joined widths can cover almost any size window.
- A Panel is a single drapery unit of one or more widths, used for one-way (o/w) draw, stack left, or stack right and stationary units.
- Pair is two equal panels that cover the desired area — unless an offset pair is necessary
- Return is the measurement from the rod to the wall; in other words, the projection.
- The "overlap" is the measurement when draperies are fully closed, of the right leading edge and the left leading edge overlapping each other. This overlapping helps balance the pleats and reduce light seepage.

Options available on draperies

- Pinch pleated with 4" or 5" buckram.
- Box-pleated or box pleated with tabs for the rod. Add the diameter of the rod to the finished length. For flat tab draperies, use 2 to 1 fullness.
- Rod pocket gathered, smocked, goblet, flounced, blouson, or cuffed.
- Self-lined, interlined or lined with polyester-cotton, black-out, or thermal suede.
- Pleat spacing varies according to the widths of material used to achieve a specified finished width. For example, three widths of material pleated to 59" to the pair will not have the same pleat spacing as three widths of material pleated to 72" to the pair. If the pleats and pleat spacing are to look alike on draperies of different widths, you should specify "comparable fullness" when you order custom draperies. Vertically striped fabrics will not fabricate to allow an identical stripe to fall between pleats.

Ordering custom draperies

Since "made-to-measure" draperies are to your exact specifications, measurements must be made with extra care and with a steel tape only. Double-check all measurements for accuracy as it is often more expensive to remake draperies than make new ones! Measure each window separately even if they appear to be the same size. If length varies, use the shortest length, especially for ceiling to floor length. Follow this rule or a portion of the drapery may drag on the floor.

Drapery Width

- Measure the width of the drapery rod from end to end.
- Add 12" to this figure to include the allowance for standard traverse rod returns and overlap.
- Standard returns are 3". For outer or "over," draperies allow for an additional 3" clearance of undertreatment.
- When ordering panels that draw o/w (one-way), specify which direction the leading edge is on: left or right. Right means drapery moves toward the right. Left means drapery moves toward the left.

Drapery Length

- Measure from top of the rod to floor or carpet.
- The under treatment should be at least .5" shorter than outer treatment.
- For floor-length draperies, measure the length at each side and in the center. Use the shortest figure for your measurements.
- Rod should be placed a minimum of 4" above the window so that hooks and pleats will not be visible from the outside.
- If sill-length, allow 4" to 6" below sill so that the bottom hem will not be visible from the outside.
- When using pole rings, measure the length from the bottom of the rings.

Yardage chart

Yardage chart for 4" or 5" heading FL (finished length) plus 20", plain fabrics only
Total number of widths per pair or panel

Finished length

	2W	3W	4W	5W	6W	7W	8W	9W	10W	11W	12W	13W	14W	15W
36"	3.25	4.75	6.25	7.75	9.25	10.75	12.25	13.75	15.25	16.75	18.25	19.75	21.25	22.75
40"	3.50	5.00	6.50	8.00	9.50	11.00	12.50	14.00	15.50	17.00	18.50	20.00	21.50	23.00
44"	3.75	5.50	7.25	9.00	10.75	12.50	14.25	16.00	17.75	19.50	21.25	23.00	24.75	26.50
48"	4.00	5.75	7.50	9.25	11.00	12.75	14.50	16.25	18.00	19.75	21.50	23.25	25.00	26.75
52"	4.00	6.00	8.00	10.00	12.00	14.00	16.00	18.00	20.00	22.00	24.00	26.00	28.00	30.00
56"	4.25	6.50	8.50	10.75	12.75	15.00	16.75	19.00	21.25	23.25	25.50	27.50	29.75	31.75
60"	4.50	6.75	9.00	11.25	13.50	15.75	18.00	20.00	22.25	24.50	26.75	29.00	31.25	33.50
64"	4.75	7.00	9.50	11.75	14.00	16.50	18.75	21.00	23.50	25.75	28.00	30.50	32.75	35.00
68"	5.00	7.50	10.00	12.25	14.75	17.25	19.75	22.00	24.50	27.00	29.50	32.00	34.25	36.75
72"	5.25	7.75	10.25	13.00	15.50	18.00	20.50	23.00	25.75	28.25	30.75	33.25	36.00	38.50
76"	5.50	8.00	10.75	13.50	16.00	18.75	21.50	24.00	26.75	29.50	32.00	34.75	37.50	40.00
80"	5.75	8.50	11.25	14.00	16,75	19.50	22.25	25.00	28.00	30.75	33.50	36.25	39.00	41.75
84"	6.00	8.75	11.75	14.50	17.50	20.25	23.25	26.00	29.00	32.00	34.75	37.75	40.50	43.50
88"	6.00	9.00	12.00	15.00	18.00	21.00	24.00	27.00	30.00	33.00	36.00	39.00	42.00	45.00
92"	6.25	9.50	12.50	15.75	18.75	22.00	25.00	28.00	31.25	34.25	37.50	40.50	43.75	46.75
96"	6.50	9.75	13.00	16.25	19.50	22.75	26.00	29.00	32.25	35.50	38.75	42.00	45.25	48.50
100"	6.75	10.00	13.50	16.75	20.00	23.50	26.75	30.00	33.50	36.75	40.00	43.50	46.75	50.00
104"	7.00	10.50	14.00	17.25	20.75	24.25	27.75	31.00	34.50	38.00	41.50	45.00	48.25	51.75
108"	7.25	10.75	14.25	18.00	21.50	25.00	28.50	32.00	35.75	39.25	42.75	46.25	50.00	53.50

Pleat-to-fullness chart

(48–54" fabric) 2.5 times fullness

Pleat to widths														
19	38	57	76	95	114	133	152	171	190	209	228	247	266	285
1	2	3	4	5	6	7	8	9	10	11	12	13	14	15

(48–54" fabric) 3 times fullness

Pleat to widths														
15	30	45	60	75	90	105	120	135	150	165	180	195	210	225
1	2	3	4	5	6	7	8	9	10	11	12	13	14	15

(55–60" fabric) 2.5 times fullness

Pleat to widths														
21	42	63	84	105	126	147	168	189	210	231	254	273	294	315
1	2	3	4	5	6	7	8	9	10	11	12	13	14	15

(55–60" fabric) 3 times fullness

Pleat to widths														
17	34	61	68	85	102	119	136	153	170	187	204	221	238	255
1	2	3	4	5	6	7	8	9	10	11	12	13	14	15

Calculating yardages

General calculations
(for detailed terms and information see next page)

With drapery calculations, one must consider the following: width and length of the window, area to be covered, amount of fullness desired, width and type of fabric, allowances for hems and headings, and pattern repeat, if applicable. And after obtaining accurate measurements, proceed with the following steps.

Step 1:
Determine the number of fabric widths required. Calculated by multiplying the width of the area to be covered by the given fullness factor: 2.5 for two and a half times fullness or 3.0 for triple fullness, for example. Divide this by the width of the fabric used. The result is the number of widths of fabric that are required to achieve the desired fullness. Since fabric suppliers will not sell a part of the width (or cut a roll of fabric vertically down the middle), this figure must be a whole number.

Step 2a:
Calculate the yardage. Add to the length of the treatment, the allowances for hems, headings, and where applicable, styling allowances, such as cuffs or blouson tops (such as the image below). Allowances listed on the item page under the corresponding yardage calculation. Next, multiply these amounts by the number of widths required and divide by 36 to obtain the number of yards. This calculation applies only to solid fabrics or to fabrics that have a pattern repeat of fewer than six inches. (Or, to calculate the yardage for a fabric with a pattern repeat of more than six inches.)

Step 2b:
With pattern repeat:
Add the length and applicable allowances together and divide by the pattern repeat. This figure is the number of patterns repeats that are required to achieve the desired length. If this number is a fraction, it must be rounded upward to the nearest whole number.

Step 2c:
Determine the cut length—this is the actual length that the workroom will cut the fabric after allowing for pattern repeats, hems cuffs, puddling, etc. Multiply the number of repeats required by the size of the pattern repeat. This number is the cut length.

Step 2d:
Multiply the number of widths required (as calculated in Step 1), by the cut length (in Step 2c) and Divide by 36 to obtain the total yardage.

Special note:
I have tried to ensure the accuracy of the calculations and yardage charts of the items in this book. However, variations in fabrics or workroom specifications may require certain modifications to the yardage calculations. For complex or elaborate style treatments such as swags, cascades, and arched treatments, please consult an interior designer or professional drapery workroom. But, most professional drapery workrooms do not work with do-it-yourselfers. This limited information is provided for those who want to figure out how much fabric is needed for a specific treatment. Some books specialize in the fabrication methods of custom draperies. *The Complete Photo Guide to Window Treatments: DIY Draperies, Curtains, Valances, Swags, and Shades*, for example.

This information is also provided for designers who want to figure out their own quantities of fabric needed for various window treatments.

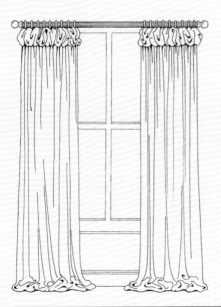

Puddled blouson drapery panels hung with rings offer casual elegance.

Drapery terms and calculations chart

Bishop's sleeve lengths = Add 5" to 15" per pouf, depending on the desired effect and quantity of poufs. .

CD = Cascade Drop. Length (top to bottom) of cascades. The cascades are most visually pleasing when they are 3/5, the length of the undertreatment.

CL = Cut Length. The length of fabric to be cut, including the allowance for headings, hems, and specialty items such as bishop sleeves or cuffs.

C/O = Center opening drapery.

F = Fullness. The fullness after pleating or gathering of drapery; usually 2x for flat panel or tabbed draperies, 2.5x for pinch-pleated or box pleated, and 3x for sheers

FL = Finished Length. The length of pairs or panels before adding for headings and hems (what the finished length of the drapery will be after fabrication). Fullness minimum = To be considered "custom" draperies usually need 2.5 to 3x fullness. Sheers require triple fullness.

FW = Finished Width. The total width of a pair or panel of draperies including returns and overlap.

HH = The Heading and Hem allowances. Custom draperies require doubling wrapping the heading and hems. Therefore, you must add 18" for drapery with 4" headings and hems and 22" for drapery with 5" heading and hem.

OL = Overlap(s). 6" per pair of single hung (no sheers) draperies and 3.5" for a single hung panel.

O/W = Single panel, one-way drapery.

R = Repeat. The total inches before a pattern repeats itself.

RFW = Rod Face Width, the total rod width, not including the return to the wall.

RT = Return(s). Rod projection from the wall. Add 6" (3" for each side) for standard single hung draperies and 12" for double-hung (over sheers) draperies. Example: A 102" Rod (RFW) single hung pair of draperies would require an additional 12". 3" for returns to the wall and 6" for overlap in the middle. A double-hung pair of draperies would require an additional 18". 12" for returns to wall and 6" for OL.

SB = Stack-back. The amount fabric that stacks back when you open the pair or panel of draperies, usually one-third of the rod face.

SBGC = Stack-back with full glass clearance = rod face x 1.5.

SD = Swag Drop. Use the "rule of fifths law" (ratios of 5 or 6 are more pleasing to the eye). When deciding how long a swag drop should be — one-fifth of the length of the undertreatment is best.

TW = Total Width. The total width of drapery fabric required after multiplying the fabric widths required.

TY = Total Yardage. Total yardage required.

WOF: Width of Fabric. Fabrics usually come in rolls of fabric. This is the width of the fabric roll from one side of the roll to the other side of the roll, usually 45 inches, 54 inches, 60 inches, or even 120 inches.

Try it! Calculate based on a 70" RFW (rod face width) and 84" FL (finished length) single hung, center opening drapery. 70" RFW + 12" for RT & OL (returns and overlap) = 82" FW (finished width). 82 x 2.5 = 205 TW (total width). 205 ÷ 54 (width of fabric used) = 3.79. Round to the next whole number because fabric stores do not sell half widths of fabric. Now figure the length. 84" FL + 18" HH (heading and hem allowance) = 102" CL (cut length). Now multiply 4 (fabrics widths required) x 102" (CL) for a total of 408". 408" ÷ 36 = 11.3 (total yards required).
Always round this number up to the next whole number, in this case, 12. It's always good for the workroom to have a little extra fabric.

French Pleated

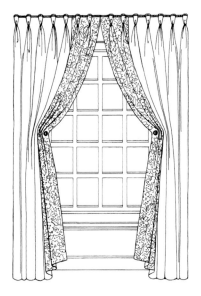

Photo: Pinch pleat; illustration: goblet pleat

A traditional panel drapery topped with a series of narrow, "pinched" folds. Also called French pleats, this type of drapery requires a good bit of stackback space, as pinching the top of the fabric results in a greater fabric fullness at the bottom.

Yardage (*including Pinch Pleat, Goblet, Cartridge, Bell, Euro, Box, and Fan pleated*)

Without pattern repeat:

Step 1 – RFW (rod face width) + 12" for RT & OL (returns and overlap) x 2.5 or 3.0 ÷ width of fabric = number of widths required (round up to the whole number) Three times fullness recommended for very lightweight fabrics such as silk.

Step 2a – FL (finished length) + 18" for HH (headings and hems) x widths required ÷ 36 = yardage (round up to the whole number).

With pattern repeat:

Step 2b – FL (finished length) + 18" for HH ÷ pattern repeat = the number of repeats required (round up to the whole number).

Step2c – Number of repeats x pattern repeat = CL (cut length)

Step 2d – Number of widths (from Step 1) x new CL (from Step 2c) ÷ 36 = yardage with pattern repeat (round up to the whole number)

Things to Consider
> Alternate lining color
> Center opening or one-way panel
> What type of rod?
> Tiebacks required?

Special Notes
1. A check measure recommended for all full-length draperies.
2. See page 90 for detailed calculating terms.

Shirring Tape / Smocked

Photo: Smocked pleat; illustration: pencil pleat

This very attractive heading exhibits even gathering across the width of the drapery heading to great feminine appeal.

Yardage *(including Pencil, Diamond, Accordion and other patterns)*

Without pattern repeat:

Step 1 – RFW (rod face width) + 6" for RT (returns) x 2.5 or 3.0 ÷ width of fabric = number of widths required (round up to the whole number) Three times fullness recommended for very lightweight fabrics such as silks and sheers.

Step 2a – FL (finished length) + 16" for HH (headings and hems) x widths required ÷ 36 = yardage (round up to whole number).

With pattern repeat:

Step 2b – FL (finished length) + 18" for HH ÷ pattern repeat = number of repeats required (round up to the whole number)

Step 2c – Number of repeats required x pattern repeat = cut length

Step 2d – Number of widths (from Step 1) x new CL (from Step 2c) ÷ 36 = yardage with pattern repeat (round up to the whole number)

Things to Consider

> Alternate lining color

> Tiebacks required?

> Center opening or one-way panel

Special Notes

1. A check measure recommended for all full-length draperies.
2. Smocked treatments should stay stationary due to the nature of the header.
3. See page 90 for detailed calculating terms

Tab Top & Grommet

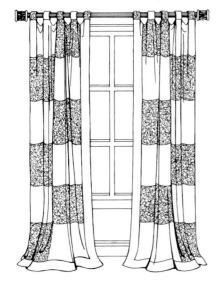

Photo & illustration: Tab top

This simple style has been popular for many years, as it has many options for decoration and celebrates the beauty of the decorative rod from which it hangs.

Yardage *(Including Tab Top, Pleated Tab Top, Gathered Tab Top, and Grommet Top)*

Without pattern repeat:

Step 1 – RFW (rod face width) + 6" for RT (returns) x 2 ÷ width of fabric = number of widths required (round up to the whole number) Two and a half times fullness recommended for very lightweight fabrics such as silks and sheers

Step 2a – FL (finished length) + 20" for HH (headings and hems) x widths required ÷ 36 = yardage (round up to whole number).

With pattern repeat:

Step 2b – FL (finished length) + 20" for HH ÷ pattern repeat = number of repeats required (round up to the whole number)

Step 2c – Number of repeats x pattern repeat = CL (cut length)

Step 2d – Number of widths (from Step 1) x CL (from Setp 2c) ÷ 36 = yardage with pattern repeat (round up to the whole number).

Things to Consider

> Alternate lining color
> What type of rod?
> Center opening or one-way panel

Special Notes

1. Yardage calculations include tabs.
2. Only two times fullness is required on this treatmentto obtain the proper effect.
3. See page 90 for detailed calculating terms

Rod Pocket

Photo: Unembellished rod pocket; illustration: rod pocket with ruffled top

A style of drapery made with an open pocket at the top. It can be dressed in a ruffle above the rod and also, depending upon the amount of fabric used, create a "shirred" effect.

Yardage *(including Rod Pocket, Double Rod Pocket, Rod Pocket with Standup and Rod Pocket with Belt Loops)*

Without pattern repeat:

Step 1 – RFW (rod face width) + 6" for RT (returns, if used) x 2.5 or 3.0 ÷ width of fabric = number of widths required (round up to the whole number) ÷ 36 = yardage without a pattern repeat. Three times fullness recommended for lightweight fabrics.

Step 2a – FL (finished length) + 16" for HH (headings and hems) x widths required ÷ 36 = yardage (round up to whole number).

With pattern repeat:

Step 2b – FL + 16" for HH ÷ pattern repeat = number of repeats required (round up to the whole number)

Step 2c – Number of repeats x pattern repeat = CL (cut length)

Step 2d – Number of widths (from Step 1) x CL (from Step 2c) ÷ 36 = yardage with pattern repeat (round up to the whole number)

Things to Consider
> Alternate lining color
> Center opening or one-way panel
> What type of rod and tiebacks?
> Ruffle or frill needed on top of treatment?

Special Notes
1. Rod pocket draperies are usually stationary but can slide across the rod with some difficulty.
2. This treatment is usually not mounted up to the ceiling.
3. See page 90 for detailed calculating terms

Box Pleated

Photo: Rod mounted box pleat; illustration: board-mounted box pleat

Crisp folds that resemble the corners of a box are the hallmark of this tailored drapery treatment.

Yardage (including Box pleated, Inverted Box Pleat)

Without pattern repeat:

Step 1 – RFW (rod face width) + 12" for RT and OL (returns and overlap) x 2.5 or 3 ÷ width of fabric = number of widths required (round up to the whole number) Use 2.5 fullness if using a traverse rod

Step 2a – FL (finished length) + 16" for HH (headings and hems) x widths required ÷ 36 = yardage (round up to whole number).

With pattern repeat:

Step 2b – FL (finished length) + 16" for HH ÷ pattern repeat = number of repeats required (round up to the whole number)

Step 2c – Number of repeats x pattern repeat =CL (cut length)

Step 2d – Number of widths (from Step 1) x CL (from Step2c) ÷ 36 = yardage with pattern repeat (round up to the whole number)

Things to Consider

> Alternate lining color
> Center opening or one-way panel
> What type of rod, if any?
> Tiebacks required?

Special Notes

1. A check measure recommended for all full-length draperies.
2. Reduce fullness to 2.5 if using a traverse rod.
3. See page 90 for detailed calculating terms

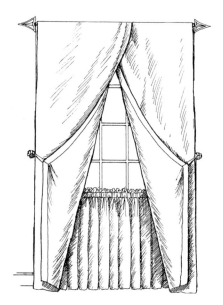

Tuxedo/Tent Fold

Photo & illustration: Tent fold

A tuxedo drapery is more about the mid-section of the treatment than the header as its most recognizable aspect is the way it folds back to reveal a contrast lining.

Yardage *(including Tuxedo, Tent Fold, and Stationary Flat Panel)*

Without pattern repeat:
Step 1 – RFW (rod face width) + 10" for RT and OL (returns and overlap, if used) ÷ width of fabric = number of widths required (round up to the whole number)

Step 2a – FL (finished length) + 12" for HH (headings and hems) x widths required ÷ 36 = yardage (round up to whole number).

With pattern repeat:
Step 2b – FL (+ 12" for HH ÷ pattern repeat = number of repeats required (round up to the whole number)

Step 2c – Number of repeats x pattern repeat = CL (cut length)

Step 2d – Number of widths (from Step 1) x CL (from Step 2c) ÷ 36 = yardage with pattern repeat (round up to the whole number)

Step 3 – Calculate with the same formula for contrast lining

Step 4 – Allow 1/2 yard for tiebacks

Things to Consider
> Alternate lining color
> What type of rod?
> Center opening or one-way panel

Special Notes
1. Large returns not recommended.
2. Tuxedo draperies limit the amount of light entering the room.
3. Not recommended for windows that are proportionately wider than high.
4. See page 90 for detailed calculating terms

Athena/Flat Panel

Photo: Clip-hung, traversing Athena; illustration: stationary Athena

The simple but stylish Athena drapery consists of a flat panel drapery with generous rings or clips attached to a rod or medallions, creating a swagged effect at the heading. This type of treatment often puddles.

Yardage *(including Athena/Flat Panel)*

Without pattern repeat:

Step 1 – RFW (rod face width) + 12" for RT (returns) x 2 or 2.5 ÷ width of fabric = number of widths required (round up to the whole number) Two and one-half fullness recommended for lightweight fabrics such as silks and sheers

Step 2a – FL (finished length) + 16" for HH (headings and hems) x widths required ÷ 36 = yardage (round up to whole number).

With pattern repeat:

Step 2b – FL + 16" for HH ÷ pattern repeat = number of repeats required (round up to the whole number)

Step 2c – Number of repeats x pattern repeat = CL (cut length)

Step 2d – Number of widths (from Step 1) x CL (from Step2c) ÷ 36 = yardage with pattern repeat (round up to the whole number)

Things to Consider

> Alternate lining color
> What type of rod, ring, and clip?
> Center opening or one-way panel?

Special Notes

1. A puddle of 6" has been allowed in the yardage.
2. Soft fabrics with good drapeability are preferable.
3. Lining or contrast lining equals drapery yardage
4. See page 90 for detailed calculating terms

Hemlines & embellishments

Short fringe edging

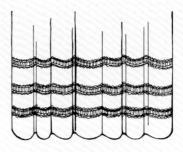

Triple fringe

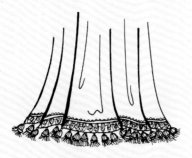

Tassel fringe

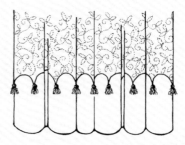

Banding with tassels

Puddled bullion fringe with beads

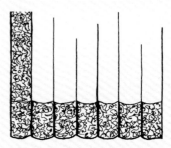

Edging variation

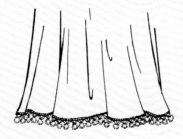

Fringe variations

Hemlines & embellishments

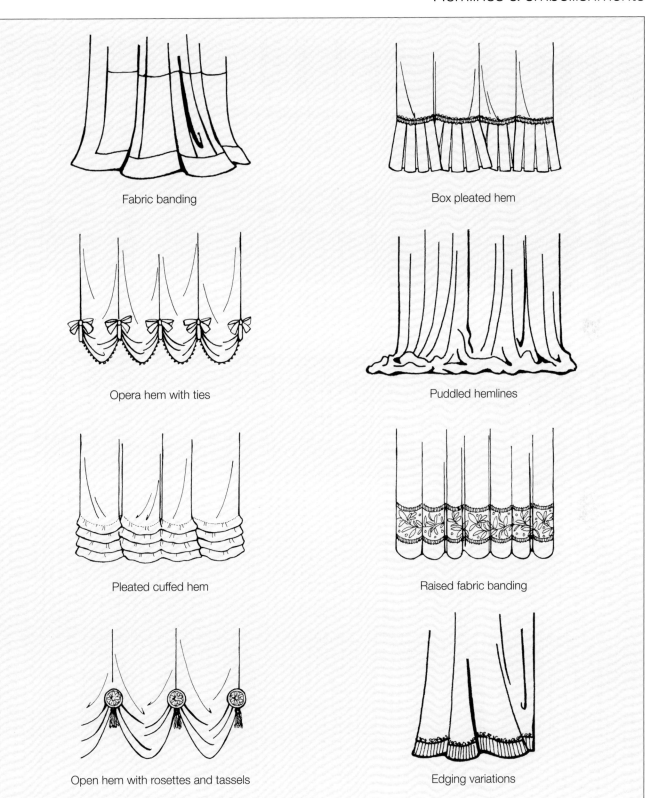

Fabric banding

Box pleated hem

Opera hem with ties

Puddled hemlines

Pleated cuffed hem

Raised fabric banding

Open hem with rosettes and tassels

Edging variations

Heading styles

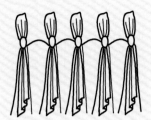

Button accented tabs with
extended fabric jabot

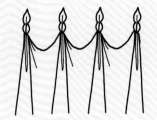

Knotted tabs

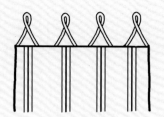

Flat panel drapery with
switchback loops

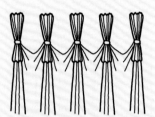

Hourglass gathered tabs

Tab panel with bows on
individual hardware

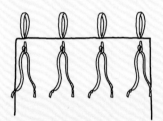

Buttonhole panel w/looped
skinny tabs

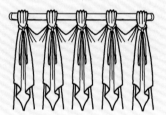

Flip over rod jabot tab header

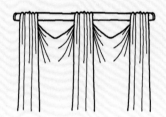

Waterfall-style gathered tab
with swags

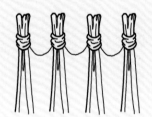

Gathered tabs

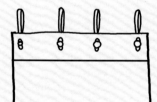

Looped tab top

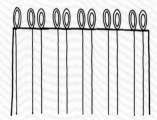

Looped tab top

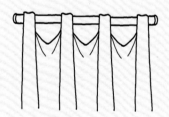

Tab top variation

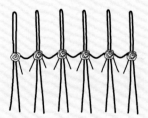

Extended tab loop panel
with rosette detail

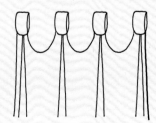

Tab top variation

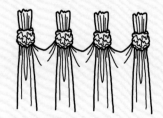

Gathered tabs

Heading styles

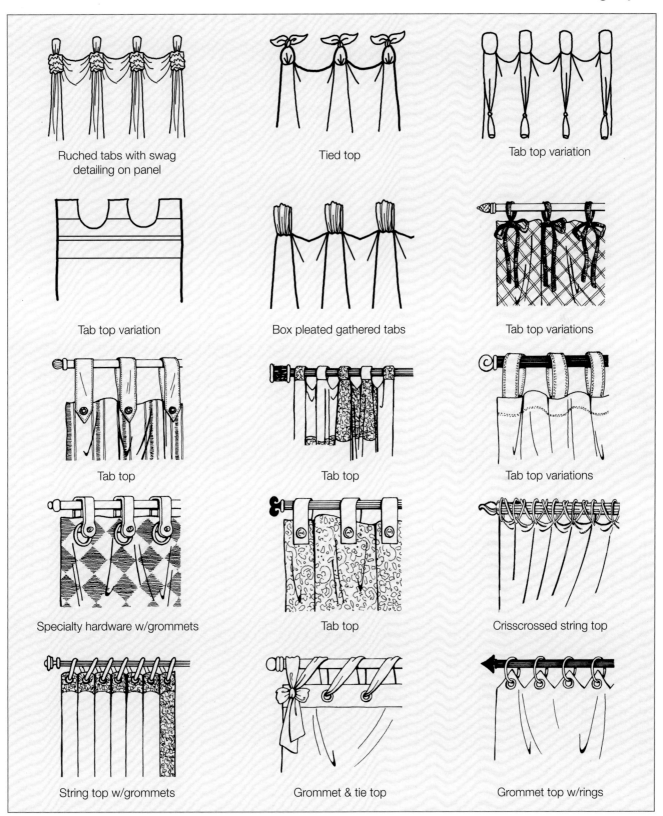

Ruched tabs with swag detailing on panel

Tied top

Tab top variation

Tab top variation

Box pleated gathered tabs

Tab top variations

Tab top

Tab top

Tab top variations

Specialty hardware w/grommets

Tab top

Crisscrossed string top

String top w/grommets

Grommet & tie top

Grommet top w/rings

Heading styles

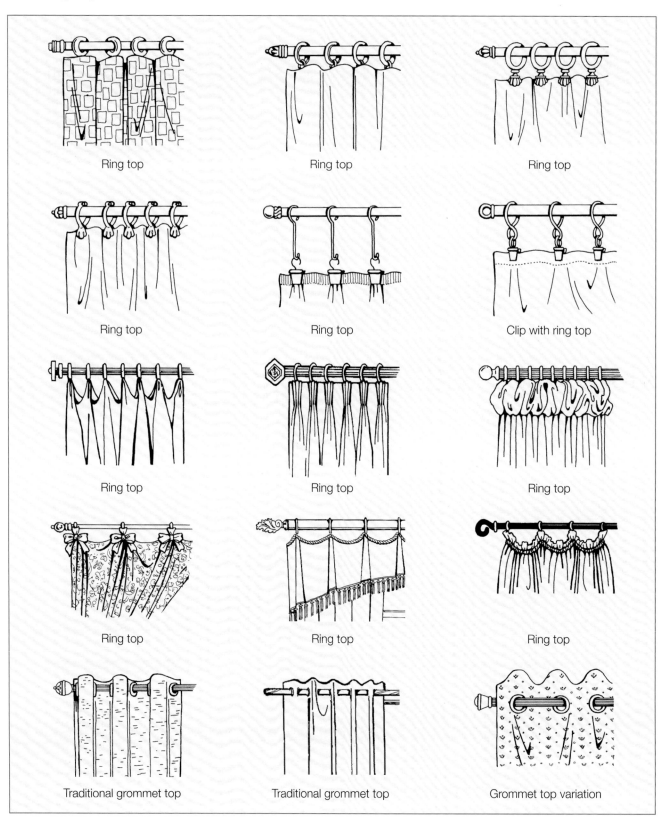

Ring top

Ring top

Ring top

Ring top

Ring top

Clip with ring top

Ring top

Ring top

Ring top

Ring top

Ring top

Ring top

Traditional grommet top

Traditional grommet top

Grommet top variation

Heading styles

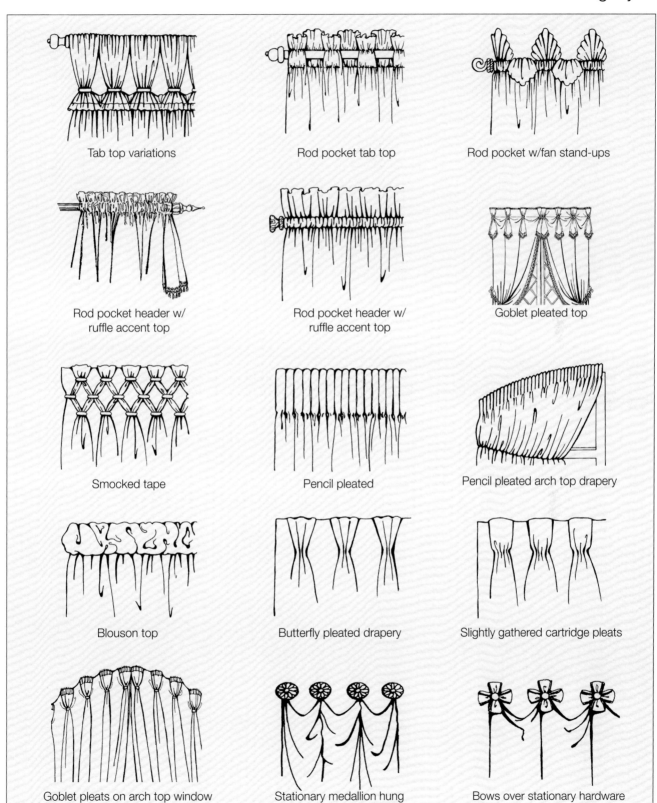

Tab top variations

Rod pocket tab top

Rod pocket w/fan stand-ups

Rod pocket header w/
ruffle accent top

Rod pocket header w/
ruffle accent top

Goblet pleated top

Smocked tape

Pencil pleated

Pencil pleated arch top drapery

Blouson top

Butterfly pleated drapery

Slightly gathered cartridge pleats

Goblet pleats on arch top window

Stationary medallion hung

Bows over stationary hardware

Rosettes & ties

Folded spiral w/ choux	Daffodil rosette	Petal rosette	Accordion fan	Bunched fan	Peacock
Choux	Shirred spiral	Double choux	Knot	Shirred pouf	Twisted knot
Pleated rosette	Pleated double rosette	Shirred rosette	Maltese Cross	Padded Maltese cross	Maltese cross w/rosette
Pointed petal rosette	Accordion bow	Multi-ribbon bow	Ruched square	Ruched doughnut	Bow tie
Straight ribbon bow	Hanging ribbon bow	Shirred bow	Triple petal bow	Bow with rosette	Thin ribbon bow
Double Maltese cross	Trefoil	Pointed trefoil	Flame trefoil	Pointed cross	Pointed petal cross
Wired ribbon bow	Knotted tie	Single pointed tie	Double clipped tie	Double angled tie	Pointed tie

Various flag styles

Triangle flag with ties, tassels

Custom shaped flag with banding and tassel

Triangle flag with rings and tassel

Tab top triangle flag with flounce

Square flag with hooks and fringe

Chevron flag with hooks and tassel fringe

Flared flag with hooks

Cascade flag

Chevron flag with hooks, banding

Custom flag with ties, fringe

Custom flag with rings, applique

Square flag with scalloped hem, fringe on medallions

Tab top flag with scalloped hem

Austrian shaped flag with knife edge banding

Arched gathered flag

Tab top Chevron flag with jabots and banding

Tiebacks

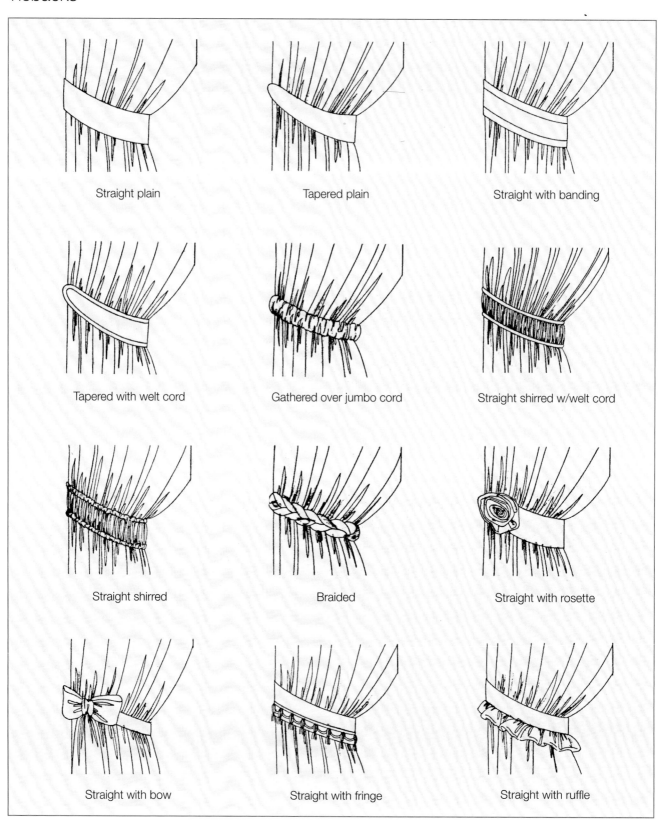

Straight plain

Tapered plain

Straight with banding

Tapered with welt cord

Gathered over jumbo cord

Straight shirred w/welt cord

Straight shirred

Braided

Straight with rosette

Straight with bow

Straight with fringe

Straight with ruffle

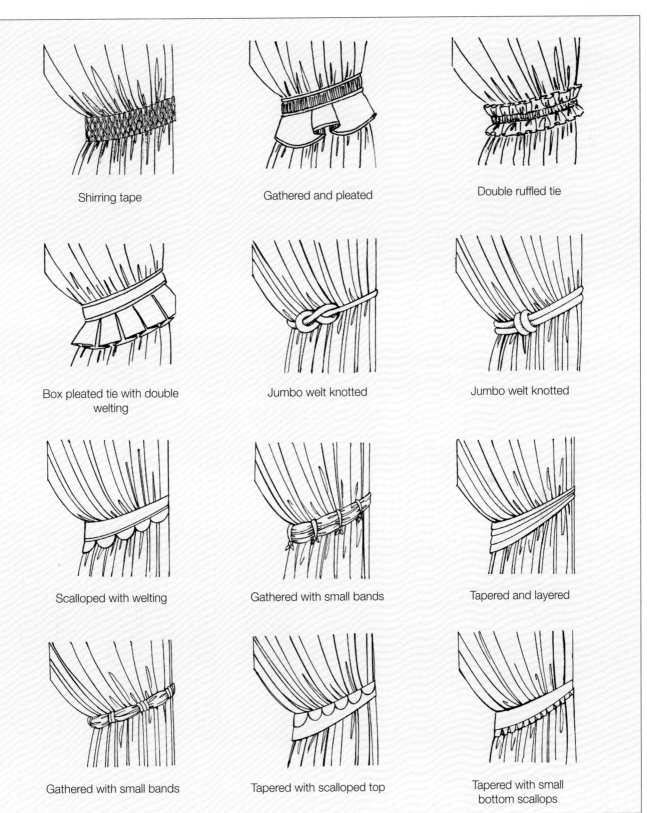

Shirring tape

Gathered and pleated

Double ruffled tie

Box pleated tie with double welting

Jumbo welt knotted

Jumbo welt knotted

Scalloped with welting

Gathered with small bands

Tapered and layered

Gathered with small bands

Tapered with scalloped top

Tapered with small bottom scallops

Tiebacks

A decorative accent by which draperies and curtains are held back from the window panes. The various styles give a personal touch to the window treatment.

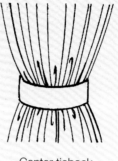
Center tieback

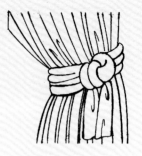
Knotted tieback

Yardage
Standard – 1/2 yard

Standard with piping – 1/2 yard + 1/2 yard piping

Standard with banding – 1/2 yard + 1/2 yard banding

Standard with bows – 1/2 yard + 1 yard bows

Contour – 3/4 yard

Ruched tieback – 1 yard

Ruffled tieback – 1 yard + 1.5 yard ruffle

Streamer tieback – 2 yards
Braided tieback – 1/2 yard each strand
  (three strands)

Collar with hook & loop fastener – 1/2 yard

Things to consider
- Style
- Fabric (if contrasts are used)

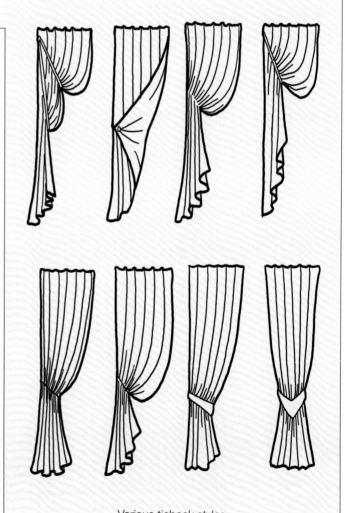
Various tieback styles

Banding & tieback styles

There are many details that may be added to personalize a window treatment. Ruffles add charm and romance to the look of a room. Use on draperies, tiebacks, cushions or comforters for a country-style look.

Inset banding adds dramatic contrast to a window treatment. A band of two inches or more is sewn inset from the edges.

Reverse lining is a decorative facing sewn to the lining, then folded outward to reveal the contrast and held in place with tiebacks.

Fringe and braids used decoratively on a window treatment echo the elegance of past eras.

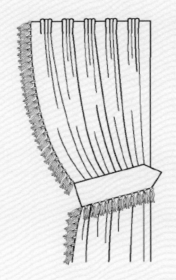

Tassel banding on leading edge

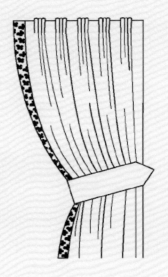

Banding on leading edge

Yardage
Ruffles
- 1/4 yard for each 24" ruffles

Inset banding
- Length + hem allowances

Reverse lining
- Length + hem allowances

Fringe & braids
- Length + additional 10%

Things to consider
- Treatment
- Fabrics

Banding set back from leading edge

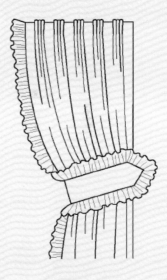

Ruffled banding

Round table covers

Ruffled overlay and skirt with tassels

Round overlay tied with bows

Plain round cover; lined or unlined

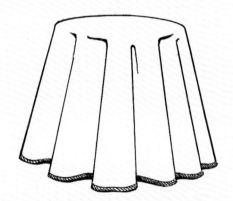

Plain round cover with welt edge

Lace square over skirt

Austrian style table cover

Sunbursts & dressing tables

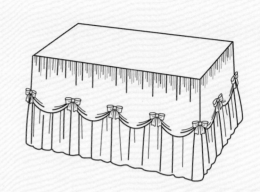

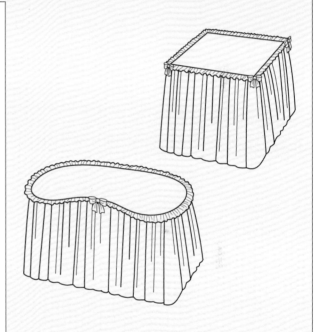

Sunburst
A decorative accent for an arched window. The sunburst is softly gathered into the center and is usually made in a sheer or lace fabric to enhance (rather than block) the window and filter the light.

A rosette may be added.

Yardage
- For 118" sheer or lace: 1.5 yards
- For 48" lace: 3.5 yards
- Windows up to 48" diameters

Things to consider
- Specify fabric
- Specify if a rosette is desired
- A template of the window should be provided

Dressing tables & stools
A romantic detail to add to the most feminine bedroom. The separate cover is gathered in two styles, balloon or ruffled. Upholstered stools coordinate with either style.

Yardage
Balloon Style
- Top and balloon skirt: 7 yards
- Underskirt: 5 yards
- Bows: 2 yards

Ruffled style
- Skirt: 10 yards
- Contrast bow: 1/2 yard

Stool
- Skirt: 3.5 yards
- Bows: 1/2 yard (for two)

Things to consider
- Style of table
- Fabric details

Table linens

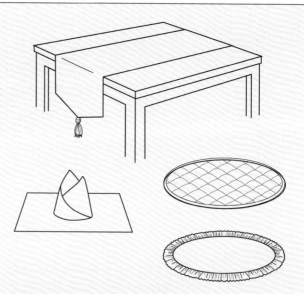

Tablecloths & toppers

Decorative tablecloths and toppers can complement any room décor. The tablecloth may be finished at the bottom with piping (welting), ruffles, or banding. Table toppers complete the look in a basic square handkerchief, stylish Austrian or box pleated.

Yardage

Round table-cloth with	Up to 74" diameter	Up to 90" diameter
Regular piping	4.75 yards	6 yards
Jumbo piping	add 1.5 yards	add 1.5 yards
Ruched band	add 2.5 yards	add 3 yards
Ruffle	add 4 yards	add 5 yards

Toppers	Up to 74" diameter	Up to 90" diameter
Square handker-chief (50")	1.5 yards	1.5 yards
Austrian	2.75 yards	3.5 yards
Pleated	2.75 yards	3.5 yards

Things to consider
- Diameter of table
- Drop measurement to the floor
- Style of tablecloth or topper
- Fabric details

Napkins, placemats & runners

Quilted placemats can be custom made to your color scheme and can be finished with piping or a one-inch ruffle. Coordinating 18" square dinner napkins are double hemmed and stitched. Runners add a decorative touch and display a fine wood or glass table to its best advantage.

Yardage
Placemats
- Print fabrics: 18–27" pattern repeat; allow 1 repeat per placemat
- Plain or small prints: allow 1/2 yard per placemat
- For ruffle, add 1/4 yard per placemat

Napkins
- Print fabrics: 18–27" pattern repeat
- 1.5 yards = 4 napkins
- Plain or small print: 1.25 yards = 4

Runners
- Length of table + 24" ÷ 36 = number of yards

Things to consider
- Fabric details
- Sizes

Fabric covered rods & mirrors

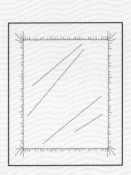

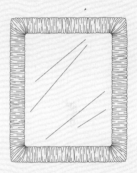

Upholstered mirrors

The ultimate in custom décor—fully upholstered mirrors. Fabric may be ruched onto a frame or pulled flat and finished around the edges with matching piping or ruffles.

Yardage
Ruched – 2 yards

Flat – 1.25 yards

Piping – add 1/2 yard

Ruffle – add 1.25 yards

Things to consider
- Style of mirror
- Size of mirror
- Fabric details

Covered rods

For a truly customized window treatment, fabric-covered wood rods and finials add decorative flare. A swag casually draped over a rod or drapes on café rings are excellent ways in which this treatment can be used.

Yardage
For rod & finial
- Up to 60" wide: allow 1 yard
- Up to 108" wide: allow 1.5 yards
- Up to 144" wide: allow 2 yards

Things to consider
- Size and diameter of rod
- Fabric details

TOP TREATMENTS

When your heart says, "beautiful window covering," but your room says, "not enough space!" the solution is a stunning top treatment. From a soft swag dipping gracefully across a window to the hard edges of a wood cornice, the function of a top treatment is to provide beauty to a home, hide the mechanics of combined window treatments, disguise architectural flaws and also to emphasize and draw focus to a window. By itself or as beautiful punctuation, valances, cornices, and swags (the lion's share of the top treatment category) are excellent choices when dressing a window.

Left: The stationary drapery panels and valances are in striped silk, and all the passementerie in the room are from "The Vintage Collection by Jamie Gibbs" for D'Kei Inc. The center-draw burn-out sheer fabric is from Kravet. The valances are board-mounted with the traverse rod attached underneath to hold the sheers. Stationary drapery panels are lined and inter-lined, adding fullness and protection from the elements. Upholstery fabrics are Scalamandre and Schumacher. *Jamie Gibbs, Jamie Gibbs Associates, www.jamiegibbsassociates.com*

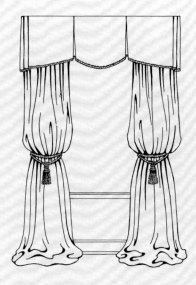

A box pleated valance tops Bishop sleeve panels accented with tassels.

DecoratingDen.com

History in the Making

The earliest recorded history of interior design is rooted in the Renaissance Era, a time of great change and rebirth in the world of art and architecture. Much of this era saw understated, simple treatments, moving toward more elaborate bed coverings and portieres (fabric panels between doors, or used to separate rooms), and onto multiple layered treatments, including, toward the end of this period, valances, swags, and pelmets. By the Baroque and Early Georgian Period (1643–1730), elaborate and theatrical treatments placed a high emphasis on the cornice and pelmet to finish off the top of window treatments.

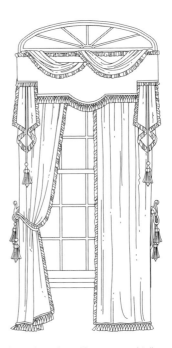

Elaborately trimmed cornice with swags and tails cap trimmed drapery panels with tassel tiebacks. *Custom rendering by DreamDraper® design software, www.dreamdraper.com © 2009 Evan Marsh Designs, Inc.*

Left: It is the upholstered cornice that ties this bedroom together with its harlequin pattern — such an ideal complement to the checked and toile fabric used in the bedding and drapery panel. The scalloped lower edge displays stylish beading, popping nicely against the white of the hard treatment. Note also that the cornice hides all the hardware and mechanisms associated with the hard treatment and the toile drapery panel.
Decorating Den Interiors, Barbara Elliot & Jennifer Ward Woods, www.decoratingden.com

Today's Top Treatments

Today, there are almost unlimited choices for top treatments, allowing for more creative exploration for the designer and workroom due to their smaller scale. "Theme" cornices (pages 206 & 207, for example) are often a favorite in children's rooms: baseball pennants at the top of a cornice or ballet slippers used as a decorative element to secure the corners of a small swag. A single handkerchief swag will punctuate a bathroom window, and elaborate padded and upholstered cornice will add beautiful emphasis to sumptuous draperies.

Below: Green silk scarves swag gently over decorative poles to soften the window area without impeding the view. It is their simplicity that is so appealing. While there is certainly room for drapery panels — or multi-layered treatments for that matter — the simplicity of the treatment is pleasing to the eye.

Scarf swag hangs asymmetrically for maximum impact. *Custom rendering by DreamDraper® Design software, www.dreamdraper.com © 2009 Evan Marsh Designs, Inc.*

SmithandNoble.com

Top treatments are important to a luxury and lush finish. *Designed and made by Custom Drapery Workroom, Inc., www.draperyavenue.com*

The Facts: **Top Treatments**

Advantages: Perfect for areas that cannot accommodate larger treatments. Above kitchen sinks and limited space areas. A top treatment can hide architectural flaws such as windows placed at different heights. They can also soften hard window treatments and introduce a beautiful focal point to any room.

Disadvantages: Not particularly useful for privacy or sun control. They can gather dust due to their stationary nature. They can overpower a small window if not designed carefully.

Cost: Top treatment costs can vary significantly. Wood or wrought iron cornices will be more costly than a padded fabric-covered cornice. A swag and tail treatment is usually more costly than a scarf top treatment.

Lifespan: 7-15 years.

Most Appropriate Locations: Anywhere that a window needs softening, but space is at a premium. As always, do keep fabric away from areas of extreme moisture to cut back on issues of mold growth and fabric discoloration.

Care & Cleaning: Depending upon the type of treatment, you may be able to vacuum or dust at the window, or remove and dust, or remove and have cleaned professionally. Do not attempt to wash your top treatments conventionally.

Pleated swag and stacked cascade with center jabot. Note coordinating buttons.

Above and Right: A stunning combination of swags, jabots, drapery panels, and Austrian shades. Austrian shades, with their swag like style, are the perfect complement to swags & cascades. Volume is very important to top treatments, the right amount of fullness and fabric completes the overall harmony. *Designed and made by Custom Drapery Workroom, Inc., www.draperyavenue.com*

119

Good to Know: A Few Top Treatment Terms

What's the difference between a cornice and a lambrequin? A valance and a pelmet? Here's a look:

Balloon: A soft fabric valance that is billowy and lush, drooping in graceful, looping folds across the top of a window. Also known as a cloud, though the shape varies slightly.

Box pleat: A flat, symmetrical fold of cloth sewn in place to create fullness, spaced evenly across the top of a drapery. The fabric can be folded back on either side of the pleat to show, for example, a contrasting fabric.

Cascade: A zig-zagged or cascading shaped piece of fabric falling gracefully from the top of a drapery or top treatment. It can also be called a jabot, depending upon the size and shape.

Cornice: A rigid treatment that sometimes serves as a mask for holding attached stationary draperies or for hiding various window treatment hardware or even masking architectural flaws. Constructed of a chipboard-style wood or lightweight material, over which some padding (usually polyester fill), is added then covered with a fabric of choice and finished with trim. Cornices fit across the top of a window frame and can be a terrific focal point, usually mounted on the outside of a window frame.

Jabot: A stationary panel, decorative in nature, used in tandem with a swag (festoon). Also known as a tail.

Lambrequin: An extended version of the cornice, the lambrequin, not only fits across the top of the window frame but also extends down on either side, resembling legs. Shaped or straight, this three-sided piece is created in much the same manner as a cornice but is typically more elaborately decorated. See the first page of Top Treatments: Cornices, for example.

Pelmet: The British term for top treatment.

Rosette: Fabric gathered into the shape of a flower or something similar. Typically placed at the top right and left corners of a window frame to accent an existing treatment, such as a scarf or drapery panel.

Scarf: A single, lengthy piece of lightweight fabric that either wraps loosely around a stationary rod or loops through decorative brackets placed on either side of a window frame.

Swag: There are many kinds of swag top treatments. The prevalent styles are basic pole swags or board mounted swags. See pages 123-123 for more information.

Valance: A simple to elaborate treatment, the valance is a piece of decorative fabric usually hung from a rod, a piece of decorative hardware, or aboard. Valances can take on many shapes: poufed, scalloped, pointed, arched, and rectangular and can also be pleated or gathered.

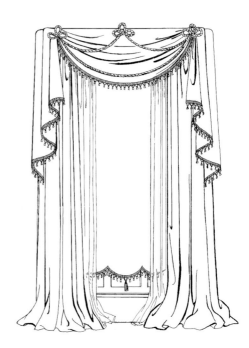

Trim on the scalloped fabric shade is echoed in the soft swag and cascade. Note, too, that this is a four-part treatment—both sheer and regular drapery panels are employed.

Two-story draperies are always impressive. Adding swags and double cascades make the room go from impressive to extraordinary.
Designed and made by Custom Drapery Workroom, Inc., www.draperyavenue.com

Top Treatments:Swags & Cascades

As diverse as they are versatile, swags and cascades can assume many roles, taking the lead role in a dramatic and eye-popping capacity—or perhaps just a supporting role or bit part. At its most subtle, a swag and cascade combination can take shape as it winds itself around a pole in a slouchy and casual way; for a more involved installation, look to a swag accompanying drapery panels. No matter how it's installed, however: board mounted, pole mounted, multilayers or just a single, this time tested top treatment is certain to make a statement.

Left: Short, narrow windows were corrected visually with the placement of an unusual arch top decorative rod, which adds height and drama. The blend of pink and blue can sometimes be polarizing, but this combination exudes style and elegance, with the pink banding allowing the treatment to distinguish itself from similarly colored walls. Notice, too, that the vine-like scrolling on the hardware echoes the floral fabric motif.
Emily B. Walser, ASID, photograph courtesy of Dustin Peck, Dustin Peck Photography

Above: This Scandinavian-style scarf treatment is casual and easy. Also appreciated is the use of complementary fabrics, rather than using the same fabric for both doorways. ADO-USA

Right: Sheer handkerchief swags with long, flowing tails accentuate the tall window wall without detracting from the view outside. Kenny Greene, Greene Designs

Multiple scarf swag treatments accent the window without over-powering it. *Custom rendering by DreamDraper® design software, www.dreamdraper.com © 2009 Evan Marsh Designs, Inc.*

This complicated bay window needs accuracy and precision for the top treatment to flow seamlessly. *Designed and made by Custom Drapery Workroom, Inc., www.draperyavenue.com*

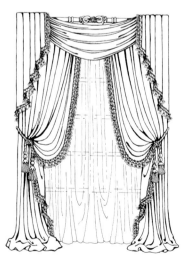

Open swag and cascades with trim, on a decorative rod, tiebacks and tassels finish this extraordinary treatment.

Pole gathered swags with decorative knots, cascades, and trimmed panels.

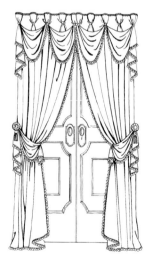

Goblet pleated panels, with swag flags and small cascades.

Unique and creative ideas for top treatments open an array of luxury. *Designed and made by Custom Drapery Workroom, Inc., www.draperyavenue.com*

Rod pocket pole swag and gathered drapery with trimmed flounce.

Gathered linear swags over traditional overlapping swags with stacking cascades make for an elegant and expensive treatment. Finished with rosettes and tassels.

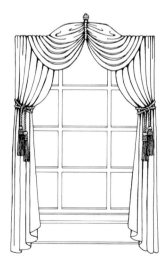

Large tassels dangling from braided tiebacks create visual interest in this simple but stunning treatment.

Regal blue and gold fabrics made for a foyer with double light sheers to complement and control sunlight. *Designed and made by Custom Drapery Workroom, Inc., www.draperyavenue.com*

DraperyAvenue.com

Unique top treatment for the master bedroom, the fullness made it cozy ready for the Chicago winters. *Designed and made by Custom Drapery Workroom, Inc.,www.draperyavenue.com*

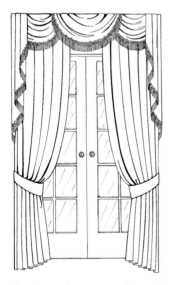

Board mounting swags and cascades with tied back panels.

Sheer under treatment, swags, cascades, and panels.

Fabric hangs in shabby chic swag and cascade style, layered over lush, puddled stationary drapery panels.

Balloon shades are also a natural complement to swags and cascades. Why not throw in a specialty valance under the swags for a luxurious finish? Don't forget the trim and banding. *Designed and made by Custom Drapery Workroom, Inc., www.draperyavenue.com*

Double swags with petite bow accents cap a set of double drapery panels, one patterned, one plain. Lovely tassel tiebacks hold the fabric away from the window until night falls.

Elaborately styled swags hang gracefully from a wooden cornice, ending in lushly fringed cascades. Underneath, draperies contained by braid fringe and trimmed tieback complete this designer window treatment.

129

Turban-style swags grace these contrasting drapery panels. These swags are hybrids of sorts: they are part swags, and part cornice boxes with their vertical wood support on each side and above. I love it when designers combine two different style window treatments into one genuinely creative design. *Decorating Den Interiors, www.decoratingden.com*

130

Swags and cascades over Austrian shade. *www.draperyavenue.com*

Open pole swags. *Decorating Den Interiors, www.decoratingden.com*

Linear swags and stacked cascades. *www.draperyavenue.com*

The drapery and swag style is one of the workroom's favorite and ultra popular designs. *Designed and made by Custom Drapery Workroom Inc., www.draperyavenue.com*

CarletteCormier.com

A classic swag and tail arrangement are naturally beautiful over drapery panels and sheer undertreatment. *Carlette Cormier, photograph by Richard Leo Johnson, www.carlettecormier.com*

DonnaHovisInteriors.com

An elaborately swagged board-mounted valance is a graceful accent in this music room.

Note the lovely crystal finial and tassel midway, and the lovely rosettes on the tiebacks — an ideal means to provide a display of decorating details. *www.donnahovisinteriors.com*

Swags & cascades

Traditional swags and cascades with bullion trim. Note the cascades are under the swags. Sheer undertreatment and puddled drapery panels finish this exquisite design.

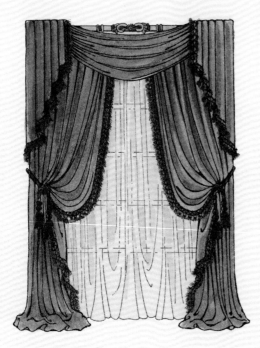 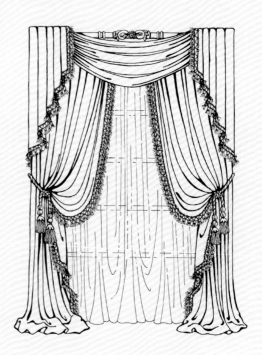

Gathered single swag under pleated cascades mounted on designer drapery rod and finished with trim and tassels.

Swags & cascades

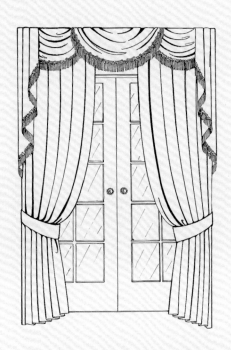

Classic (pleated and overlapping) swags and cascades are trimmed in heavy fringe.

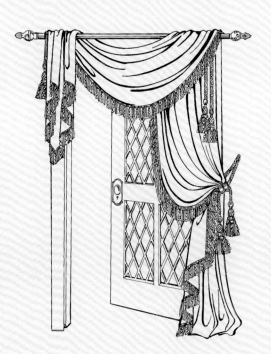

An asymmetrical swag treatment is lushly detailed with bullion, tassels, and plenty of thick, drapeable fabric. This treatment consists of three different parts but looks like one continuous piece of fabric.

Swags & cascades

Gathered swags with rope and tassel heading. Raised jabots add a dramatic touch.
Tiebacks with banding finish this formal treatment.

A two-layered treatment incorporates a sheer side panel, held back with tassel tieback and
asymmetrical pole swag with bullion fringe and tassel tieback. The panel is easily released from
its tieback to offer additional sun filtering.

Swags & cascades

Tab top gathered open flag swags are anchored on a decorative wood rod. Since the pleated under draperies cover the entire window, the ties can be undone for privacy.

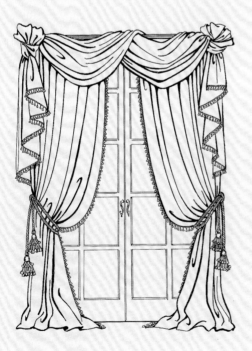 

A pole swag exhibits large decorative knots, which heightens the treatment visually and draws the eye upwards. Side panels held back with braided tassel trim complete this elegantly casual look.

Swags & cascades

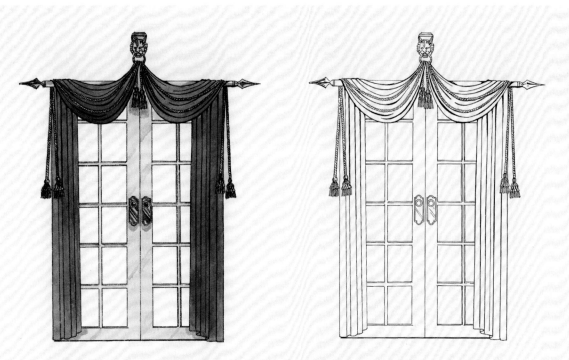

A simple but elegant top treatment, perfect for French doors: A pole swag with lovely detailing draws attention but does not impede egress.

Trim on the scalloped fabric shade is echoed in this swag and cascade design. Note, too, that this is a four-part treatment—both sheer and regular drapery panels are employed.

Swags & cascades

Two linear swags raised slightly in the middle cover a small flat jabot. Two gathered cascades with contrasting lining match nicely with the stationary banded panels.

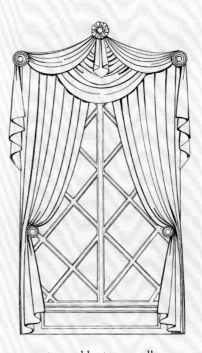

This eye-pleasing treatment is achieved by using one large swag topped by two smaller swags and jabot. Medallion holdbacks complement the use of medallions atop the cascades.

Swags & cascades

A simple but elegant treatment is achieved by adding bullion fringe and rosettes to a gathered swag and extra-long stacked cascades.

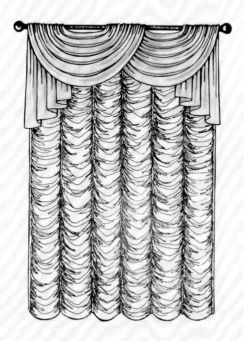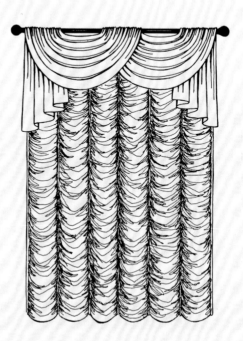

An Austrian shade looks lovely under pole swags and cascades.

Swags & cascades

For creative use of swags this treatment uses two large and one small gathered swag;
extra-long pleated trimmed cascades add an extra custom look to this treatment.

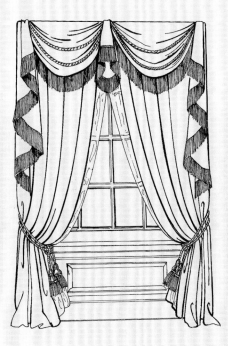

Long stacked cascades tumble down the sides of stationary drapery panels,
enhanced by the linear swags above.

Swags & cascades

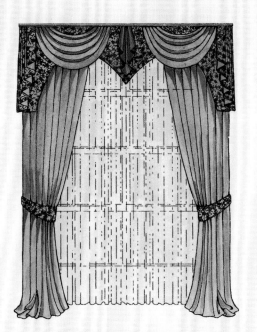

A possible unsightly view can be diffused with sheer draperies. To draw focus, an elaborate swag, jabot, and cascade treatment are a lovely distraction.

A classic pole swag is offset by pleated drapery panels and flip-top bell pull-style ornaments.

Swags & cascades

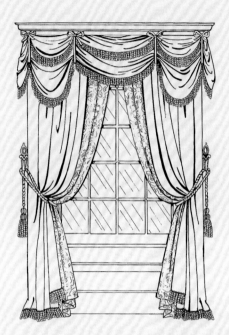

A double set of swags cap a double set of drapery panels—one patterned,
one plain. Lovely tassel tiebacks hold the fabric away from the window until night falls.

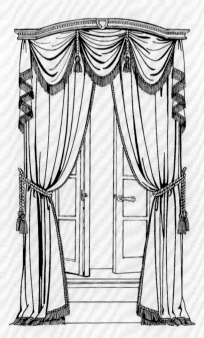

A detailed wood cornice houses a fringed swag and cascade top treatment, accented with tassel embellishments. Braid follows the leading edge of the drapery panels with bullion trim brushing the floor.

Swags & cascades

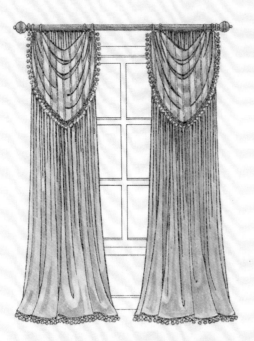
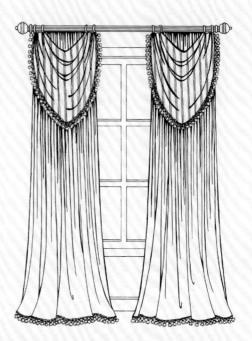

Open pleated and trimmed swags are pole-mounted to rings. Fringe added to the puddled hem of the pencil pleated drapery add a touch of drama.

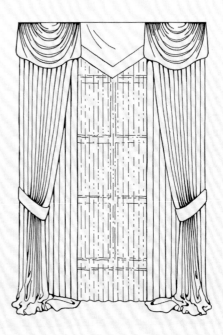

A five-part treatment: Sheer under draperies, traversing over draperies, stationary side panels, swags and a triangle valance.

Swags & cascades

A wood cornice with sconce embellishments holds scalloped swags, trimmed in bullion fringe, and accented with brush fringe. Matching drapery panels are held back with braided tassels.

Elaborately styled swags hang gracefully from a small wood cornice, ending in lushly fringed cascades. Underneath, draperies contained by braid fringe and trimmed tiebacks complete the treatment.

Board mounted swags & cascades

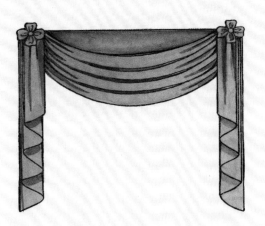 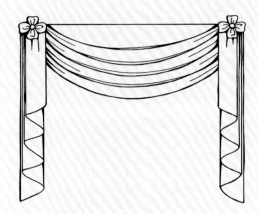

Classic board mounted swag with stacked cascades and Maltese cross accents.

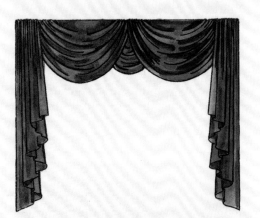 

Classic gathered swags and cascades—board mounted.

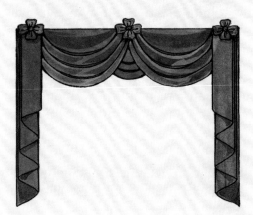 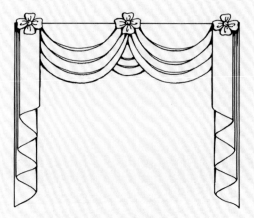

A classic board mounted swag and cascade treatment with Maltese crosses.

Board mounted swags & cascades

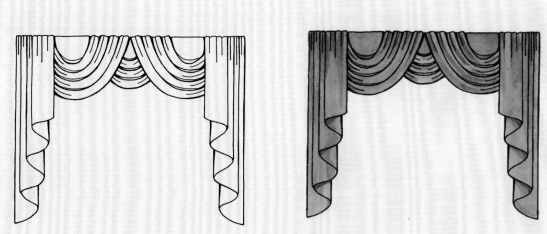

Simple board mounted swag and cascade.

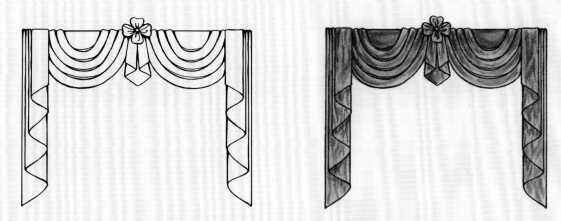

Board mounted swag and cascade top treatment with jabot and Maltese cross accents.

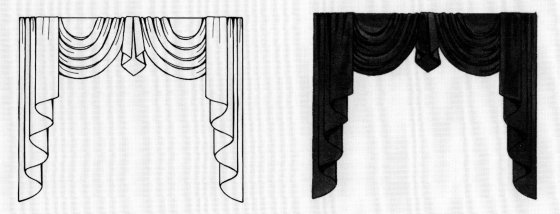

A simple board mounted swag, cascade and jabot treatment

Pole mounted swags & cascades

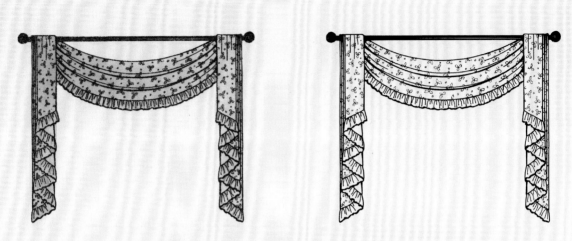

A simple pole swag and cascade with ruffle trim.

Pole mounted swag and cascades with contrast underlining and rosette accents.

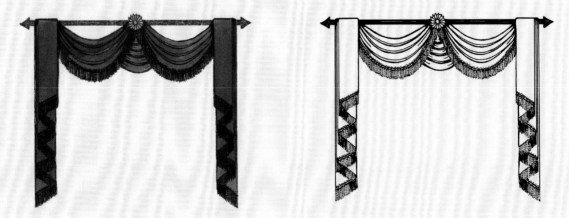

Stacked cascades over pleated swags, pole-mounted, brush fringe, and rosette.

Pole mounted swags & cascades

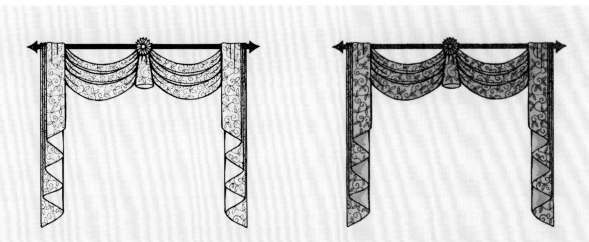

Pole swag and jabot with contrast underlining and center rosette accent.

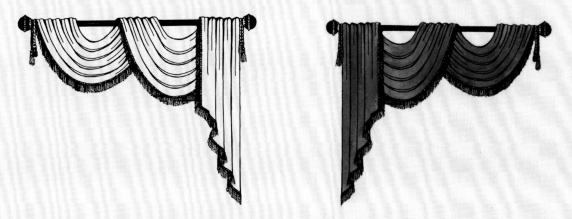

Asymmetrical pole swags with bullion fringe.

Casual pole swags with knotted and tied corner detailing.

Swag & cascade arrangement styles

Various cascade/jabot styles

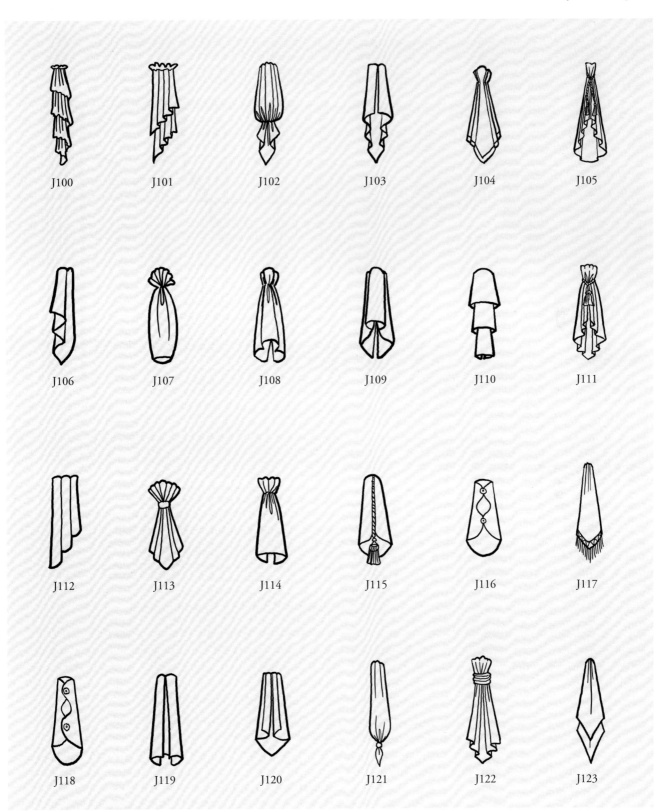

J100   J101   J102   J103   J104   J105

J106   J107   J108   J109   J110   J111

J112   J113   J114   J115   J116   J117

J118   J119   J120   J121   J122   J123

Swags & Cascades

This classic pole swag exhibits all of the fine characteristics of a venerable top treatment. The brush fringe is a terrific choice for decorative trimming, and the petite polka dot adds interest. An exceptionally well-done window covering. *Decorating Den Interiors, Design by Ruth Zerbe, www.decoratingden.com*

This crisp treatment includes a gathered swag and pleated cascade, stationary drapery panel, all edged in petite tassel trim, and a fabric covered three-inch pole.

Good to Know

From the previous pages on top treatments, you have probably discerned that swags are a special kind of top treatment, capable of standing alone or as accents to other treatments. There are many kinds of swags: pleated, gathered, and stacked, for example. They are hung in a variety of ways, including on cornice boxes, on draperies, on rod poles, or attached directly to the inside of a window frame, to name a few.

Since they are crafted into soft, graceful folds, it's best to use fabrics that drape easily, rather than stiff and unyielding fabrics. Also, when using swags in multiples, odd numbers usually look better than even numbers for better symmetry. Finally, be sure to line your swags, not just for sun protection, but also so that the sun doesn't leak through the fabric unevenly. By lining your fabric, you create a sturdier swag and one that remains the same color throughout.

Over the next couple of pages, we will look at a variety of swag and cascade treatments, and what you need to know to create a wonderful accent in your home. Later on, we'll also cover valance and cornice box styles.

Swag & Cascade Specifications

For standard room and window sizes, the preferable swag width size is 20" to 40" wide and has a vertical drop (finished length) of 16" to 24". Swags in this range only require 1.5 yards of fabric if lined, or three yards if self-lined (recommended). Swags between 40" and 60" require two yards of fabric if lined, or four yards if self-lined. These yardages are for plain fabrics only. For swags wider than 60" or with patterned fabrics, especially stripes, please consult a professional designer or drapery workroom.

The area to be covered and windows behind the swags are important considerations. Does the area to be covered include one, two, or three separate windows? Balancing the swag placement in front of multiple windows is an important design element. If only one large window is to be covered, then swag placement is much easier.

Swag Widths & Board Face

Since swags vary in width and length, the folds will also vary in quantity and size. Very small swags have only a few folds, and extremely wide swags will have a limited drop length. You will determine the width of the swags by the area to be covered.

Traditional (overlapping) Swag Sizes and Quantities

Traditional swags overlap; therefore, you will need to add an allowance for overlapping into your calculations. Swag overlaps will start approximately one-half, or less, of the width of the swag face. Swag widths when overlapped = length of board face divided by the number of swags plus 8" in many cases.

For example, let's say your board face is 127" wide, and you want five swags: 127 ÷ 5 = 25.4 (round to the whole number of 26); 26 + 8 = 34", or the width of each swag face. This method allows for 8" overlapping for each swag. Since the final swag width of 34" is between 20" and 40" this would make five swags an excellent choice for an area to be covered of 127". Caution: the 8" overlap rule may need to be adjusted down to 4", 2" or 0" for a small board face with multiple swags. For example, a 40" board face with three swags would result in reducing the overlap to 2". 40 ÷ 3 = 14. 14 + 2 = 16" swag face widths. That's plenty of overlap.

Linear (non-overlapping) Swag Sizes and Quantities

Linear swags don't overlap; therefore, you don't need to add for overlapping allowance. It's easier to figure swag face widths for linear swags because you divide the board face by the number of desired swags. Example: A board face of 127 ÷ 5 equals five swags that are 27" wide. Since 27" is between 20" and 40",

that would be appropriate for swag face widths. But since 127 ÷ 4 = 31, that would also be appropriate for swag face widths. Keep in mind that fewer swags mean less cost. You could also use three swags: 127 ÷ 3 = 42" swag face widths. Jabots or horns are usually required to hide the open spaces left when using linear swags.

Standard Drop Lengths

Since swag length, or drop, is usually one-fifth of the drapery length, or a close approximation, the standard drop lengths of swags are 16" for an 84" drapery treatment, and 20" for a 96" long drapery treatment.

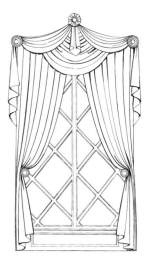

This eye-pleasing treatment is achieved by using one large swag topped by two smaller swags and jabot. Medallion holdbacks complement the use of medallions atop the cascades.

Swags, cascades, and center jabot over puddled panels with matching trim.

Cascades & Jabots

An elaborately swagged board-mounted valance is a graceful accent in this music room. Note the lovely crystal finial midway — an ideal means to provide a flourish of detail. *Carlette Cormier, CC's. Designs, photograph by Richard Leo Johnson*

Swag valance over drapery panels on a French door. *Custom rendering by DreamDraper® design software, www.dreamdraper.com © 2009 Evan Marsh Designs, Inc.*

There are many varieties of swags, cascades, and jabots; unfortunately, many professionals use different terms used to describe the same thing. While in the UK, the term "tail" is used to describe a cascade or jabot, in the US, the term jabot is used to describe a cascade. Both are correct; it is simply a matter of personal preference. I like the term jabot to describe smaller decorative pieces of fabric. Jabots usually adorn swags or swag-like valances: including, Kingston, Empire, or Austrian valances. Jabots may be tie-shaped, cone-shaped, rounded at the bottom, or even look like a smaller cascade.

A cascade is a folded piece of fabric that falls from the top of a drapery heading, swag, valance, or board to create a sort of zig-zagging, or cascading effect. Because you will no doubt see the interior side of the cascade as it folds back onto itself, cascades are either self-lined or have contrast lining.

Yardage: Cascades

For self-lined cascades, double the longest length or point of the cascade, then add four inches (for tack or attaching strip) then divide by 36 to supply you with the proper amount of yardage needed for a single pair of cascades. This calculation is for a cascade width (face) up to 14". For contrast-lined cascades, add 4" to the longest point of the cascade and divide by 36.

Swags & Cascades

Multiple board mounted swags. *Custom rendering by DreamDraper® design software, www.dreamdraper.com © 2009 Evan Marsh Designs, Inc.*

Traditional swags and cascades in cream-colored satin. Note the extra-long cascades and beautifully matching trim. *Photo courtesy Charles Randall*

Overlapping swags are draped gracefully above and across a window, making an elegant and formal statement. A section of draped fabric at the top of the window that typically resembles a big sideways "C" shape. A swag is sometimes coupled with a vertical cascade or "tail," which hangs gracefully on either side.

Yardage

Swags, plain fabric – 1.5 yards for contrast lined swags up to 40" and 3 yards if self-lined — two yards for swags between 40" and 60" and 4 yards if self-lined. For swags over 60" consult a professional drapery workroom as these swags may need to be "railroaded," and yardage calculations can be complex.

Things to Consider

> Swag type: Pleated, gathered or stacked
> Color of lining or self-lined
> Bay and Bow windows are more difficult to cover
> Clearance for passage doors
> Returns

Special Notes

1. Swags look best between 20" and 40" on standard windows
2. A re-measure by the workroom recommended
3. Linear swags are a better choice for bay windows
4. See page 90 for detailed calculating terms

Contemporary Swags

Single pole mounted swag with contrast lining. *Decorating Den Interiors* *www.decoratingden.com*

Asymmetrical pole-mounted swags.

Swags are draped across the window on a decorative pole and constructed to appear as if the fabric is thrown casually over the rod or constructed as one large swag.

Yardage

One swag
Width of area to be covered + 3" ÷ 36 = yardage

More than one swag:
Width of area to be covered x 1.5 ÷ 36 = yardage

Things to Consider

> Color of lining
> Width and drop of swags
> Number of swags
> Mounting on medallions, wrought iron or poles

Special Notes

1. Usually cut on the straight grain of the fabric. Any fabric with an obvious directional print should be constructed by a professional drapery workroom.
2. Proportions are important for this type of swag
3. A check measure by the workroom recommended.
4. For bay windows consult a professional
5. See page 90 for detailed calculating terms

Linear Swags

Bullion trimmed board mounted linear swags.

Linear swags with a double cascade in coordinating fabric.

These swags are butted together, without overlapping, a good choice for bay windows, where overlapping swags are difficult to design and install. Linear swags need not touch each other; they can be separated by a few inches, thus saving on yardage and labor.

Yardage

Swags, plain fabric – 1.5 yards for contrast lined swags up to 40" and 3 yards if self-lined. Two yards for swags between 40" and 60" and 4 yards if self-lined. For swags over 60" consult a professional drapery workroom as these swags may need to be "railroaded," and yardage calculations can be complex.

Things to Consider

> Color of lining, or self-lined
> Contrast or self-lined jabots, cascades
> Width and length in relations to other windows in the same room
> Number and type of swags
> Returns, if any

Special Notes

1. To achieve proper proportions, consult with professional drapery workroom
2. See page 90 for detailed calculating terms

Top Treatments: **Valances**

DecoratingDen.com

Top treatments, such as this versatile inverted box pleated valance, have the wonderful capability to be infinitely casual or completely elegant. Take the feminine cloud valance, for example; it will step into a supporting role alongside an elegant set of draperies or a modest vertical or sheer shading shade. Other styles will command a room, drawing the spotlight upon themselves so all may enjoy their standalone beauty. From the most petite bathroom window to a large picture window, a soft valance may be the answer to any window dressing question.

An inverted box pleated valance with luxurious white cotton fabric accented with decorative sun-inspired banding near the bottom of the valance, and the leading edge of the drapery is an inspired choice: a beautiful combination of formal and modern. A closer look reveals the coordinating welt and tassels atop and below this fabulous drapery treatment. Add a scalloped Roman shade, and you have a truly designer treatment. *Decorating Den Interiors, Barbara Tabak, Harrisburg, PA., www.decoratingden.com*

The clean lines of the cream flat-panel valances with decorative teal banding add elegance to the room and flow nicely with the drapery panels in this dining area. *Decorating Den Interiors, Mary Elliott, Indian Trail, NC., www.decoratingden.com*

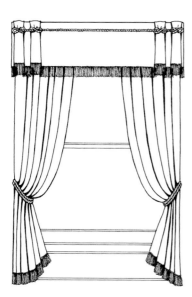

A soft flat valance with simple side pleats enhanced with bullion fringe and tiebacks.

Beige/green and white checked cloud shades, trimmed in small tassel fringe, complement stationary drapery panels, and are echoed as a valance above the bed with graceful style. *Beth Hodges, Beth Hodges' Soft Furnishings, window design by Pam DeCuire, photograph by Rob Garbarini*

Richly patterned fabric is highlighted with a contrast silk cuff. The raised center swags draw the eyes upward and add a unique custom finish. *Design and fabrication by Gillian Wendel, The Wendel Works.*

This gorgeous valance was created with tab tops hanging on a golden decorative rod with beautifully matching finials. Custom shaped bottom with trim adds the drama. Add striped silk draperies and sheers and you have a timeless window coverings masterpiece.
Decorating Den Interiors, Tonie Vanderhulst, Wellington, FL., www.decoratingden.com

This simple but elegant treatment is composed of a flat-panel valance which allows for lots of warm natural light diffused by the graceful sheers. The treatment perfectly frames the geometric medallions in the Vern Yip fabric. For the contrast inserts, buttons, and banding on the drapery panels. The designer used an unusual Tilton Fenwick tweed of seafoam and navy. These fabrics pick up the accent colors from the traditional oriental rug under the table. While not exactly whimsical, they do keep the dining room from becoming too stuffy.

Decorating Den Interiors, Heidi Sowatsky, St. Louis, MO., www. decoratingden.com

DecoratingDen.com

This lovely flat-panel valance with blue banding and cascades hangs gracefully over cafe shutters, allowing for privacy and light. *Decorating Den Interiors, Gretchen Curk, Cincinnati, OH. www.decoratingden.com*

CynthiaPorcheInteriors.com

A beautiful flat-panel asymmetrical valance with coordinating banding and medallions. *Cynthia Porche Interiors www.cynthiaporcheinteriors.com*

Three Asymmetrical flat-panel valances with kick pleats. Bottom banding with pom-pom trim finishes this custom creation. *Decorating Den Interiors, Barbara Elliott and Jennifer Ward Woods, Stone Mountain, GA., www.decoratingden.com*

DecoratingDen.com

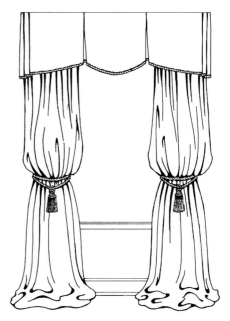

A box pleated valance tops Bishop sleeve panels accented with tassels.

Color-blocked drapery panels with button accents complement the inverted box pleated valance.

Right: With tails approximately five inches lower than the center, this valance is well constructed and stylish. Note, too, that the fabric is picked up in accent pillows, a common but delightful design trick. *Fabritec LLC., www. fabritecdesigns.com*

Bottom Right: A simple box pleated valance is perfect for this small area. *Decorating Den Interiors, Design by Jeanne Sallee, photo by Jeff Sanders, www.decoratingden. com*

Opposite page: A pretty pencil pleated cloud valance with billowing folds enhance this luxurious sunroom. Long wooden beads alternating in black and white is an elegant contrast.
Decorating Den Interiors, www.decoratingden.com

DraperyAvenue.com

Kingston valance with subtle color-matched banding, tassel trim, and bishop sleeve tiebacks make a stunning breakfast nook. *Designed and made by Custom Drapery Workroom, Inc., www.draperyavenue.com*

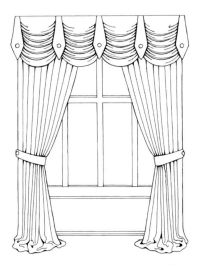

An Austrian valance with buttoned jabots. Drapery panels with matching fabric tiebacks puddle onto the floor.

Arched Austrian valance with stationary panels.

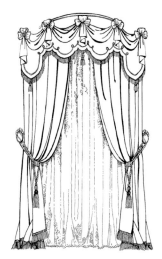

Tassel fringed Kingston valance with rosettes over tieback draperies.

I love it when designers create new custom window coverings. This hybrid relaxed cloud/balloon valance, with ribbon tape trim tabs in between each swoop, is a good example. *Willow Drapery & Upholstery. Designer: Leigh Anderson, Glenview, IL., www.willowglenview.com. Photographer: Dennis Jourdan Photography & Video, Inc, Buffalo Grove, IL., www.DJphoto.com*

A top treatment with a lot of detail, from the graceful curves to the jabot pleats to the detailed rosettes. *Decorating Den Interiors, www.decoratingden.com*

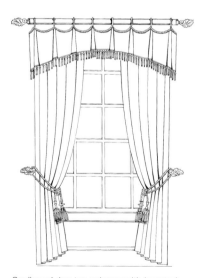

Scalloped ring top valance with inverted pleats and tied-back panels.

Pleated valance with swags and rosettes over tied-back draperies with rosettes.

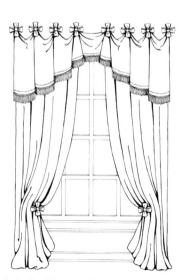

Arched soft inverted box pleated valance with Maltese crosses and bullion trim. Note matching Maltese holdbacks.

DecoratingDen.com

Queen Ann style valance with jabots work perfectly in the bay window. Note how the jabots/tails line up with the bay angles. Piping along the top of the valance adds extra detail. *Decorating Den Interiors, www.decoratingden.com*

Valance & drapery combinations

Tassel fringed Kingston valance with rosettes over tieback draperies.

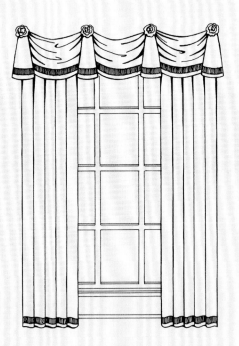

An open Kingston valance works perfectly with flanking stationary drapery panels.

Valance & drapery combinations

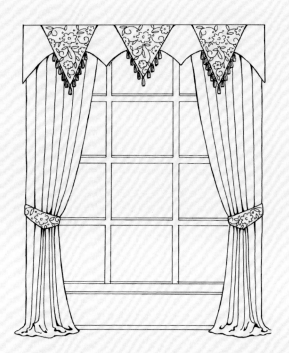

A soft cornice with flags pulls the eye up with the contrast fabric. Note that the drapery panels have matching contrast fabric tiebacks.

An offset arched non-pleated valance with a triangle flag is an unusual twist. Pleated stationary panels complete the treatment.

Valance & drapery combinations

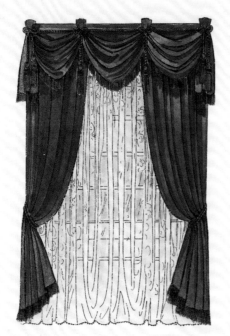 

Empire valance top treatment adorned with bullion fringe and rope tassels over sheers
and tieback pleated draperies.

Arched swag style valance with rosettes and jabot accents. Simple side panels with
bullion fringe along the hemline keeps the eye focused on the beauty of the arch.

Valance & drapery combinations

Gracefully arched soft cornice valance with accent welting and cascades over puddled tieback draperies with rosettes.

Arched wide swag style valance with cascades, center jabot, and rosettes.

Valance & drapery combinations

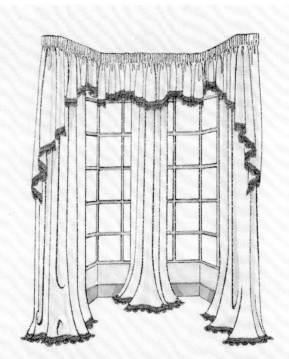 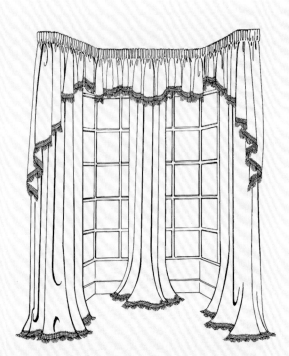

A scalloped pencil pleated valance enhances the shape of the bay window and hides the hardware for the stationary drapery panels.

 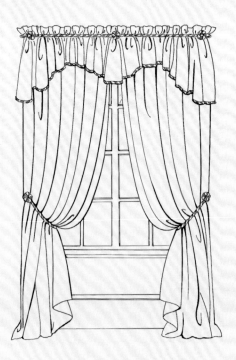

Double arched gathered valance with decorative rope and ties and coordinating trim make a simple but elegant treatment.

Valance & drapery combinations

A rod pocket valance with cascades top simply pleated, traversing drapery panels. Brush fringe is a terrific, eye-catching accent.

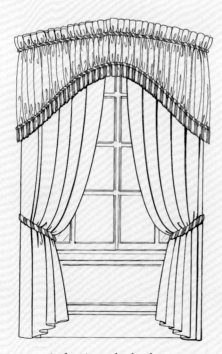

A classic arched valance creates a comfortable country style window treatment.

Valance & drapery combinations

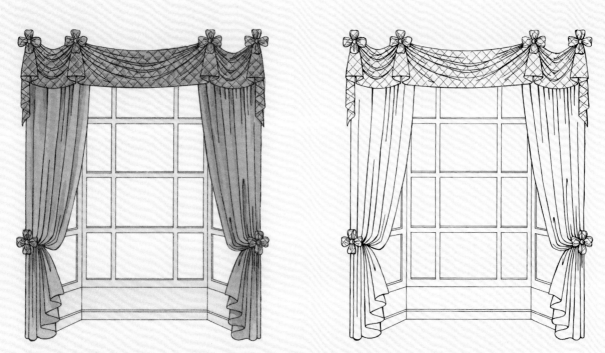

This graceful treatment is created by using a non-pleated valance and adding Maltese cross jabots and ties.

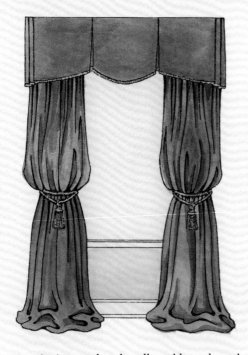 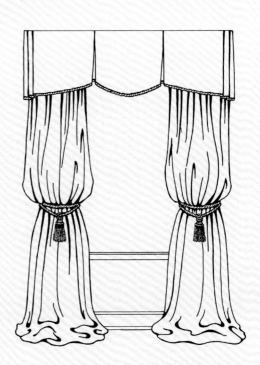

An inverted and scalloped box pleated valance tops Bishop sleeve panels accented with tassels.

Valance & drapery combinations

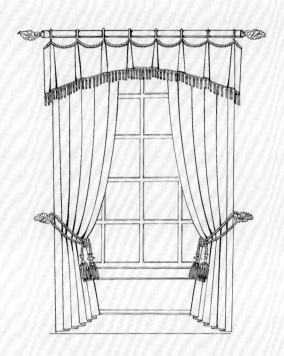 

A scalloped ring top space pleated valance edged with small tassel fringe complements the pleated drapery panels—which can easily be released from their holdbacks to provide privacy.

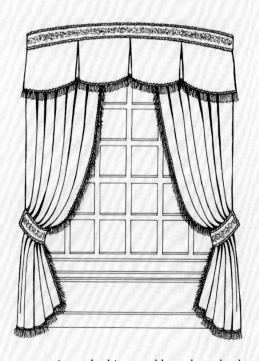 

An arched inverted box pleated valance edged with brush fringe, paired with pleated, matching drapery panels.

Valance & drapery combinations

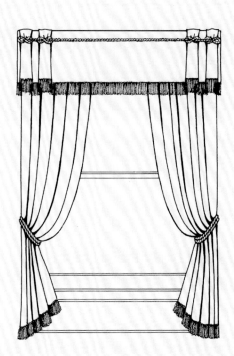

A soft cornice with simple side pleats enhanced with bullion fringe and tiebacks.

A deep goblet pleated top treatment works perfectly in this bay window with flanking, stationary drapery panels.

Valance & drapery combinations

An arched box pleated valance with bullion fringe over tied back draperies with rope ties.

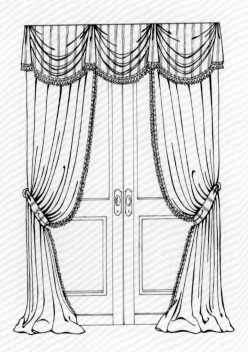

Kingston valance with tassel fringe over pleated and puddled draperies with fabric tiebacks.

Pleated valance styles

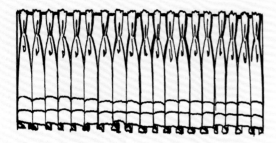 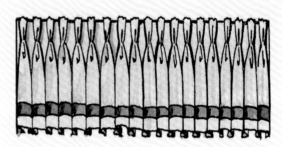

A simple pinch pleated valance with banding

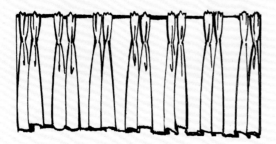 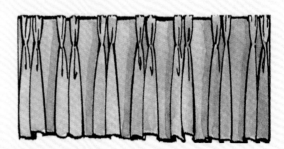

Double pinch pleat

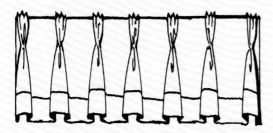 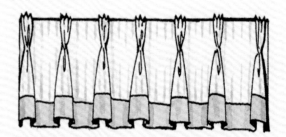

Space pleated valance with bottom banding

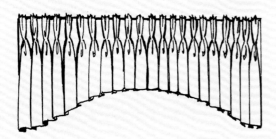 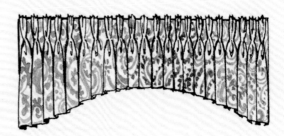

Arched pleated valance

Pleated valance styles

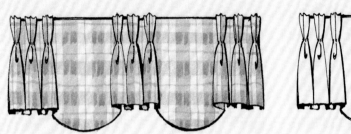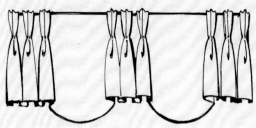

Space pleated Queen Ann valance with three pleats and scalloped bottom

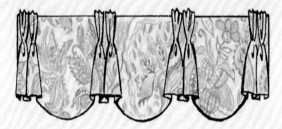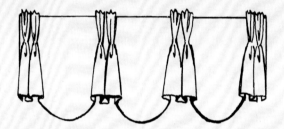

Double pleated Queen Ann

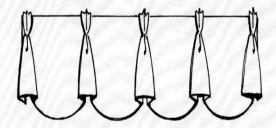

Queen Ann valance

Queen Ann valance with extra wide space in the middle with rope accent and fringe

Rod pocket/gathered valance styles

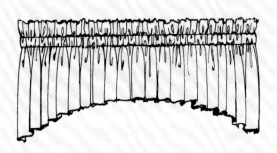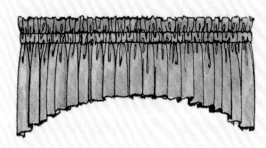

Arched rod pocket valance

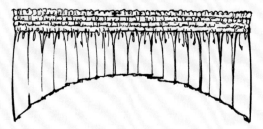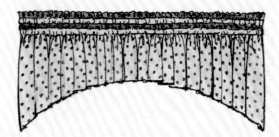

Arched shirred heading valance

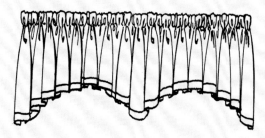

Multiple arched rod pocket valance

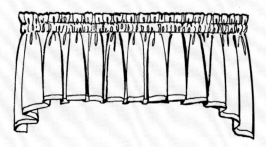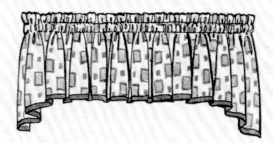

Rod pocket with arched valance

Rod pocket/gathered valance styles

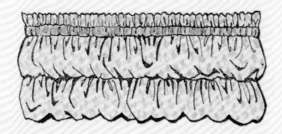
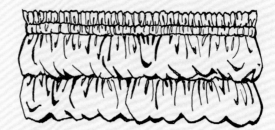

Double cloud rod pocket valance

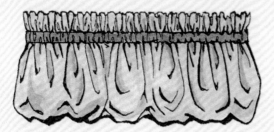
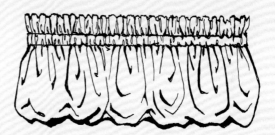

Cloud valance with rod pocket heading

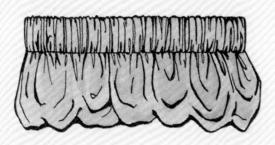

Rod pocket cloud valance

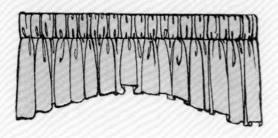
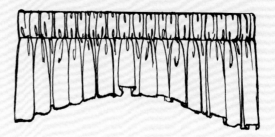

Arched rod pocket

Specialty valance styles

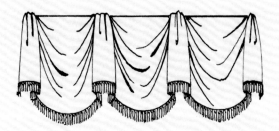

The elegant Kingston valance

Open Kingston valance on decorative rod

Louis XV valance

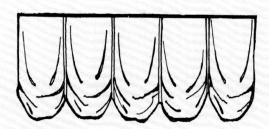

Balloon valance with matching welting

Specialty valance styles

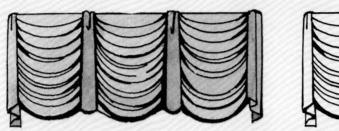

Austrian valance with jabots

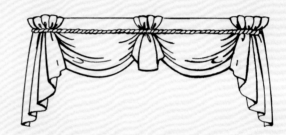

Murphy valance

Bordeaux valance

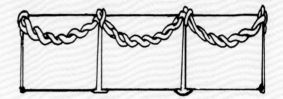

Inverted box pleated valance with twisted cording

Outside mounted balloon valance

Balloon & Cloud Valances

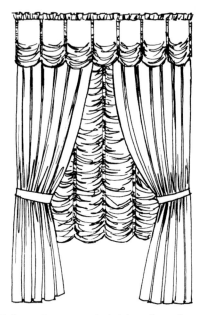

Balloon valance over pleated draperies and Austrian shade.

This valance has large, inverted pleats that create a more tailored effect than a cloud valance. It can stand alone or cover undertreatments; it's soft and pretty poufs add a feminine touch.

Yardage *(including Balloon or Cloud valance)*

Without pattern repeat:

Step 1 – Width of valance + RT (returns) x 2.5 ÷ width of fabric = number of fabric widths required (round up to whole number).

Step 2a – Valance length + 16" for HH (heading and hems) x widths required ÷ 36 = yardage

With pattern repeat:

Step 2b – Valance length + 16" for HH ÷ pattern repeat = number of repeats required (round up the whole number)

Step 2c – Number of repeats required x pattern repeat = CL (cut length)

Step 2d – Number of widths, (from step 1), x CL (from step 2c) ÷ 36 = yardage with pattern repeat (round up to the whole number)

Things to Consider

> Width, length and color of the lining
> Placement: inside, outside, or ceiling mounted
> Size of returns and mounting: board or rod?

Special Notes

1. For valances shorter than 16", a functional balloon that can be raised to the correct height is recommended.
2. See page 90 for detailed calculating terms

Box Pleated Valance

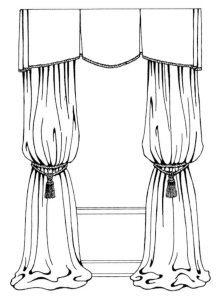

Box pleated valance over Bishop sleeve panels.

Contrast lined inverted box pleated valance.

Crisp and tailored, this top treatment lends itself well to pairings with many different kinds of under-treatments, both hard and soft.

Yardage *(including Box Pleated, Inverted Box Pleated)*

Without pattern repeat:

Step 1 – BFW (board face width) + 6" or 12" for RT (returns) x 2.5 ÷ width of fabric = number of widths required (round up to whole number) Step 2a – FL (finished length) + 8" for HH headings and hems) x widths required ÷ 36 = yardage (round up to the whole number)

Step 2a – FL (finished length) x 2 + 6" for HH (headings and hems) x widths required ÷ 36 = yardage (round up to whole number)

With pattern repeat

Step 2b – FL (finished length) + 8" for HH ÷ pattern repeat = the number of repeats required (round up to the whole number).

Step 2c – Number of repeats x pattern repeat = CL (cut length).

Step 2d – Number of widths (from step 1) x CL (from 2c) ÷ 36 = yardage with pattern repeat (round up to the whole number)

Things to Consider

> Width, length and returns
> Contrast fabric color if "open throat" (as shown above)

Special Notes

1. A check measure and installation are strongly recommended.
2. Pleats are sized to window and pattern usually 5" to 16".
3. See page 102 for detailed calculating terms

Mock Roman valance.

Mock Roman Valance

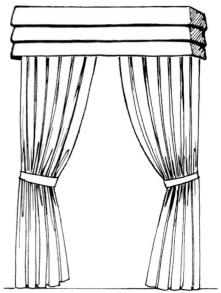

Mock Roman valance over tieback panels.

This top treatment suggests the look of a Roman Shade, yet it cannot be raised or lowered. A variety of decorative trims or contrasting bands can be employed to create interest.

Yardage

Without pattern repeat:

Step 1 – BFW (board face width) + 6" or 12" for RT (returns) + 4" ÷ width of fabric = number of widths required (round up to the whole number)

Step 2a – FL (finished length) x 2 + 6" for HH (headings and hems) x widths required ÷ 36 = yardage (round up to whole number).

With pattern repeat:

Step 2b – FL (finished length) x 2 + 6" for HH ÷ pattern repeat = number of repeats required (round up to the whole number)

Step 2c – Number of repeats x pattern repeat = CL (cut length)

Step 2d – Number of widths (from step 1) x CL (from 2c) ÷ 36 = yardage with pattern repeat (round up to the whole number).

Things to Consider

> Width, length, the color of the lining, and returns
> Inside or outside mount

Special Notes

1. See page 90 for detailed calculating terms

Pinch Pleated Valance

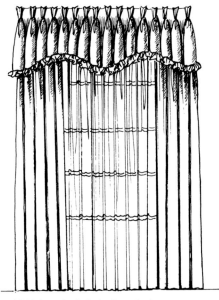

Multiple arched pinch pleated valance over draperies and sheers.

Color blocked French pleated valances. *Decorating Den Interiors, Kathie Golson, Orlando, FL., www.decoratingden.com*

The French pleated valance is the most common top treatment. It can be arched on top or bottom for additional interest.

Yardage *(Including French, Euro, Fan, Smocked, Box, and arched)*

Without pattern repeat:

Step 1 – RFW (rod face width) + 6" or 12" for RT (returns) x 3 ÷width of fabric = number of widths required (round up to whole number)

Step 2a – FL (finished length) from longest point + 16" for HH (headings and hems) x widths required ÷ 36 = yardage (round up to the whole number)

With pattern repeat:

Step 2b – FL (finished length) from longest point + 16" for HH ÷ pattern repeat = number of repeats required (round up to the whole number)

Step 2c – Number of repeats x pattern repeat = CL (cut length)

Step 2d – Number of widths (from step 1) x CL (from 2c) ÷ 36 = yardage with pattern repeat (round up to the whole number).

Things to Consider

> Width and returns
> Longest point, shortest point and mid-point
> Standup or no standup, type of rod

Special Notes

1. A check measure and installation are strongly recommended.
2. Use a hook and loop fastener for shirred headings.
3. See page 90 for detailed calculating terms

Top Treatments: **Cornices**

JCandlerDesign.com

Whether alone or as an accompaniment to an existing window treatment, cornices can be a wonderful addition to any home decor. Though they are a permanent window treatment usually installed snugly next to a window frame, a cornice box is anything but sedentary.

Situated atop a tall window, an intricately carved cornice box can transport the room to a time when kings and queens lived in opulence. Conversely, a shaped cornice above a child's window (page 207, for example), adorned with a favorite animal or icon, can contribute to a playful theme in a big way.

Upholstered cornices provide a classic topping for windows of any size, making an excellent overtreatment for draperies, vertical blinds, or sheer shadings. The cornice is constructed of a wooden frame that is padded and upholstered in a decorative fabric and usually finished with piping on the top and bottom edges.

These Moroccan inspired lambrequins are a perfect choice for this two-story breakfast nook. Note the abundant floor pillow seating in keeping with Moroccan dining tradition. Motorized flat Roman shades in aqua add the final flair to this enchanted space. Private residence, Bel Air, California, Jeanne Candler Design, *www.jcandlerdesign.com,* Photo: Charles Randall

This Moorish inspired cornice, coupled with multiple sheer treatments, is a visual delight. With 18-foot ceilings, this was a treatment that needed to pull out all the stops. Taking inspiration from engravings of the Victorian era)there was a proclivity toward Moorish design in that period, six and a half foot wide by seven-foot-high cornices, covered in subtle iridescent silk, designed to anchor the room). Two layers of sheers come down from behind the cornices. *Marcye Philbrook, Marcye Philbrook Design Studio, photograph by Marcye Philbrook*

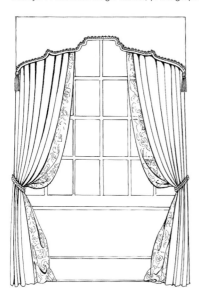

A padded, upholstered cornice with unique detailing is the perfect foil for double drapery panels.

StitchAboveTheRest.com

Two-story bay windows covered with a custom one-piece cornice box. The bay window is seventeen feet wide with one-hundred and fifty-degree angles. What makes this design so attractive is the elimination of butting corners that would have been necessary with three cornices. The cornice box was mounted halfway up the wall to provide a cozier feeling. Underneath are three drapery panels, made of the same fabric and tied back with custom tassel holdbacks that coordinate with the small key tassels hanging off the ends of the cornice — trimmed in black and ivory cord shaped into circular decorative designs at each end. *Design by Elizabeth Gerdes, Stitch Above the Rest, Woodstock, GA., www.stitchabovetherest.com Photography by Woodie Williams.*

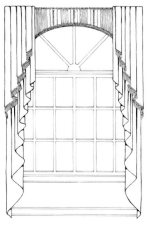

Arched cornice box with double pleated cascades; note trim on cornice box and outer cascades.

Multi jumbo welting creates this arched custom designer cornice box. Cord and tassels over stationary panels finish this treatment beautifully. A one of a kind window treatment.

Bishop sleeve draperies with thickly braided ties and arched cornice follow the window shape without masking it.

An asymmetrical upholstered cornice with bold upholstered hold-back exhibits stunning workmanship. *Decorating Den Interiors, Design by Barbara Elliott/Jennifer Ward Woods, photo by Jeff Sanders, www.decoratingden.com*

Upholstered silk taffeta cornice with crystal
chandelier beads swaged across. Silk formed
rosette at top. *Willow Drapery & Upholstery.*
Designer: Leigh Anderson, Glenview, IL.,
www.willowglenview.com. Photographer:
Barry Rustin Photography, Wilmette, IL.,
www.barryrustinphotography.com

GailaniDesigns.com

These tall narrow windows are covered in elegant sheer panels and topped with curved cornices. These custom designed cornices have LED lights installed in two rows: the top row creates a reflective curve on the ceiling, and the lower row directs light onto the draperies. Light dimmers were used to allow the homeowner to create the desired ambiance. *Susan Gailani, ASID Allied, Gailani Designs Inc., www.gailanidesigns.com*

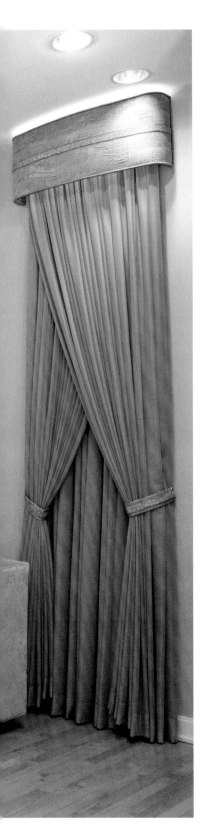

Above: A beautiful wood cornice, intricately carved, emphasizes the bay window and houses the mounting hardware for the classic swag and tail top treatment, as well as the fabric/vane privacy treatment. *Rainbow Woods Inc.*

Elaborately detailed real wood cornice with stationary panels puddled and trimmed.

Contoured and detailed real wood cornice over puddled drapery panels with holdbacks.

Straight cornice box in black velvet with silver nailhead trim and matching dining room chairs: a beautiful modern masterpiece. *Designed and made by Custom Drapery Workroom Inc., www.draperyavenue.com*

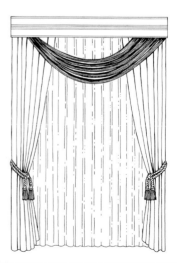

A straight cornice with banding and welting houses all the hardware needed for hanging the sheer under drapery, side panels, and single swag.

A shaped cornice with a black fabric bottom makes an interesting design. The matching banding on the leading edge of the drapery and the matching welting on the headboard make a wonderful custom design. *Decorating Den Interiors, Bohnne Jones, Nashville, TN., photographer Reed Brown, www.decoratingden.com*

DecoratingDen.com

On this sweeping window wall, trillion-shaped chocolate brown upholstered cornices encase lengthy drapery panels. Pleated shades installed in the lower bank offer privacy when needed. *Decorating Den Interiors, Design by Barbara Elliot & Jennifer Ward Woods, www.decoratingden.com*

Flip-top stationary draperies cascade over the top of upholstered cornices, accentuated with delicate passementerie. *Decorating Den Interiors, Design by Alisa Lankenau/Heidi Sowatsky, St. Louis, MO., photo by Bob Hill, www.decoratingden.com*

Intricate cornices, lush swags, and Bishop sleeved drapery panels make for an unforgettable treatment.

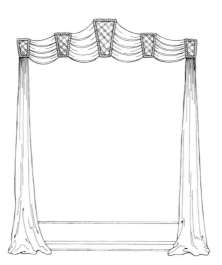

Upholstered trillion-shaped cornices accentuate the view; swagged fabric in between boxes softens, while the puddled drapery adds the final touch.

Trillion-shaped cornices at top and bottom flank the doorway and hold the single swag at the top.

Left: Huge yellow tassels on the sheer drapery treatments are designed to play off the large floral motifs and tie in with the wall color.
Decorating Den Interiors, www.decoratingden.com

Right: To cover the off-center arched windows, designer Charla Traugot used ceiling to floor lambrequins and added twenty-inch depth to the design. This stroke of genius design decision allowed for a small faux dressing room and puppet stage to encourage the child's imagination to run wild. Crystal pullbacks added some "bling" to this magical window treatment. *Decorating Den Interiors, Charla Traugot, www.decoratingden.com*

Left: An awning valance in pink and cream trellis pattern ties in perfectly with the look of the room. The trellis pattern flows over the edge and into the pennant edging, creating a youthful fun look.
Decorating Den Interiors, Terri Ervin, Dacula, GA., www.decoratingden.com

Right: The focal point of the room is the crib and the dramatic statement of a circus tent surrounding it. In a variation from the traditional red of a circus tent, a burnt orange stripe as the drapery panels under a geometric print crowns the cornice. Metal curved tiebacks add the finishing touch as well as a safety application. This wonderful space is the child's first window to the world.
Decorating Den Interiors, Abby Connell, Mason, OH., www.decoratingden.com

Cornices & lambrequins

An arched quilted cornice box is mirrored on the deep bottom hem of the pleated draperies.

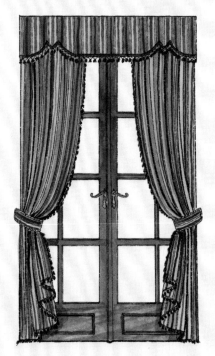 

Vertically striped drapery panels coordinate well with a matching, upholstered cornice and horizontally striped fabric tiebacks crafted from the same fabric.

Cornices & lambrequins

Sometimes the fabric pattern will help in choosing the cornice box design. Note the checkered pattern is lined up with the sides of this custom shaped cornice.

Stationary drapery panels puddle slightly on the floor. An upholstered cornice with unique detailing is the perfect foil for color-blocked drapery panels.

Cornices & lambrequins

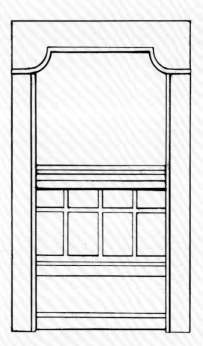

Lambrequin with welt edge over a flat Roman shade.

Shirred full-length lambrequin over pleated draperies.

Cornices & lambrequins

Horizontally striped fabric cornice plays off the vertically striped and plain fabrics.

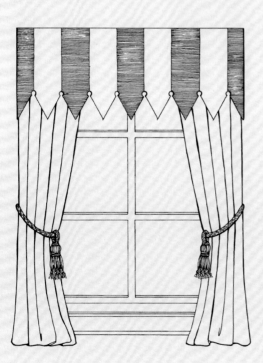 

Wide striped fabric adds an interesting touch to this deep custom cornice box. Finished with cord tassel tiebacks.

Cornices & lambrequins

A large arched upholstered cornice with matching trillion-shaped cornices showcase this large window as well as hold small swags and Bishop sleeve drapery panels.

Upholstered trillion-shaped cornices accentuate the view; swagged fabric in between vertically softens, puddled drapery enhances the design.

Cornices & lambrequins

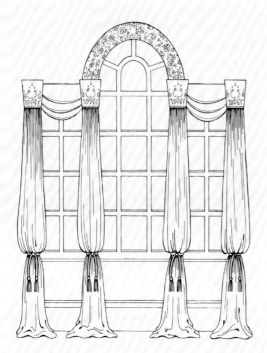 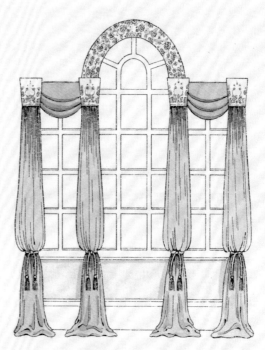

A variation of the treatment on the opposing page. Note that by changing a few elements, one can have a totally custom window covering.

Trillion-shaped cornices at top and bottom flank the doorway and hold a single swag at the top and the shirred vertical fabric treatments.

Cornice shapes, styles & embellishments

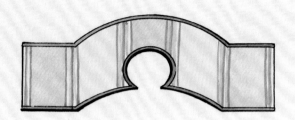

Arched cornice with a circular center.

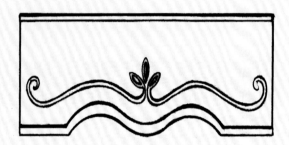

Cornice with accent welting and custom appliqué.

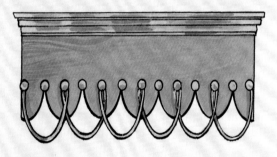
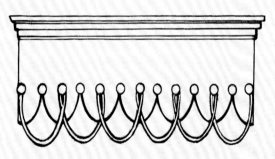

Wood top cornice box with gilded top and rope tassels.

Wood top designer gilded cornice.

Cornice shapes, styles & embellishments

Cornice box with large rope top and custom appliqué.

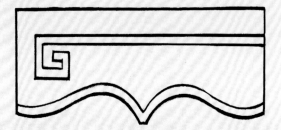 

Cornice box with custom banding.

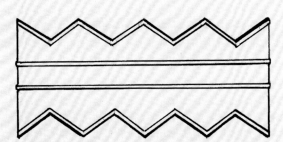 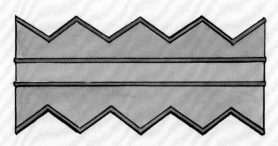

Chevron top and bottom cornice.

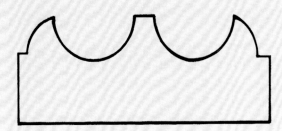 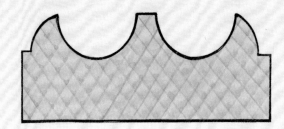

Pagoda top cornice box.

Cornice shapes, styles & embellishments

Arched cornice with fabric ruffles.

Custom design cornice with bottom ruffle.

 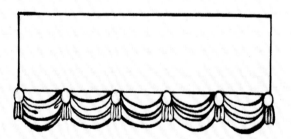

Straight cornice with small swags and buttons.

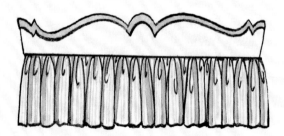 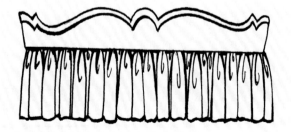

Shaped crown cornice with gathered valance.

Cornice shapes, styles & embellishments

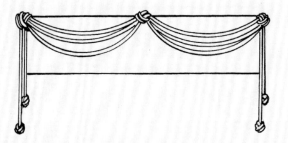
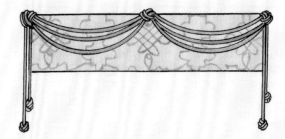

Straight cornice with ropes and knots.

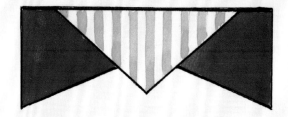

Multi fabric chevron cornice box.

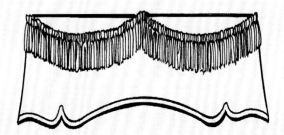
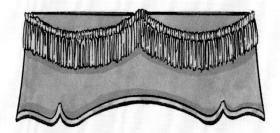

Pagoda cornice box with heavy bullion fringe.

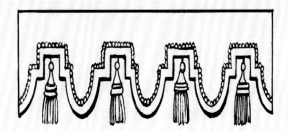
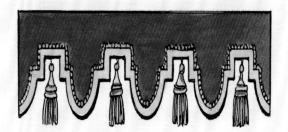

Shaped cornice with large tassels.

Cornice shapes, styles & embellishments

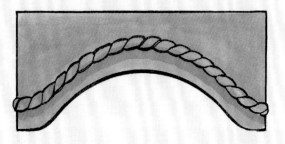
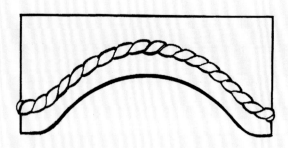

Arched cornice with large twisted rope.

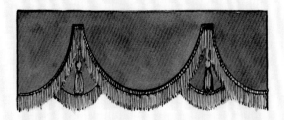
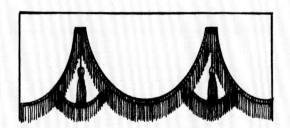

Shaped cornice with bullion fringe.

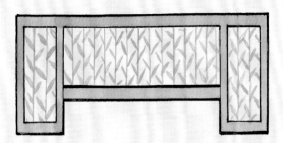
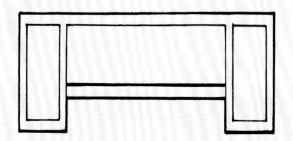

Custom shaped cornice with short side drops.

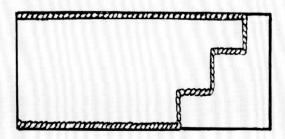

Multi-fabric cornice with rope design.

Cornice shapes, styles & embellishments

Sunburst pleated cornice.

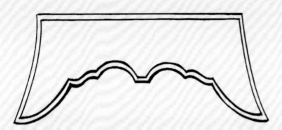
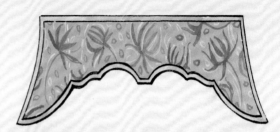

Custom shaped pagoda-style cornice.

Straight bottom cornice with a custom shaped crown.

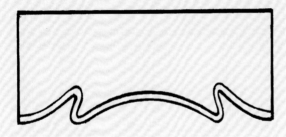

Custom shaped cornice with coordinating banding.

Cornice shapes, styles & embellishments

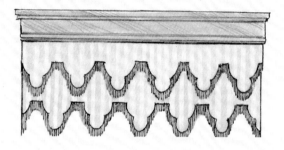
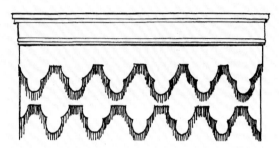

Double rows of fringe with a real wooden crown.

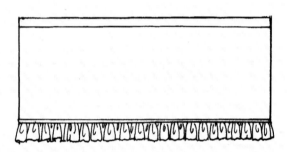

Cornice box with banding on the top and a ruffle on the bottom.

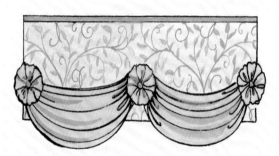
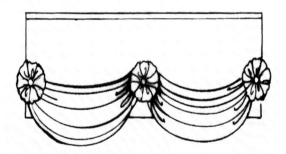

Cornice box with swag and rosettes.

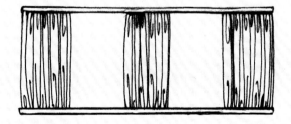

Cornice box with alternating shirred and flat fabric.

Cornice shapes, styles & embellishments

 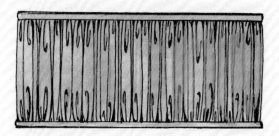

Shirred cornice box with jumbo welting.

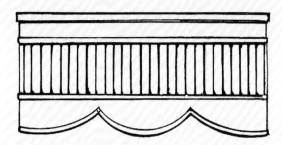 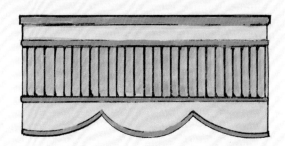

Cornice box with pleated fabric in the middle.

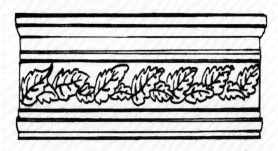 

Real wood cornice with painted leaf design.

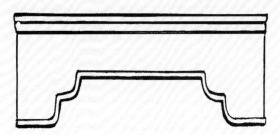 

Cornice with wood header and wallpapered front and sides.

Cornice shapes, styles & embellishments

Straight wood painted cornice with a stenciled design.

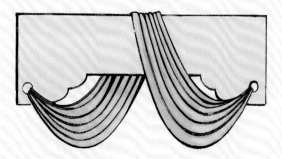
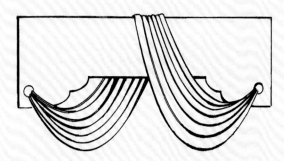

Cornice with over and under swags.

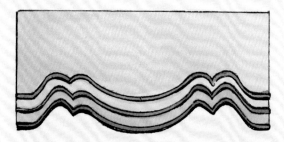
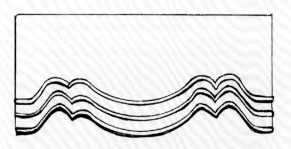

Cornice with double shaped and raised banding.

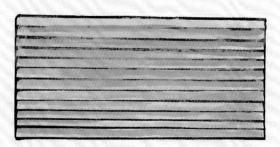

Cornice with horizontal pleating.

Cornice shapes, styles & embellishments

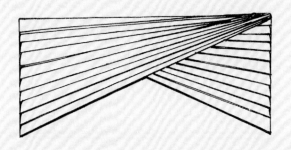

Cornice with diagonally arched pleating.

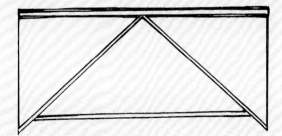
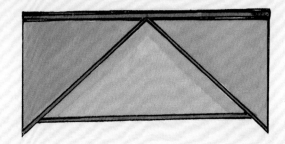

Cornice with unique angled welting.

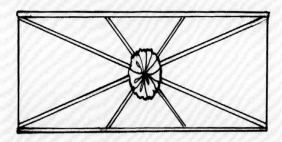
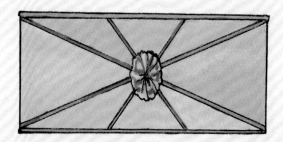

Straight cornice with diagonal welts and center rosette.

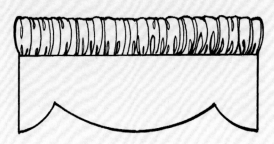
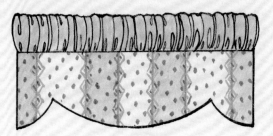

Cornice with rounded gathered top and large scalloped bottom.

Cornice shapes, styles & embellishments

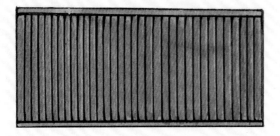
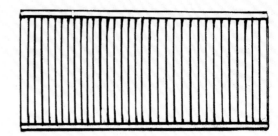

Cornice box with one-inch pleats.

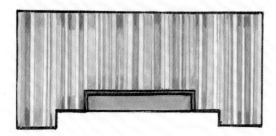
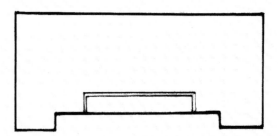

Cornice box with coordinating fabric insert.

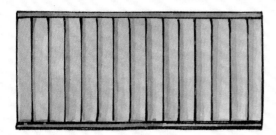
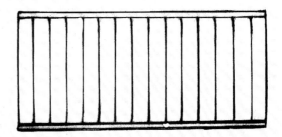

Cornice box with two-inch vertical pleats.

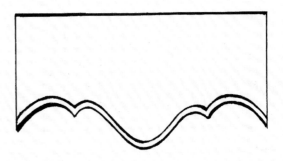

Custom shaped cornice box with coordinating welting.

Cornice shapes, styles & embellishments

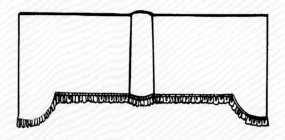 

Custom shaped cornice box with coordinating welting.

Cornice box with a shirred bottom.

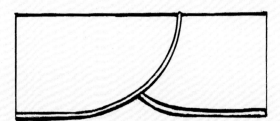 

Custom shaped cornice box with welting.

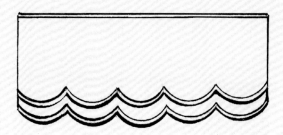 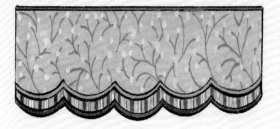

Scalloped bottom with coordinating fabric and welting.

Lambrequin shapes

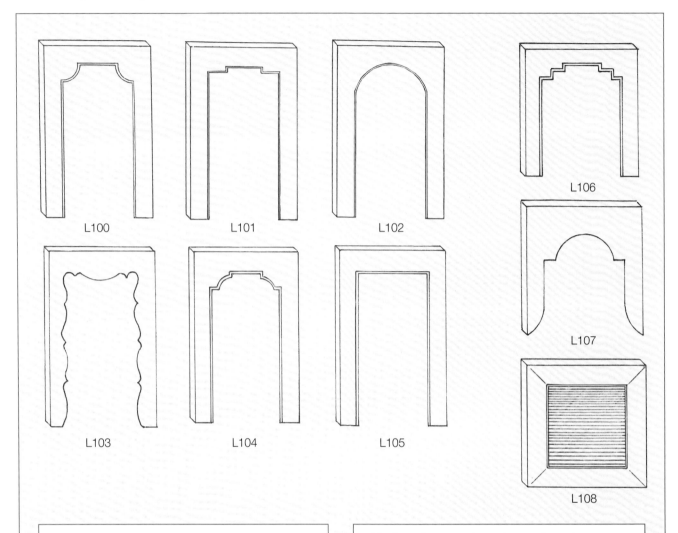

L100 L101 L102 L106

L103 L104 L105 L107

L108

Things to consider

- Width
- Color of lining
- Return
- Length: shortest + longest points
- Fabric details

Special notes

1. A check measure and installation are strongly recommended.
2. Off center prints may create an unbalanced effect, so choose fabric carefully.

Yardage for non-pleated or gathered Cornice boxes only (opposite page). For Lambrequins (above) please consult a professional drapery workroom.

Style	Width		
	48" to 84"	84" to 120"	120" to 144"
Tailored	2 yards	3 yards	3.5 yards
Scallop	2 yards	3 yards	3.5 yards

Cornice box shapes

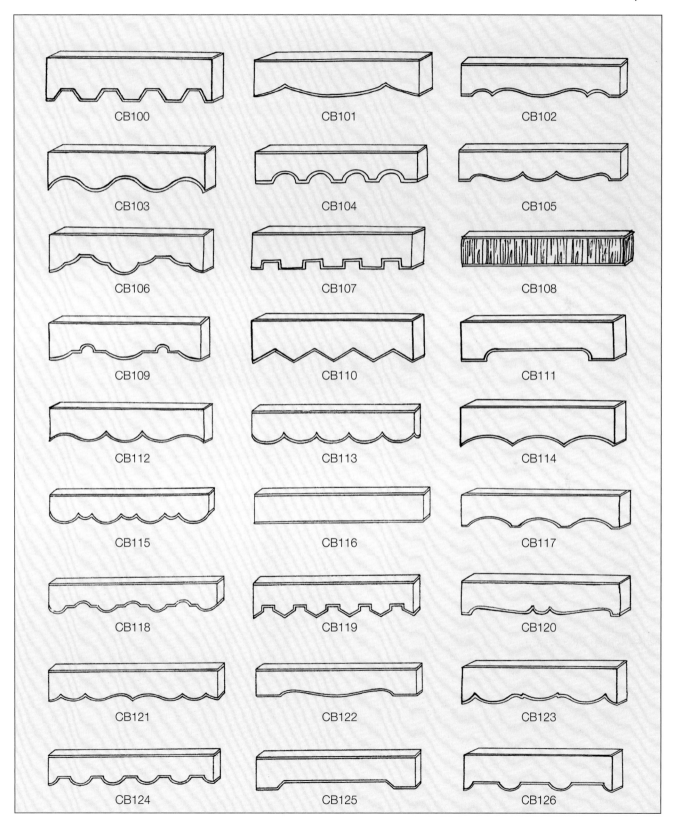

CB100

CB101

CB102

CB103

CB104

CB105

CB106

CB107

CB108

CB109

CB110

CB111

CB112

CB113

CB114

CB115

CB116

CB117

CB118

CB119

CB120

CB121

CB122

CB123

CB124

CB125

CB126

SHADES: MODERN & FABRIC

Alone or as dramatic accompaniment to other window treatments, shades come in all shapes and configurations.

Modern Shades, also known as "hard" shades, such as honeycomb, roller, solar, and woven woods, are capable of fitting into awkward areas and inaccessible windows, like skylights, and sometimes used as unique room dividers.

Fabric Shades, also known as "soft" shades, are clean-edged and neat and can take a back seat to beautiful architectural details when up and out of the way or add stunning emphasis. They are typically an economical alternative to draperies, providing the beauty of fabric with less volume of yardage. In areas where full-length draperies are not practical, shades are ultimately suited.

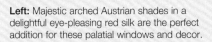

Left: Majestic arched Austrian shades in a delightful eye-pleasing red silk are the perfect addition for these palatial windows and decor.

This very formal Kingston treatment with an Austrian shade underneath displays gorgeous tassel trim punctuated with gold studs along the trim edge.

History in the Making

As you may have suspected, shades have long been known for their function — to protect the home from damaging solar heat and to provide privacy. At first appearing as a piece of fabric stretched over various wooden frames, which was attached to the window and was sometimes hinged. Evolving into custom constructed draped fabric, the shade pulled up and out of the way with a simple cord system, then progressed to the popular Austrian shade, among others. The eighteenth-century witnessed the invention of the roll-up shade, as well as the Roman shade, with its unique operating system offering folds of fabric from stiff to graceful. Flat shades of that time, such as the roll-up shade, were decorated with painted scenes and florals. Since then, shades have been a popular part of our interior spaces.

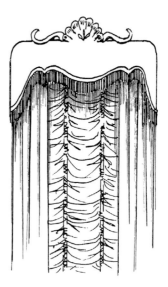

Austrian shades were popular window coverings in the Rococo period. A trimmed Cornice box with faux shell crown tops this elegant window treatment.

Left: A traditional Empire valance in lavish gold silk complements the Austrian shade beautifully. Add gorgeous tassel trim punctuated with gold studs along the trim edge, and you have a window treatment masterpiece. While not for just any home, this quasi-period-piece is picture-perfect in its execution of detail.

Today's Shades

Today, there are so many shade choices, it's astonishing. From roller shades to honeycomb (cellular) to pleated to woven wood to fabric, there's a shade to fit almost any window. One must first determine whether one wants a Modern shade or a Fabric shade. Modern shades are categorized as: pleated, honeycomb, woven wood, sheer shadings, roller, or solar shades. Fabric shades are constructed from drapery fabric, or in rare cases, upholstery fabrics. Look over both sections of this chapter: Modern Shades & Fabrics Shades to quickly see which style appeals to you. Consider your options, analyze your needs, and plan how you want your new shade to fit into your décor.

Below: Semi-sheer fabric makes a unique flat fold Roman shade, allowing the sweeping view to filter through while shielding furnishings from UV rays. This modern shade is more about enhancing décor rather than providing privacy.

Specialty fan shade with banding and chevron top. If privacy is important, then shade should be longer than the window to hide the light gaps.

Modern Shades: **Sheer Shadings**

Pirouette® Window Shadings *by Hunter Douglas, www.hunterdouglas.com*

The Facts: **Modern Shades**

Advantages: Top-down/Bottom-up features in most applications add to their flexibility, such as in areas like bathrooms and bedrooms. They can work in difficult spaces such as skylights, angled windows, arched windows, and more. The cordless option is usually the best option for convenience and safety. Shades are available for inside or outside mount, and multiple shades can be installed on one headrail.

Disadvantages: Most Modern shades, when closed (except for sheer shadings), cannot manipulate how much light enters the room. Check with your window decorating professional for details. Some archtop shades are stationary; woven wood shades are not private unless they have a privacy backing.

Cost: It can vary widely depending upon the type of shade selected. Roller shades are still the least expensive type of shade.

Lifespan: Ten years or more. Technology has vastly improved the mechanisms.

Most Appropriate Locations: Just about any window in your home.

Care & Cleaning: Depending upon the type, good judgment must be used. Always check manufacturers' cleaning suggestions.

Good to Know: Modern Shades

What's right for your design situation? Here's a look at your options:

Modern Shades

Accordion: see Pleated

Cellular: see Honeycomb

Sheer Shadings: Most of these products are better known by their brand names: Silhouette®, Luminette® and Shangri-La®, but also by generic names such as Zebra and Banded, to name a few. In basic terms, they are vanes between which fabric has been suspended. Closed, these products look like regular shades; open, they look like strips of fabric magically levitating across the window. With the treatment in a closed position but with the vanes rotated open, they filter the light, thus allowing more control than other shades.

Honeycomb: Named after the cellular shape of the comb of the honeybee, honeycomb shades are a flexible, forgiving material that will accommodate unusually shaped windows. With the option of single, double, or triple honeycomb, these cells trap air, making them perfect for homes requiring sound and thermal insulation. Best, they can be installed either horizontally or vertically, and

Zebra/Banded shades have recently become very popular.

are available in a variety of material weights, from sheer to complete light blockage. Honeycombs are available in a variety of sizes: from 3/8" to three inches.

Matchstick Shade: Like woven wood and grass shades. Horizontally placed sticks of toothpick-thin bamboo are woven together and then will fold up in pleats like a hobbled Roman shade or operate as a standard flat shade. Better used in a sun porch area where the issue of sun filtering, rather than privacy, is most important.

Mesh: Synthetic materials of various densities of weave and color options offer a high-tech look. Typically, a roll-up, these shades can be motorized to add to their futuristic appeal.

Pleated: A single layer of sturdy fabric with crisp pleats that fold up like an accordion when raised and offer a slight zigzag look when closed. Fabrics can range from sheer to opaque, and the pleats are usually one to four inches. Also known as accordion shades.

Roller: Vinyl or fabric, this shade is operated with a spring or clutch system that rolls up into a tube when open. Today, there are many options to add individual design flourishes to the bottom, including lace, fringe, and decorative pulls. Available in sheer, designer light filtering fabrics, and blackout. There have been improvements made throughout the years, and the clumsy mechanisms of the past have been replaced with the capability for precise positioning with zero snapbacks. Decorative valances to hide the top of the roller are now commonplace.

Solar: A spectacular tool to control the harmful rays of the sun, solar shades filter and diffuse bright sunlight without sacrificing your view of the outdoors. A downside is that most solar shades are not meant to offer privacy, so they are best used in conjunction with another treatment, such as draperies if privacy is important to you.

Woven Woods: Beautiful blends of wood, bamboo, reeds, and grasses make woven shades a natural, warm choice. Many require more stacking space than the thinner honeycomb and pleated shades. Banding options add a beautiful finishing touch. Request a privacy backing if you want them to do more than filter light. See also Matchstick blinds.

Silhouette® Window Shadings by Hunter Douglas, *www.hunterdouglas.com*

Left: Sheer Shadings are an excellent choice for angled windows and French doors. Motorization recommended for high windows.

Above: I love the bold red color used in this window decor. Add some matching pillows and art, and you have a pleasant modern style. *www.hunterdouglas.com*

Right: Sheer shading is the perfect window treatment for those who prefer clean, modern lines. *www.hunterdouglas.com*

Pirouette® Window Shadings, Fabric: Satin, Color: Champagne

Modern Shades: **Woven Woods**

SmithandNoble.com

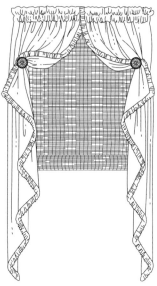

Rod pocket curtains held back with medallions, over woven wood shade. *Custom rendering by DreamDraper® design software, www.dreamdraper.com; © 2009 Evan Marsh Designs, Inc.*

Above left: Top-down/bottom-up woven wood shade with small wood valance. *Smith+Noble, www.smithandnoble.com*

Below left: Flat fold Roman shades in a top-down/bottom-up style are a brilliant solution for hard to treat French doors. The natural tones are a complementary shoo-in — perfect for blending with woodwork.

Below right: A woven wood shade with green contrast fabric banding is a natural beauty.

HunterDouglas.com

Woven wood shades in a Roman fold style are the height of fashion in this modern style living area where privacy is not an issue. *www.hunterdouglas.com*

Above: Woven wood shades can cover large expanses of window with relative ease.

Left: The basketweave texture on this tabbed hem roller shade enhances the natural decor and complements the wood finial and metal rod accent. The rod accent is a means to draw the shade without touching the shade material (and thus possibly dirtying the fabric through repeated handling). *Smith+Noble, www.smithandnoble.com*

Below: Scarf valance over woven wood shade. *Custom rendering by DreamDraper® design software, www.dreamdraper.com © 2009 Evan Marsh Designs, Inc.*

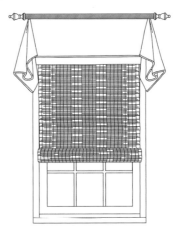

Right: The exotic patterning in this woven wood shade is exceptionally eye-catching and stylish.
Century Shades and Blinds Co. www.centuryblinds.com

Below: Ring topped valance over woven wood shade.
Custom rendering by DreamDraper® design software, www.dreamdraper.com © 2009 Evan Marsh Designs, Inc.

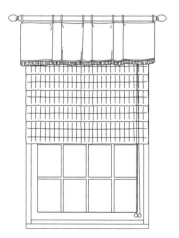

Custom fabric banding on woven wood shade.

Modern Shades: **Pleated & Honeycomb**

Give yourself ultimate control with Duolite®, by Hunter Douglas, a system that combines two fabrics—one light filtering, the other room darkening—into a single shade. It's the ideal option for controlling light and privacy in your home. *www.hunterdouglas.com*

Multiple sets of cellular shades can be installed on a single headrail. Notice how well the shade blocks the sun. Honeycomb shades: light and sturdy with exceptional privacy and light blocking capabilities. *Smith+Noble, www.smithandnoble.com*

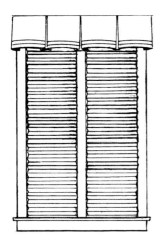

Box pleated valance over pleated shade.

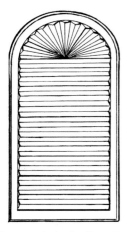

Honeycomb shade with arched honeycomb shade above.

Flat drapery panels pulled back over the pleated shade. Consider a different color lining for a more dramatic design.

Top-down/bottom-up shades are a popular choice for a reason. They provide superior privacy and light control. *Duette® Architella® Honeycomb Shade: Fabric: Opalessence™, Color: Silver Sheen www.hunterdouglas.com*

Pleated shades are light and airy and are capable of conforming to many different applications, from small to large to odd shapes as well. Note the great width they can span, due to solid but lightweight construction. *Hunter Douglas, www.hunterdougles.com*

Modern Shades: Roller, Solar & Screen Shades

Hunter Douglas Designer Screen Shades. These are the kinds of windows that are better with motorization. Fortunately, motorization is now affordable.
Hunter Douglas, www.hunterdouglas.com

Blackout roller shades have clean lines and are still the most cost-effective window treatment. *www.blinds.com*

Gathered valance with bows over roller shade with an appliqued bottom.

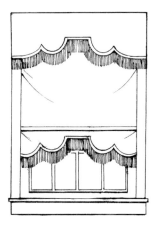

Fringed scalloped roller shade with valance.

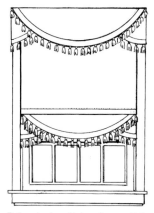

Roller shade with banding and trim.

HunterDouglas.com

Hunter Douglas Designer Screen Shades are available in a variety of colors and lifting options. *www.hunterdouglas.com*

HunterDouglas.com

Hunter Douglas Designer Roller Shades. Fabric: Giovanni, Color: Silver Dust, *www.hunterdouglas.com*

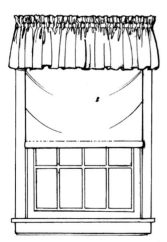

Rod pocket valance over roller shade.

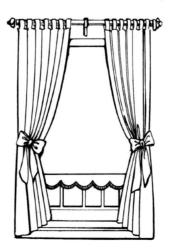

Tab top curtain on a decorative rod over roller shade with a scalloped and fringed bottom.

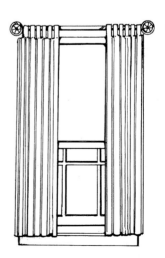

Tab top curtain on a decorative rod over roller shade.

Fabric Shades

Flat Roman shades offer a simple, serene space. Most Roman shades can be ordered in light filtering or room darkening. *Decorating Den Interiors, Deb Betcher, West Chester, PA., www.decoratingden.com, photography by Jon Friedrich*

The Facts: **Fabric Shades**

Advantages: One can use COM (Customer's Own Material) to coordinate with existing fabrics in a room. Decorative fabric offers a softer look and a greater variety of colors and patterns than modern shades. They are recently available in the popular top-down/bottom-up feature.

Disadvantages: Being fabric, this kind of shade is susceptible to environmental factors such as smoke, sunlight, and moisture. Decorative fabric material will break down more quickly than some of the modern product shades

Cost: Typically, more expensive than a modern shade, being the are often created in a workroom rather than a fabricating facility. Fabric shades can vary greatly in price depending upon the style. A flat fold or hobbled Roman shade 36" wide by 42" high, can cost $400 or more.

Lifespan: About six to ten years, if it is lined with a quality lining.

Most Appropriate Locations: Any area that needs softening, although drapery fabric, is not well suited for areas with high moisture, sun, or smoke. Lined shades will last much longer and are better for insulation.

Care & Cleaning: As with any kind of fabric-style product, consult with either the workroom who created the treatment or with a professional drapery/shade cleaner.

Simple flat Roman shades in a translucent fabric invite the sunlight indoors and protect from glare when lowered. The royal blue banding is an inspired touch. *Decorating Den Interiors, Jan Bertin and Lorin Petit, Alexandria, VA., www.decoratingden.com, photography by Jenn Verrier*

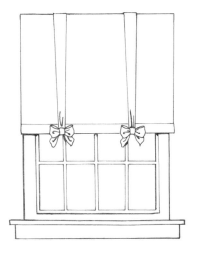

Stagecoach shade with bow ties.

Stagecoach shade with contrast straps and buttons.

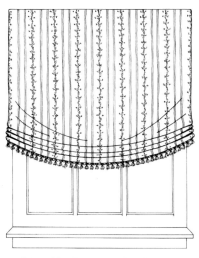

Relaxed flat Roman shade with trim.

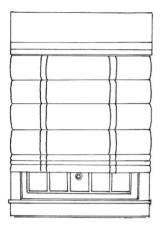

Roman shade with banding on shade and valance.

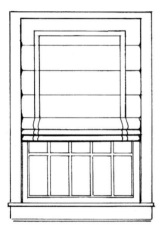

Roman shade with coordinating banding.

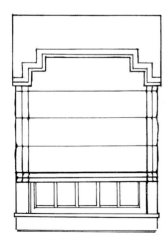

Roman shade with coordinating banding on shade and cornice box.

Blinds.com   Roman shades provide a clean, classic, elegant look.

Good to know: Fabric shades

Fabric shades offer a softer touch at the window, perfect for those rooms where fabric is a must, but draperies may be too much.

Of course, this does not mean that fabric shades can't be used in tandem with draperies or curtains. You will find fabric shades were often used in Victorian interiors, to Art Deco, to today's most fashionable interiors. You will find fabric shades in just about every style — from the very tailored look of a flat Roman shade to the femininity of a cloud shade. Add beads, fringe, bows, or ruffles, should you choose to dress it up.

One important aspect to keep in mind, of course, is the lift mechanism and how you will access the cord, be it on the left or right side. Fabric shades can also be motorized, on the off chance that the lift cord is hard to reach (this might be in the case of a window being behind a piece of furniture, for example).

Popular styles of fabric shades are the Austrian, known for its lovely vertical shirring. Roman, probably the most popular as it can have a pleasant tailored look. The Balloon/Cloud, both of which are softer looking with plenty of folds. And, finally, Roller shades, which you will also see in a modern style but can also be made of fabric. This shade will draw up from the bottom and into a tight roll. Of course, there are variations on the shades. The London shade and the Empire, both of which have similarities to the Cloud/Balloon. Fabric Shades can also have a modern look.

Flat Roman shade with grommets. Private residence, Bel Air, California, *Jeanne Candler Design, www.jcandlerdesign.com, Photo: Charles Randall*

One of my favorite designs. Succulent silk shades with trim. No need for the draperies to be opaque because the shades offer privacy. I also like the fun finial at the end of the black wrought iron decorative rod. *Decorating Den Interiors, Tonie Vanderhulst, Wellington, FL., photographer Paul Emberger, www.decoratingden.com*

253

DraperyAvenue.com

Balloon Shade with tassel trim works perfectly with this old-world classic style kitchen. *Designed and made by Custom Drapery Workroom, Inc., www.draperyavenue.com*

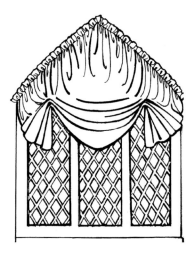

Cathedral A-frame cloud shade.

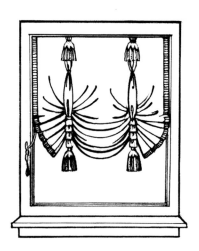

London shade with side banding and tassels.

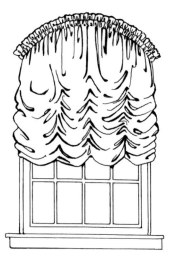

Arched top cloud shade.

London shades with tassel trim. Note the custom tops with buttons lined up with pleats. Attention to detail makes these shades warm and inviting.
Designed and made by Custom Drapery Workroom Inc., www.draperyavenue.com

Bottom arched balloon shade.

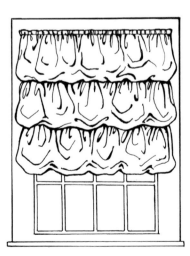

Tiered cloud shade.

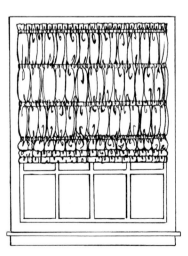

Triple fullness shade gathered on horizontal rods.

Good to Know: Fabric shades

Austrian: A formal treatment that offers shirred, vertical panels (versus the horizontal panels of the Roman shade). Note that this treatment, when created improperly, will tend to pull in on the sides. Only use professional drapery workrooms with experience in Austrian shades.

Balloon: Light and airy, this shade can be lined or unlined. A soft, malleable, lightweight fabric is best, in my experience. Completely operational, it resembles its cousin, the cloud valance, when open, and also offers the operational capability of being able to provide privacy and protection from the sun when closed. Billowy and lush, this is a beautiful fabric treatment. It closes vertically and is out of the way when open.

Cloud: This fabric shade has a gathered heading that cascades into soft poufs when opened. Like the balloon shade, it can be finished with or without a decorative skirt at the bottom edge.

Roman: This corded shade can have rods set horizontally on the backside of the fabric, which, when raised, form a series of horizontal pleats, usually about four to six inches deep. The beauty of a Roman shade is that it implies the look and feel of drapery, but it raises and lowers horizontally. It can be made with either flat folds or overlapping folds. Not recommended for window applications wider than 60" or longer than 84".

Smocked/Shirred: A traditional Roman shade with special smocked heading (also called shirring tape) at the top of the shade. An elegant style. For the best effect, soft drapery fabrics are suggested.

English turret with leaded glass windows shows three inside mount flat stitched Roman shades, rib on the backside, with black wrapped banding along the edges. Custom made one piece window seat with matching pillows. *Willow Drapery & Upholstery, Designer: Leigh Anderson, Glenview, IL., www.willowglenview.com. Photographer: Barry Rustin Photography, Wilmette, IL., www.barryrustinphotography.com*

WillowGlenview.com

Blackout Roman shades offer the opportunity to light a few candles and slip into an inviting bathtub after your afternoon massage. Private Residence, Bel Air, California. *Design by Diana Derycz-Kessler, Photo: Charles Randall*

A fantastic combination of swags, cascades, double cascades, drapery panels with tassels, real wood cornice, and finally, a gorgeous Austrian shade in coordinating fabric. Over the top? Not for those who enjoy stunning window treatments, like me. *Designed and made by Custom Drapery Workroom Inc., www.draperyavenue.com*

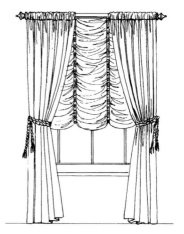

Rod pocket drapery panels with ties on a decorative pole over Austrian shade.

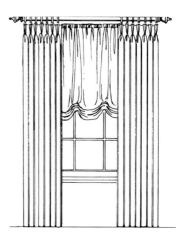

French pleated draperies on a decorative rod over cloud shade.

Flat-panel draperies with swag flags on a decorative rod over a Roman shade.

It was almost mandatory to motorize these pleated Roman shades. One can only imagine climbing over the furniture to get to the cords. And with the blackout lining used to improve television viewing, these shades became heavier. Solution: Hardwiring planned and installed while this mansion was in the building stage. Great design is always in style.

Private residence, Bel Air, California, *Jeanne Candler Design, www.jcandlerdesign.com,*
Photo: Charles Randall

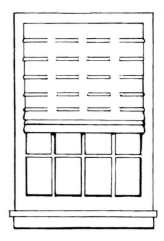

Roman shade with alternating large
and small pleats.

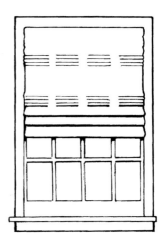

Roman shade with mini pleats.

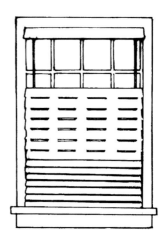

Top-down/bottom-up Roman shade.

Fabric shades

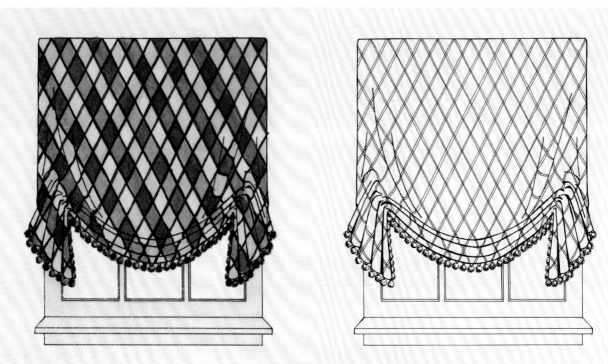

London shade with trim pulls up into graceful folds.

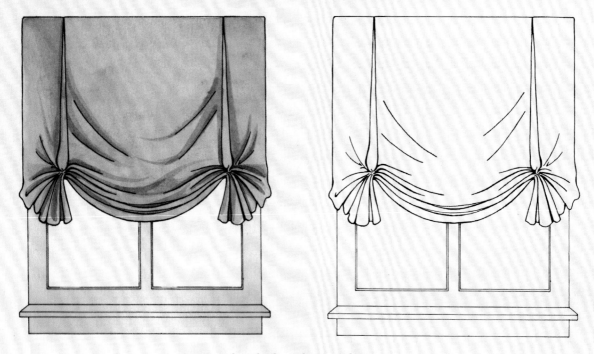

London shade with open pleats.

Fabric shades

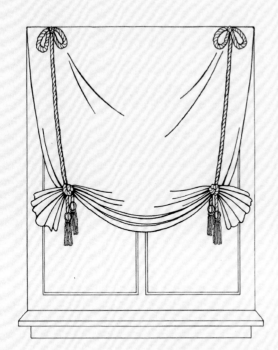
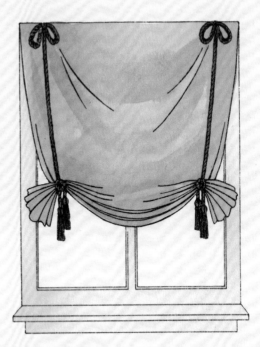

London shade with rope and tassels adds interest.

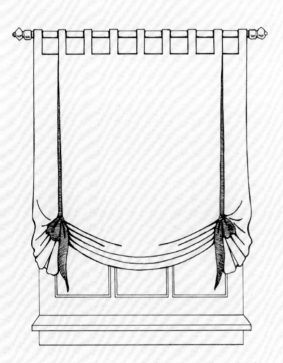
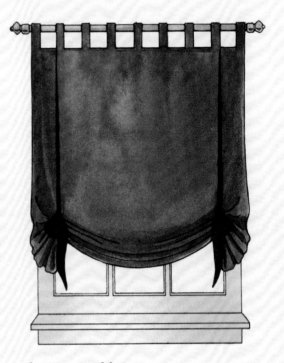

Tab top London shade with pleats and contrasting fabric.

Fabric shades

Arched rod pocket valance over a London shade with grommets.

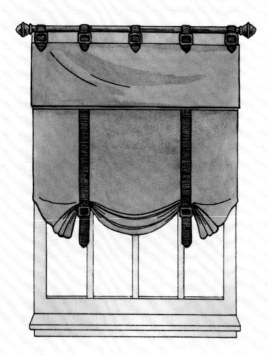
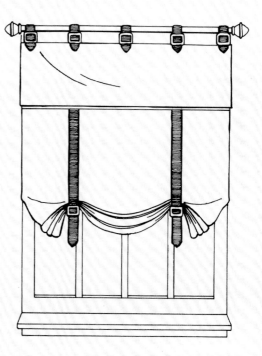

London shade on a decorative rod with leather straps and valance.

Fabric shades

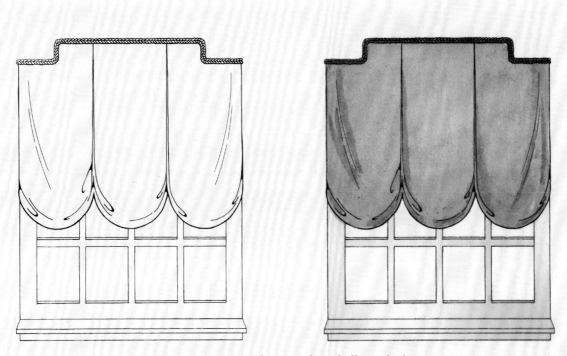

Cut out corners and rope welting balloon shade.

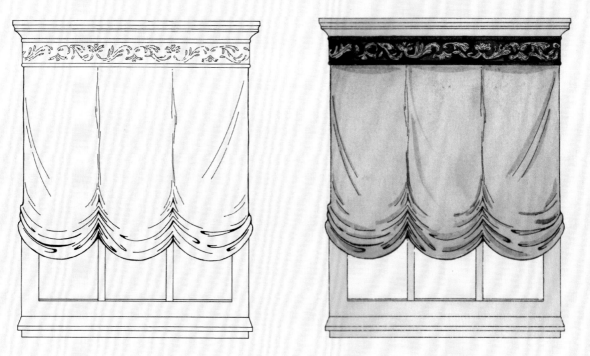

A wood cornice with stenciled design atop a balloon shade.

Fabric shades

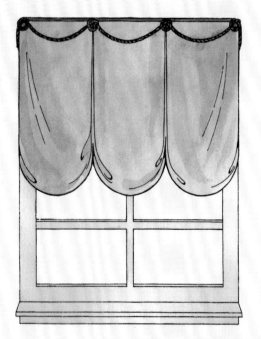 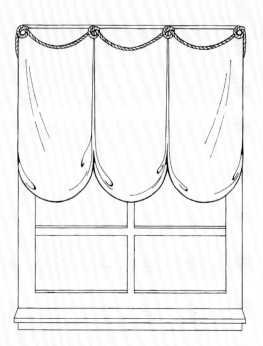

Balloon shade with knotted rope and welting accents.

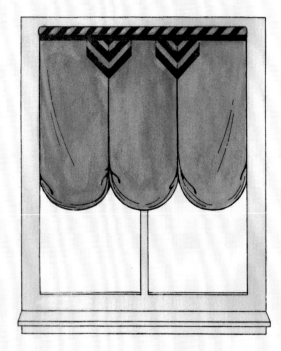 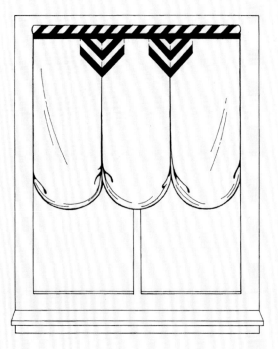

Chevron accents and stripes top this Balloon shade.

Fabric shades

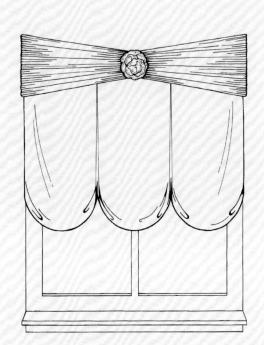
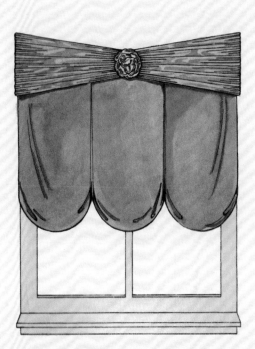

Shirred/gathered horizontal hourglass with center rosette atop a classic balloon shade.

Balloon shade with London shade style bottom.

Fabric shades

A custom shaped valance with matching banding on a flat
Roman shade.

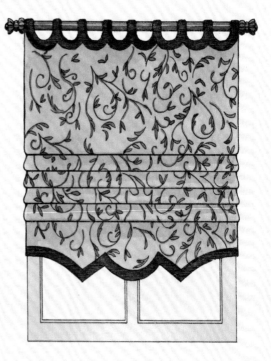

Tab top scalloped Roman shade with contrasting
banding.

Fabric shades

Flat Roman shade with bullion fringe.

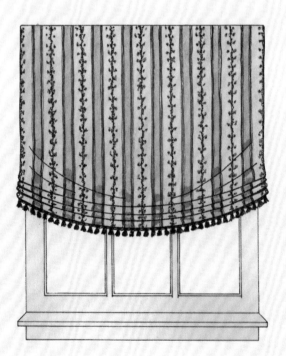
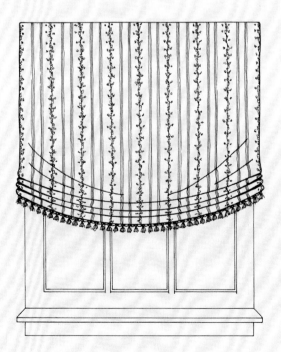

Relaxed Roman shade with trim.

Fabric shades

Stagecoach style flat shade with contrast strips and buttons.

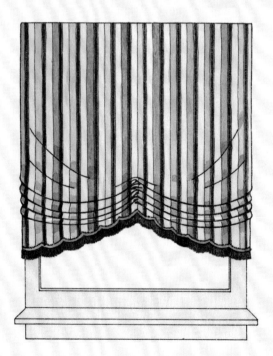
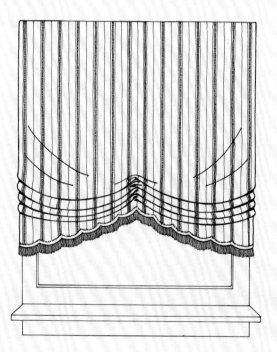

Flat Roman shade with coordinating bullion fringe.

Fabric shades

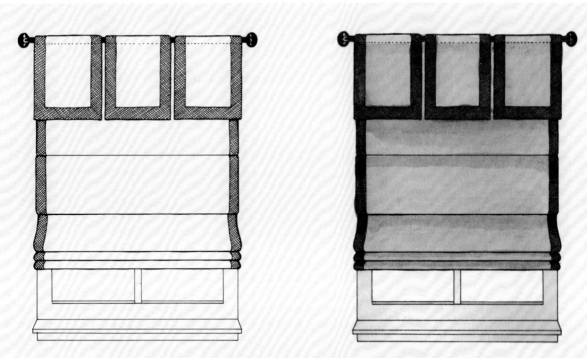

A flat Roman shade on a decorative rod. Flags and coordinating banding
make this a unique shade.

Hobbled Roman shade with inverted box pleated valance and banding
add interest.

Fabric shades

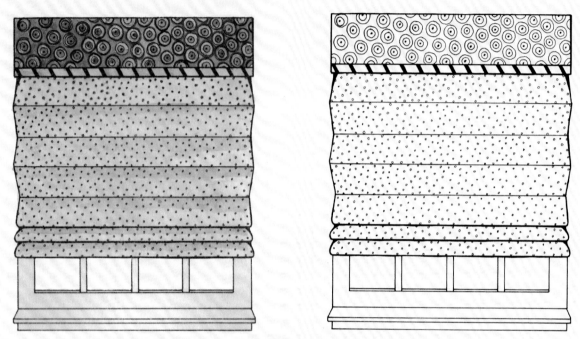

This Roman shade shows good use of multiple cheerful fabrics.

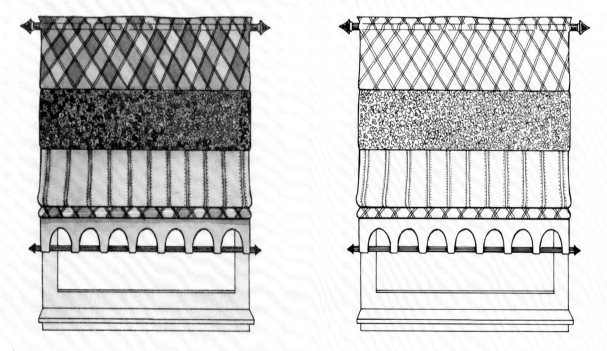

Rod pocket multi-fabric Roman shade with scalloped bottom holding
a decorative rod.

Fabric shades

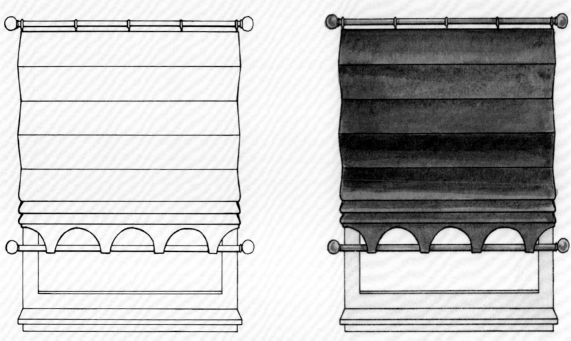

Ring and rod-top Roman shade with scalloped bottom holding a
decorative rod.

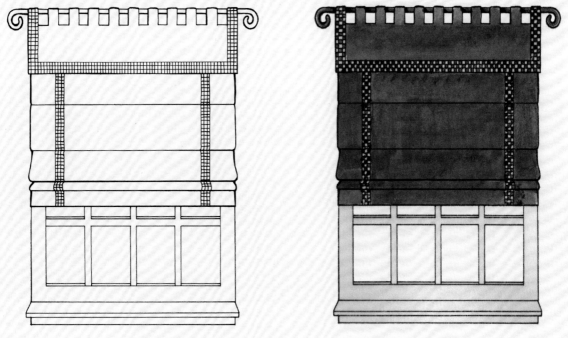

Tab top Roman shade on a decorative rod. Add a valance and
coordinating banding, and you have a unique fabric shade.

Fabric shades

A custom shade that is a combination of cloud and balloon shades with rosettes.

Rod pocket fabric specialty shade in striped fabric.

Fabric shades

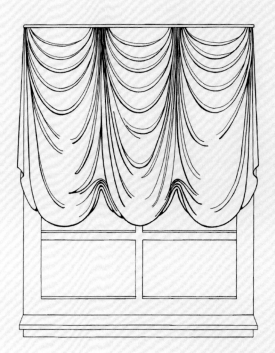

Opera cloud shade with welting top.

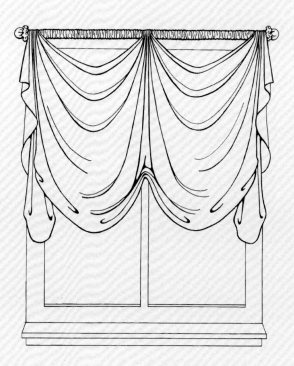

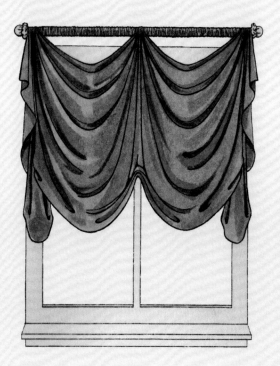

Another Opera style fabric shade with a fabric-covered rod.

Fabric Shade Measuring Information

Inside or Recessed Mounts

Width

Measure width of window at the top, center and bottom of window. Use the narrowest measurement when ordering. Specify on order form if outside clearance has been made. If no clearance has been allowed, the factory will deduct .25" from the overall width.

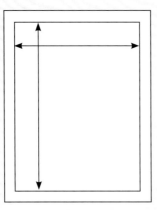

Length

Measure the height of the window from top of opening to top of sill, no allowance is made for length.

Outside or Wall Mount

Width

Measure exact width of the area to be covered. It is recommended that shades extend past actual window opening by two inches on each side. Furnish finished shade width, no allowances will be made.

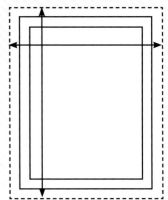

Length

Measure length of area to be covered, allowing a minimum of 3" at top and bottom of window to accommodate headerboard, brackets and light gap at bottom of shade.. At this time you may want to take into consideration stackage of shades and allow for this in your length measurement. Furnish finished shade length, no allowance will be made.

All Installations

- Specify right or left cord position.
- Specify cord length (length of cord needed for easy reach, when shade is completely down).
- For pole cloud, cloud and balloon shades, specify if length given is high or low point of pouf.

Fabric Shade Square Footage Chart

Shade Width (in inches)

	24	30	36	42	48	54	60	66	72	78	84	90	96	102	108	114	120	126	132	138	144
30	10	10	10	10	10	11¼	12½	13¾	15	16¼	17½	18¾	20	21¼	22½	23¾	25	26¼	27½	28¾	30
36	10	10	10	10½	12	13½	15	16½	18	19½	21	22½	24	25½	27	28½	30	31½	33	34½	36
42	10	10	10½	12¼	14	15¾	17½	19¼	21	22¾	24½	26¼	28	29¾	31½	33¼	35	36¾	38½	40¼	42
48	10	10	12	14	16	18	20	22	24	26	28	30	32	34	36	38	40	42	44	46	48
54	10	11¼	13½	15¾	18	20¼	22½	24¾	27	29¼	31½	33¾	36	38¼	40½	42¾	45	47¼	49½	51¾	54
60	10	12½	15	17½	20	22½	25	27½	30	32½	35	37½	40	42½	45	47½	50	52½	55	57½	60
66	11	13¼	16½	19¼	22	24¾	27½	30.¼	33	35¾	38½	41¼	44	46¾	49½	52¼	55	57¾	60½	63¼	66
72	12	15	18	21	24	27	30	33	36	39	42	45	48	51	54	57	60	63	66	69	72
78	13	16¼	19½	22¾	26	29¼	32½	35¾	39	42¼	45½	48¾	52	55¼	58½	61¾	65	68¼	71½	74¾	78
84	14	17½	21	24½	28	31½	35	38½	42	45½	49	52½	56	59½	63	66½	70	73½	77	80½	84
90	15	18¼	22½	26¼	30	33¾	37½	41¼	45	48¾	52½	56¼	60	63¾	67½	71¼	75	78¾	82½	86¼	90
96	16	20	24	28	32	36	40	44	48	52	56	60	64	68	72	76	80	84	88	92	96
102	17	21¼	25½	29¾	34	38¼	42½	46¾	51	55¼	59½	63¾	68	72¼	76½	80¾	85	89¼	93½	97¾	102

Shade Length (in inches)

Austrian Shade

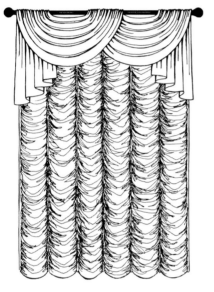

Austrian Shade combined with pole-mounted swags and cascades.

Austrian shade with trim under tied back draperies.

A soft, formal treatment created by vertical shirring/gathering between scallops.

Yardage

Without pattern repeat:

Step 1 – Width of shade x 2 ÷ width of fabric = number of fabric widths required (round up to the whole number)

Step 2a – Number of widths x shade length + 10" for HH (heading and hems) x 3 ÷ 36 = yardage.

With pattern repeat:

Step 2b – Number of widths x shade length + 10" for HH x 3 ÷ pattern repeat = number of repeats required (round up the whole number)

Step 2c – Number of repeats required x pattern repeat = CL (cut length)

Step 2d – Number of widths (from Step 1) x new CL (from Step 2c) ÷ 36 = yardage with pattern repeat (round up to the whole number)

Things to Consider

> Color of the lining (if applicable, but usually not lined)
> Right or left cord pull

Special Notes

1. This treatment tends to pull in on the sides.

2. Use heavier fabric for privacy or sheer/lace fabric for more light and less privacy.

3. Austrians can hold their own as a standalone treatment or work beautifully in combination with draperies and top treatments.

4. See page 90 for detailed calculating terms.

Balloon Shade

Balloon shade with tassel trim. *Designed and made by Custom Drapery Workroom Inc., www.draperyavenue.com*

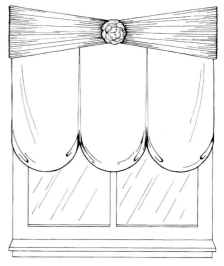

Balloon shade with hourglass valance.

This fully functional shade has large, inverted pleats for a more tailored look. While still billowy looking like the cloud shade, it has a less feminine appearance.

Yardage

Without pattern repeat:

Step 1 – Width of shade x 2.5 ÷ width of fabric = number of fabric widths required (round up to the whole number).

Step 2a – Shade length + 16" for HH (heading and hems) x widths required ÷ 36 = yardage.

With pattern repeat:

Step 2b – Shade length + 12" for HH ÷ pattern repeat = number of repeats required (round up the whole number).

Step 2c – Number of repeats required x pattern repeat = CL (cut length).

Step 2d – Number of widths (from Step 1) x new CL (from Step 2c) ÷ 36 = yardage with pattern repeat (round up to the whole number).

Things to Consider

> Color of lining
> Skirt or no skirt
> Left or right pull or motorized

Special Notes

See page 90 for detailed calculating terms

Cloud & London Shade

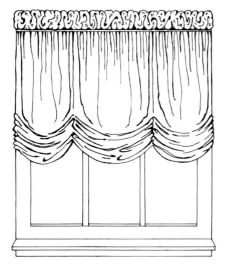

Cloud shade.

TheShadeStore.com

London shade. *Photo courtesy of The Shade Store, www.theshadestore.com*

These are fully functional shades with gathered (cloud), or pleated (London) headings that fall gracefully into soft cloud-like poufs.

Yardage

Without pattern repeat:

Step 1 – Width of shade x 2.5 ÷ width of fabric = the number of fabric widths required (round up to the whole number).

Step 2a – Shade length + 12" for HH (heading and hems) x widths required ÷ 36 = yardage.

With pattern repeat:

Step 2b – Shade length + 12" for HH ÷ pattern repeat = number of repeats required (round up the whole number).

Step 2c – Number of repeats x pattern repeat = CL (cut length).

Step 2d –Number of widths (from Step 1) x new CL (from Step 2c) ÷ 36 = yardage with pattern repeat (round up to the whole number).

Things to Consider

> Color of lining
> Embellishments
> Left or right pull, or motorized, as with all shades

Special Notes

See page 90 for detailed calculating terms

Hobbled/Waterfall Shade

Color blocked hobbled Roman shade.

Above a busy prep area, most fabric treatments would be too fussy and involved. With fabric shades, however, such as this Roman beauty, you are allowed softness up and out of the way of your workspace when necessary, and full privacy and sun control at the pull of a cord.

The Hobbled Roman shade is characterized by its overlapping folds cascading down the full length of the shade.

Yardage

Without pattern repeat:

Step 1 – Width of shade + 8" ÷ width of fabric = number of fabric widths required (round up to the whole number).

Step 2a – Shade length + 10" for HH (heading and hems) x 2 for overlapping folds x widths required ÷ 36 = yardage.

With pattern repeat:

Step 2b – Shade length + 10" for HH x 2 ÷ pattern repeat = the number of repeats required (round up the whole number).

Step 2c – Number of repeats required x pattern repeat = CL (cut length)

Step 2d – Number of widths (from Step 1) x new CL (from Step 2c) ÷ 36 = yardage with pattern repeat (round up to the whole number).

Things to Consider

> Color of lining
> Right or left pull

Special Notes

1. Folded Roman shades larger than 60" in width or 84" in length are not recommended.

2. Due to the nature of fabric construction, the folds do not always hang evenly. Use caution where two or more are hung side by side.

3. Most cannot be made with returns.

4. See page 90 for detailed calculating terms.

Flat Roman Shade

Flat Roman with decorative edging and tab top.

Flat Roman shade.

Design by Sarah Barnard, Sarah Barnard Design

This versatile shade hangs straight but collapses into folds when raised. Accommodates many different decors, from casual to traditional to contemporary, and even formal. Add interest with contrast banding, scalloped edges, pleats, and trim.

Yardage

Without pattern repeat:

Step 1 – Width of shade + 8" ÷ width of fabric = number of fabric widths required (round up to the whole number).

Step 2a – Shade length + 10" for HH (heading and hems) x widths required ÷ 36 = yardage.

With pattern repeat:

Step 2b – Shade length + 10" for HH ÷ pattern repeat = number of repeats required (round up the whole number).

Step 2c – Number of repeats required x pattern repeat = CL (cut length).

Step 2d – Number of widths (from Step 1) x new CL (from Step 2c) ÷ 36 = yardage with pattern repeat (round up to the whole number).

Things to Consider

> Color of lining
> Right or left pull

Special Notes

1. Not recommended for areas wider than 60" or longer than 84" unless a very light fabric is used. Always a good idea to ask your drapery workroom.

2. These types of shades cannot be made with returns unless small returns are used at the top sides to hide the wood they are mounted on and the brackets.

3. See page 90 for detailed calculating terms.

COMBINATIONS

Who says you can't have the best of both worlds? When one window treatment isn't enough, exploring the beauty and flexibility of combination treatments is the perfect way to proceed. Typically, modern (hard) window treatments (such as blinds or shutters) are combined with stationary drapery panels…or fabric shades…or a top treatment…or whatever your heart desires. Indeed, it is sometimes the hard treatment that stays, with the soft treatment changing as often as the homeowner wishes.

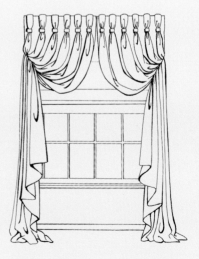

Left: Stationary panels over Zebra/Banded shades hung from acrylic rods and rings. The unique fabric adds texture and dimension. *Design by Susan A. Gailani, Gailani Designs Inc. Photography: Richard Lanenga Photography, Inc.*

Goblet-pleated Italian strung drapery panels cascade to the floor. A flat-panel Roman shade underneath provides the privacy and sun control.

HunterDouglas.com

History in the Making

By the 17th century, window treatments were a distinct and planned element in the design of an interior. Layer upon layer of fabric, created specifically for draping, unveiling complex and ornate works of window art. Coupled with flat woven braids, fringe, opulent tassels, and fanciful rosettes, combination treatments were lush beauties to behold with their rich colors in gold, red, and blue, vibrant tapestries, and heavy silks and cotton blends.

By the mid-18th century, combination treatments had begun to evolve into something more easily equated with today's interiors. Roller blinds crafted of natural linen, rather than heavy under-treatments, oversaw sun control, for example. Shutters, another favorite, were coupled with pretty curtains.

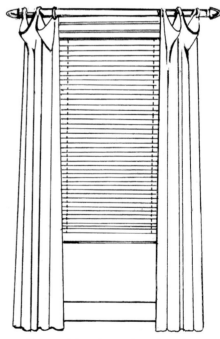

Flat-panel draperies on decorator rod over a horizontal blind.

Clever use of both horizontal and vertical fabric/vane shades add interest to this tall window wall, with a stationary drapery panel to bridge the change. A part of Hunter Douglas's Whole-Home Solution. *Hunter Douglas Luminette® and Silhouette® www.hunterdouglas.com*

Today's Combinations

Today, combinations come in many configurations, but at their best, they couple to fulfill the needs of today's consumer: a hard "under" treatment, such as a blind or shade takes care of the elements of privacy and sun control. A fabric "over" treatment softens the window, adds a splash of color and provides focus and impetus to the design of the room. Finally, a top treatment, such as a cornice or valance, finishes the top and conceals any architectural flaws or unsightly drapery hardware.

Stationary tab top panels with gathered knots hang on a decorative rod over a trimmed roller shade.

Arched cornice box with nailhead trim over sheer shading shade. Stationary color-blocked draperies hang neatly on golden decorative rod and rings.
Decorating Den Interiors, Jan Bromberek, Oswego, IL., www.decoratingden.com

DecoratingDen.com

Stationary panels over zebra/banded shades hung from acrylic rods and rings. This unique fabric adds texture and dimension. *Design by Susan A. Gailani, Gailani Designs Inc. Photography: Richard Lanenga Photography Inc.*

The Facts: **Combinations**

Advantages: Offers the functional nature of Modern shades and blinds, coupled with the beauty of fabric; in future years, you could, for example, keep the Modern treatment and have a new soft overtreatment installed, thus changing the entire look of the room without the expense of an entirely new treatment.

Disadvantages: More window treatments equal more money, and a larger space to accommodate. Treatments may not wear at the same rate.

Cost: Multi-layered treatments are the most expensive way of decorating windows. Count on your costs, reaching into the thousands of dollars.

Lifespan: Varying, depending upon the types of treatments being used. Remember that fabric has a lower life expectancy than hard treatments such as

blinds. You may find that you must replace one layer, while the other is still perfectly fine.

Most Appropriate Locations: Anywhere that there is space that will accommodate both hard and soft choices. Typically seen most often in dining and living rooms, period-style homes, elaborate sitting rooms, and bedrooms.

Care & Cleaning: Each treatment may require a different type of care. Refer to specific chapters within this book for more specialized information.

Grommet draperies have become very popular in the last few years. Deservedly so with their ability to keep well-defined folds neatly in place. Flat Roman shades in a geometric fabric finish the space beautifully. *www.blinds.com*

Made from select natural woods, including reeds, bamboo, and grasses, these woven wood shades are uniquely textured, adding casual good looks. The draperies soften and pull together the unusual wall color patterns. *www.hunterdouglas.com*

A fantastic display of decorating acumen. Arched swags flow into double cascades and then into gathered drapery panels. Sheers, drapery, swags, and cascades all supported on wrought iron decorative rods. The faux wrought iron grille is a stroke of designer inspiration. These windows are a good example of why one needs the help of an Interior Designer, or window decorating expert. *Decorating Den Interiors, Tonie Vander Hulst, Wellington FL., www.decoratingden.com. Photography: Paul Emburger*

DecoratingDen.com

Good to Know: Combinations

- If you are manipulating the shade or blind treatment regularly, it may not be necessary to have an operational outer soft treatment. Consider stationary panels flanking your window to soften the hard edges of the blinds or shades. Or, to minimize light leakage from the sides of the hard window coverings.

- Make certain your hard treatment offers the privacy and sun control you desire; otherwise, your soft treatment should be operational.

- Consider a top treatment to cover the pieces of window hardware needed to hang your other window treatments.

- To change the look of your draperies seasonally, consider a removable drapery swag, which typically attaches to the front of a stationary panel. The easiest way to achieve this is by using Velcro to hang the swags or valances. Perhaps in winter, a lushly fringed velvet swag in a deep cognac tone will add holiday cheer to a patterned drapery panel, while in summer, a small string of silk flowers or an unlined blue silk swag will coordinate and lighten the look.

- Know that while your initial expense may be higher for combination treatments, subsequent redressing of the window may only require a change of fabric, while the hard treatment stays.

This lovely design includes an arched inverted box pleated valance with brass nailheads and matching tassel trim. This fabulous treatment is the work of a creative designer and professional drapery workroom. *Decorating Den Interiors, Barbara Elliott and Jennifer Ward Woods, Stone Mountain, GA., www.decoratingden.com. Photography: Scott Jonhson.*

This combination treatment consists of a custom shaped cornice box over coordinating traversing drapery panels and woven wood shade. I like this treatment because of the way the woven wood brings in a little bit of the outdoors and matches perfectly with the dining room table. *Decorating Den Interiors, Sandy Burroughs and Allison Fikejs, Kansas City, MO., www.decoratingden.com, photography by Jeremy McGraw.*

SmithandNoble.com

Teal and gold ring top Euro pleated drapery panels with black-out lining kiss the hardwood floor — a perfect length in that the hem is much less likely to wear and also makes for easy floor maintenance. A traditional Roman shade completes this layered look. *Smith+Noble, www.smithandnoble.com*

JamieGibbsAssociates.com

What could be prettier than sunny yellow in the morning when you wake up? This three-layer treatment has it all, with cornice, sheers, and a fabric/vane combination for privacy and sun control. *Jamie Gibbs & Associates, www.jamiegibbsassociates.com*

DecoratingDen.com

This eye-pleasing straightforward design consists of an inverted box pleated valance with kick pleats. The shutters without tilt bars offer a better view and a more modern motif. Matching shutters with cutouts on the French doors harmonize the overall design. *Decorating Den Interiors, Sandy Burroughs and Allison Fikejs, Kansas City, MO., www.decoratingden.com, photography by Jeremy McGraw*

DecoratingDen.com

One of my favorite window treatment designs. This combination treatment includes silk sheers with a fun, whimsical pattern that matches the sheer shading shades and mirrors perfectly. *Decorating Den Interiors, Abby Connell, Cincinnati OH., www.decoratingden.com*

DecoratingDen.com

Layers of fabric make this master bedroom area an opulent retreat. In this application, the balloon valance is inoperable, as are the drapery panels. All privacy for this room is provided by the fabric/vane shades. The dark chocolate brown drapery folds are truly sophisticated. This is a combination that succeeds on all levels. *Decorating Den Interiors, Sharon Binkerd, www.decoratingden.com*

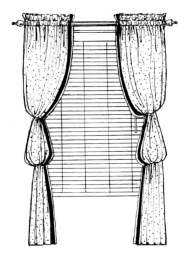

Rod pocket stationary Bishop sleeve panels over a miniblind.

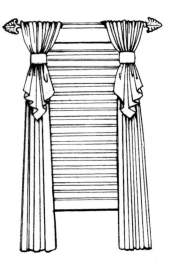

Flip topper drapery panels over a pleated shade.

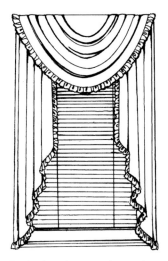

Single pleated swag and cascades with ruffles over a wood blind.

DecoratingDen.com

Stationary pleated draperies on decorative rods and rings. Sheer shading shades in off white on eight windows are window decorating perfection! *Decorating Den Interiors, Angela Carroll Ast, Coopersburg, PA., www.decoratingden.com*

This lovely breakfast nook is decorated with custom-designed valances with horizontal and vertical coordinating banding. Including the door was an inspired design decision. Wood blinds provide light control and privacy. *Decorating Den Interiors, Peggy Herrick, Missouri City, TX., www.decoratingden.com*

Design by Elizabeth Gerdes, Stitch Above the Rest, Woodstock, GA., www.stitchabovetherest.com, Photo: Woodie Williams www.woodiewilliamsphoto.com

StitchAboveTheRest.com

DecoratingDen.com

Floor to ceiling draperies on wrought iron decorative rod match the faux wrought iron grilles in the transom windows. The flat Roman shades complement the décor perfectly. *Decorating Den Interiors, Design by Mimi Wilson, Bristow, VA., www.decoratingden.com*

DecoratingDen.com

These eye-pleasing window coverings were created by using perfectly matched draperies and flat Roman shades with side banding. A white arched faux grille adds the final touch of creativity. One of my favorite treatments. *Decorating Den Interiors, Design by Cretchen Curk, Cincinnati, OH, www.decoratingden.com*

The Zebra/banded sheer shadings look fabulous in this view window. Note the geometric banding on the leading edge of the two-finger pleated draperies. Adding the white faux wrought iron grille to the arched window was an inspired choice. *Decorating Den Interiors, Gretchen Curk, Cincinnati, OH., www.decoratingden.com*

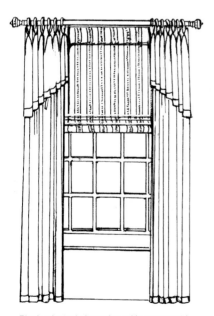

Pinch pleated draperies with asymmetrical flounces over a woven wood blind.

Stationary drapery panels soften the window frame, while the striped Roman shade provides privacy and sun control.

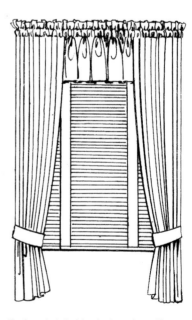

Rod pocket tied back draperies with center valance over wood blind with fabric tapes.

Flip topper drapery panels with coordinating fabric on the flipped side. Crystal finials on the wrought iron rods add more interest. The wood blind provides light control and privacy. *Decorating Den Interiors, Denise Huff, Norman, OK., www.decoratingden.com*

Butterfly pleated draperies on real wood decorative rods match the wood in this room beautifully. Flat Roman shades provide light control and privacy. *Decorating Den Interiors, Cassy Young, Athens, GA., Photographer Scott Johnson, www.decoratingden.com*

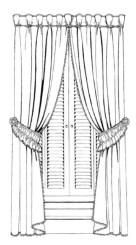

Goblet pleated panels with ruffled tiebacks over shutters.

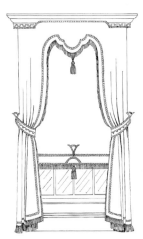

Fringed Roman shade under cornice and drapery panels.

Smocked diamond style heading over Roman shade.

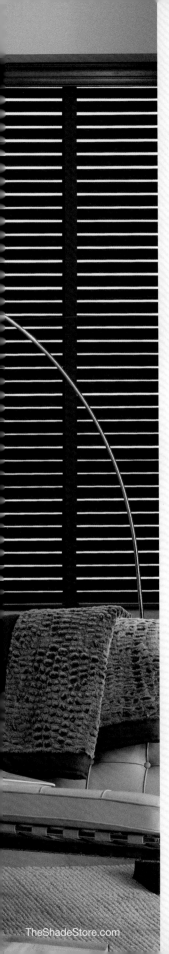

BLINDS

There is something in the structured simplicity of a blind that appeals universally. Neat, compact, and orderly, horizontal and vertical blinds fulfill a multitude of needs with the simple pull of a cord or twist of a wand, and, more recently, the push of a button. They usually consist of a headrail system, slats, louvers or vanes, and, with horizontal blinds, a bottom rail. Blinds can interface with any interior due to the full range of colors, materials, stains, and decorative tapes. Fit them inside the window to lie flush with the frame or mount them outside the frame; blinds are infinitely capable of being beautiful and functional.

Left: The bank of two-inch blinds with matching ladder tape contributes to the modern appeal of this room set. *Photo courtesy of The Shade Store www.theshadestore.com*

Two-inch wood blinds with ladder tapes under an arched window. The dramatic molding works well with the blinds.

Armstrong.com

History in the Making

While blinds have been premier window coverings within this lifetime, it is worth mentioning that they have been around for much longer. Egyptian culture has a record of the use of vertical blinds constructed of reeds. Additionally, woven bamboo blinds in ancient China were employed to filter light in elaborate palaces and lowly huts. Subsequently, they evolved into shutters, which in turn became wood slat blinds. You will find a record of the use of blinds in America as early as the mid-1700s.

In 1841, a U.S. patent was awarded to New Orleans' John Hampson, who invented a method of adjusting the angle of slats in a Venetian blind.

The 1930s and 1940s saw two-inch Venetian blinds in almost every home and office in America. Still, due to the lack of anti-static properties and their cumbersome nature, they were difficult to clean and not aesthetically pleasing.

It wasn't until modern technology came into play in the mid-twentieth century that vertical and horizontal blinds truly burgeoned. Processes for casting aluminum into strips, developed in the mid-1940s, was the beginning. Yet for our modern world, we can look to the 1960s and the 1970s, as World War II draperies began to age on their rods, that the call for blinds was truly heard. By the 1980s, mass production and thus, the use of hard window treatments in interiors were common. The sleek lines and simple manipulation of slats to control light and privacy, so modern, challenged fabric treatments for the first time.

Right: Modern Precious Metals® Aluminum Blinds. Color: Brushed Aluminum by Hunter Douglas, *www.hunterdouglas.com*

Left: Two-inch white metal blinds with black ladder tapes. Flooring by Armstrong World Industries.

Today's Blinds

Today, horizontal and vertical blinds are still enjoying their place in interiors all over the world. Wider slats, replicating the look of shutters, to vertical blinds—a virtual moveable curtain wall—offer plentiful choices. Versatile, uncomplicated, and clean, their colorways are generous, wood and faux wood products are unbelievably hard to discern from one another, and blinds work in tandem with the escalating trend toward fabric at the windows. A new hybrid, too, basically a horizontal or vertical slat meets fabric, combine for a softened window appearance.

Offering an attractive horizontal and/or vertical line from not just the interior but also the exterior of the home, the uniformity of these window treatments is attractive and suitable for any interior.

HunterDouglas.com

Good to Know: Blinds

- Consider cordless blinds, those that raise and lower with slight pressure applied to the bottom rail, for homes with children and pets. Easy to lift, they provide a sleek, modern look and the issue of safety will never arise again.

- For vibrant color, consider metal blinds. The color application on metal is bright, tough and can withstand plenty of abuse. They are also available cordless.

- Generally, the smaller the slat, the less light leakage when shut. Micro mini blinds are a great option in areas that require total darkness.

- If your goal is to enhance architectural details or create a focal point, wood blinds with a quality stained or painted finish will offer a sense of permanence.

- Be sure to select blinds treated with an anti-static finish to alleviate dust build-up.

- Consider vertical blinds if your goal is to enhance the height of a room. The vertical nature will make a low ceiling look higher.

- With vertical blinds, be sure to allow about ¾" clearance from the floor to allow for ease when traversing. Also, it is important to note that when the vertical blind has been pulled to the side, there will be stackback — i.e., a small amount of vertically stacked product — that will remain, as there is no headrail for a vertical blind to escape into.

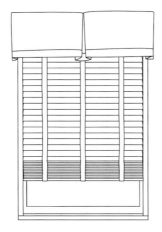

Above: Banded, box pleated valance over wood blinds. *Custom rendering by DreamDraper® design software, www.dreamdraper.com © 2009 Evan Marsh Designs, Inc.*

Right: There is something special about the simple, uncluttered lines of wood blinds. Combine those with the ultimate in light and glare control and bringing in a bit of nature to the home, and you will understand the timeless popularity of real wood blinds. *www.hunterdouglas.com*

HunterDouglas.com

Blinds: **Horizontal**

DecoratingDen.com

Horizontal Blinds

Horizontal blinds most often come to mind when considering the best method for covering a window, because they fulfill so many of the basic requirements, as well as offer a sleek, modern appearance and a low to moderate price point. Easy to acquire, fast turnaround and a wide variety of materials and slat sizes make horizontal blinds a perennial favorite. And better yet, their solid construction makes this a window treatment that will last and last.

Above: A majestic focal point is enhanced by the addition of whimsical drapery panels and horizontal blinds. The colors in this room are absolutely enchanting—while using some of the most popular colors of today, they are used sparingly. And isn't less always more? *Decorating Den Interiors, www.decoratingden.com*

Next page:
The arched wrought iron grille matching the designer wrought iron decorative rods is an inspired choice. French pleated drapery panels over wood blinds add privacy and light control. Throw in some designer inspired valances, and you have a window covering masterpiece. One of my favorite designs! *Decorating Den Interiors, Rebeca Lane, Olathe, KN., www.decoratingden.com, photography by Jeremy Mason McGraw*

DecoratingDen.com

Gorgeous beading and trim on a relaxed Roman shade over a two-inch faux white wood blind.
Decoring Den Interiors, www.decoratingden.com

The Facts: **Horizontal Blinds**

Advantages: Can control light direction by a simple twist of the slats; will harmonize with just about any type of soft treatment; can be motorized in a variety of manners; typically a fast turnaround for this kind of product; routless construction offers the ultimate privacy; hidden brackets and no valance options allow this blind to almost disappear into the inner window frame; cordless operating systems make treatments safer for children and pets

Disadvantages: Rout holes in the center of a blind will allow anyone interested to see inside your home. Be certain you buy a blind with rout holes placed at the back of the slat—or opt for the new "no hole" construction; dust will accumulate, even with a built-in dust repellant; metal blinds can bend and clank against a window when a breeze enters the room

Cost: An inexpensive vinyl product can be had for about $10 but if you are looking for a treatment that will last, expect to spend at least $50 per 30" x 42" window. As always, extras, such as valances and various blind materials such as wood, faux wood, aluminum, etc. will cause great price fluctuation.

Lifespan: Decades

Most Appropriate Locations: Any window will do, although some materials are not suitable for some areas (such as wood blinds in a bathroom). Also note that any treatment near a stove where there is airborne grease will be difficult to clean. Think about raising your blind fully when cooking to avoid coating the slats, which will in turn attract dust.

Care & Cleaning: Most blind slats are now anti-static and dust repellant, though some more than others. Clean the slats with a feather duster to remove weekly accumulation of residue. You can also have blinds cleaned sonically through a take down, clean and reinstall service that cleans blinds thoroughly with no damage or wear.

SpringsWindowFashions.com

Instead of covering a window arch completely, consider ironwork to decorate and enhance an architectural element.
Springs Window Fashions, *www.springswindowfashions.com*

Motorization is now available on almost all window treatments, even wood blinds. Motorized wood blinds are a good option when cords are hard to reach. Springs Window Fashions, *www.springswindowfashions.com*

Parkland® Wood Blinds: Fabric/Material: Basswood, Color: Espresso, *www.hunterdouglas.com*

Blinds: **Verticals**

CenturyBlinds.com

Vertical Blinds

Neat and elegant vertical blinds can cover a large expanse of glass, such as a sliding glass door or large picture window, easily. With individual stiffened cloth or vinyl (typically) louvers that can rotate 180 degrees as well as pull completely out of the way, vertical blinds are a terrific way to obtain coverage similar to that of a drapery, but with a better capability to control light. Best yet, vertical blinds can strengthen a room's focus with their strong lines and elongated structure. Beautiful colors abound, with embossed prints to fit any décor; custom valances (upholstered and wood, to name a few) to provide a pop of trendy beauty; and the vanes themselves are available from a sheer, translucent material to the hard edge of aluminum. And now, many manufacturers are creating soft fabric verticals (sheer fabric adjoining each vane), which replicate the look of draperies but offer the flexibility of a typical vertical blind.

HunterDouglas.com

Above: Skyline ® Gliding Window Panels, Fabric/Material: Constellation, Color: Bone, *www.hunterdouglas.com*

Opposite page: Panel track vertical blinds are a terrific alternative to 3 1/2 inch vertical blinds when treating a sliding glass door area. They are neat and compact — yet note that the stackback will be as wide as approximately one panel. *Century Shades & Blinds Inc., www.centuryblinds.com*

Vertical Solutions® Fabric/Material: Afton, Color: White, *www.hunterdouglas.com*

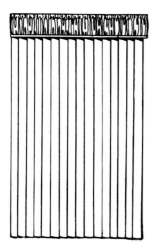

Simple shirred cornice over vertical blinds.

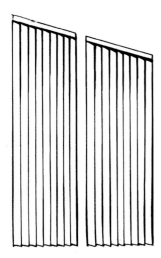

Slanted windows with custom cut vertical blinds.

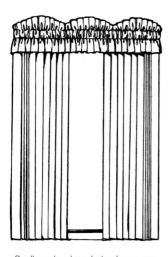

Scalloped rod pocket valance over vertical blinds.

HunterDouglas.com

Somner® Vertical Blinds, Fabric/Material: Brittmore, Color: Union Square, *www.hunterdouglas.com*

HunterDouglas.com

This is a setting in which vertical fabric/vane blinds work perfectly — covering large expanses of glass. Consider opting for a split draw so that you have equal stackback on either side of the window, versus a large, potentially clumsy stackback on just one side. *www.hunterdouglas.com*

The Facts: **Vertical Blinds**

Advantages: Can cover large expanses of glass; newer styles hang perfectly straight without any weights or bottom chains; operating systems are now quiet and smooth; some manufacturers boast over 80 colors available; can be motorized in a variety of manners; its elongated structure will augment the height of a room; allows good air circulation; some verticals have the capability of slipping strips of material (such as wallpaper) into the vanes to match a room's décor

Disadvantages: Cheaper vertical blind slats will clank and tangle together; hardware is visible without a headrail (be sure to order one); they're kid magnets (hide and seek has never been more enticing!); perception still puts them in a corporate rather than a residential setting; can be imposing in a room

Cost: Prices can vary depending upon the material selected, but a very simple version approximately seven foot tall by about five foot wide will cost around $100.

Lifespan: Decades

Most Appropriate Locations: For areas with great expanses of glass, such as sliding glass doors, as well as tall casement windows, large picture windows, arch-top and some angular windows.

Care & Cleaning: Minimum maintenance. Blind slats are now anti-static and dust repellant, though some more than others. Clean the vanes with a feather duster to remove weekly accumulation of residue. You can also have blinds cleaned sonically through a take down, clean and reinstall service that cleans blinds thoroughly with no damage or wear.

Swag with ruffled side drops over vertical blinds.

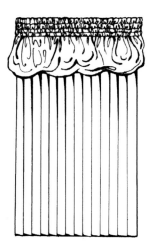

Smocked cloud valance over vertical blinds.

Pleated swags and floor-length cascades attached to a fabric-covered rod over vertical blinds.

HunterDouglas.com

Luminette® Vertical sheer shadings work perfectly when used to cover sliding glass doors.
www.hunterdouglas.com

HunterDouglas.com

Panel track verticals are a great choice for modern interiors.
Skyline ® Gliding Window Panels, Fabric: Maya, Color: Zanzibar Grey

Top: Skyline ® Gliding Window Panels and Designer Roller Shades, Fabric/Material: Barista, Color: White Mocha. www.hunterdouglas.com

Bottom: Skyline ® Gliding Window Panels, Fabric/Material: Empire, Color: Fence Post. www.hunterdouglas.com

SHUTTERS

The clean lines and perfect function of a shutter are a true joy to behold, enhancing any interior with beautiful permanence. Louvers operate smoothly to vary light penetration from full-on bright to almost complete darkness. They offer a warm, traditional appearance, and insulate effectively from cold and heat. The most beautiful wood shutters are constructed with the same attention to detail and loving care as fine furniture. The most ingenious of environmentally friendly faux shutters can withstand the dampest of environments.

It seems there's nothing that shutters can't do. As someone who owns shutters (see page 346), I can tell you I love the way they operate, block heat and light, and look.

Left: Windows on a round wall can be problematic for window treatments--especially when they include arch top windows. *Custom Polywood Shutters® by Sunburst Shutters solved this design challenge. www.sunburstshutters.com*

Designer tab top drapery panels over plantation shutters. *DreamDraper® design software, www.dreamdraper.com © 2009 Evan Marsh Designs, Inc.*

History in the Making

During the era of Europe's Tudor and Elizabethan periods, wood shutters were the primary window covering. Installed on the inside of the home, these shutters were all about function. When closed, they could cover the entire window to protect from rain, sunlight, and intruders, often standing in for an expanse of glass. When open, they folded against the inner walls to act as decorative panels.

As architecture changed and windows became increasingly recessed, shutters moved outdoors to give decoration to the exterior. Painted shutters on North American and European homes provided a pop of color. Late nineteenth-century improvements, such as the capability to manipulate louvers, presented a homeowner with additional options. Two-tier panels (also known as Dutch shutters), offered the choice of opening just part of the shutter or all of it, and hinges provided the vertical swing, bringing shutters back into the interior.

Shutters can accommodate unique shapes.

Dramatic window accents can be beautiful, but if too much light enters a room, furnishings can take a beating. Consider covering your window with a specialty shaped shutter, which will cut down on glare yet still offer a winning look. *www.hunterdouglas.com*

HunterDouglas.com

Today's Shutters

Today, shutters can be found both indoors and out, offering more than just protection from the elements: exceptional beauty, terrific insulation, a variety of light control options, and a life expectancy unmatched by most other window coverings. Plus, you can consider shutters an investment—most are appraised into the value of a home.

And, the industry is growing at a rapid pace. As reported in Window Fashions Vision, a magazine for window coverings trade professionals, shutters are a billion-dollar industry. Representing approximately 14 percent of the total window coverings market, shutters are showing signs of continued growth and consumer interest. There is a significant expansion in the affluent middle-class market population; home-owners are upgrading to this quality, high-end product without question.

Combine shutters with fabric to soften their hard lines or leave them beautifully, distinctively elegant. Comb through the options: plantation, roller, accordion, archtop, Bermuda, and more. With louvers from as little as 3⁄4" to as wide as 5 1⁄2" to suit your needs, there's a shutter waiting to improve your window décor.

HunterDouglas.com

Hardwood shutters add timeless appeal to this space, capturing the beauty of wood effortlessly. *www.hunterdouglas.com*

Above and next page: Solid wood panel shutters will have fewer light gaps and may reduce outside noise a bit better, but you will have less light control, and you will need a bit more room for clearance when opening, as opposed to just tilting the louvers. *www.theshutterstore.com*

The Facts: **Wood Shutters**

Advantages: Natural and warm; insulates well; bridges the gap between design styles; high structural integrity; recyclable; can be painted or stained to match any décor; self-squaring frames have eliminated much of the difficulty of installation; prices have dropped due to the product becoming more accessible and available; specialty sizes offer plenty of options.

Disadvantages: Not as effective in areas where water, humidity and/or moisture may be a problem, such as bathrooms; wood can warp, crack or split due to fluctuations in humidity; louvers can accumulate dust quickly if not manipulated/cleaned often; rigid; occasional unpredictable louver quality, especially with painted surfaces; lead time to acquire product can sometimes be lengthy, depending upon the manufacturer.

Cost: Costs will vary depending upon the type of shutter style selected (see "Good to Know" for descriptions), the size of the shutter needed, configurations, and finally, whether it is stained, unstained or painted.

They can also be priced by the square foot or by the square inch. However, a "normal" double-hung window approximately 30" wide by about 42" high will equate to a shutter somewhere in the area of about $200–$400.

Lifespan: Decades

Most Appropriate Locations: Kitchens, living and dining rooms, bedrooms, dens, offices. Do not install in areas of high moisture, such as a bathroom, unless you install faux wood shutters (see "Facts" section on Faux Wood shutters). Interior and exterior applications, although exterior requires regular maintenance.

Care & Cleaning: Minimum maintenance. Use a feather duster or soft cloth to remove dust accumulation between the louvers. Be sure to manipulate the louvers tilted up, then down, to remove all accumulation; washing is not recommended as, despite being sealed, the wood can discolor or warp; vacuuming with a brush attachment is also effective.

TheShutterStore.com

SunBurstShutters.com

Using Polywood ® Shutters by Sunburst Shutters gives this dining area the ultimate control of light. Matching Polywood ® Shutters on the French door harmonizes the windows. *www.sunburstshutters.com*

The Facts: **Faux Wood & Vinyl Shutters**

Advantages: Moisture and fire-resistant, these shutters can be used in areas of high moisture; will not warp, crack or split due to environmental introductions such as moisture; can insulate better than wood; environmentally friendly; bridges the gap between design styles; recyclable; vinyl-clad wood shutters have solved the paint/durability problem.

Disadvantages: Louvers can accumulate dust quickly if not manipulated/cleaned often. The cheaper brands may not duplicate the look of a wood product as much as you desire. Shutters are not as flexible when it comes to matching more unusual color tones.

Cost: Costs will vary depending upon the type of shutter style selected (see "Good to Know" for descriptions), the size of the shutter needed, config-urations, and finishes. Typically, however, a "normal" double-hung window approximately 30" wide by about 42" high will equate to a shutter somewhere in the area of $150–$300.

Lifespan: Decades

Most Appropriate Locations: Kitchens, bathrooms, living and dining rooms, bedrooms, dens, offices. Interior and exterior applications.

Care & Cleaning: Minimum maintenance. Use a feather duster or soft cloth to remove dust accumulation between the louvers. Be sure to manipulate the louvers tilted up, then down, to remove all accumulation. For more difficult soils, use a soft cloth and a mild soap/water solution; vacuuming with a brush attachment is also effective.

DecoratingDen.com

3" Plantation shutters without tilt rods are not only practical but also beautiful. The pleated draperies cover the edges of the shutters and add a warm, inviting feeling. *Interiors by Decorating Den, Suzanne Christie, Clearwater, FL, www.decoratingden.com*

CenturyBlinds.com

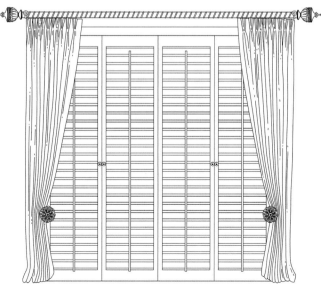

Previous page: French door cutouts within this shutter help control interference with the lever handles. Note that the shutter should be measured to fit outside the span of the window glass to allow proper installation, which may then require extension blocks or spacers to allow clearance. *www.hunterdouglas.com*

Above: Bi-fold shutters are a great way to cover larger windows, and typically are installed on a track to steady the panels when they are operated. Remember, also, when choosing solid wood shutters, that the beauty and natural variations of wood may show through a colored stain, no matter how dark. *Century Shades & Blinds Inc., www.centuryblinds.com*

Right: Stationary pinch pleat draperies soften four-paneled shutters. *DreamDraper® design software, www.dreamdraper.com © 2009 Evan Marsh Designs, Inc.*

Good to Know: Wood Versus Faux

There are a variety of shutter products on the market today: here's a look.

Metal: Typically used as an exterior product in areas of high hurricane probability, steel shutters are preferred over aluminum for better strength and protection. Large and heavy, care should be used when installing due to potentially sharp edging. Typically, these "hurricane," style shutters are removable in the non-tumultuous "off" seasons and pack together well for storage.

Polycore: An aluminum core is inserted into the center of a solid polymer as it is being extruded. A synthetic material that mimics the look of wood, this material will not chip, fade or warp over time and can be cleaned with a typical citrus-style product. The aluminum reinforcement allows shutters to be constructed in lengths up to 36" wide, maximizing light control. Its capacity to withstand the hazards moisture makes. This product is capable of being used anywhere in the home.

Polywood®: A synthetic wood substitute (exclusive to Sunburst Shutters), this material is made from natural gas products and is water and fire-resistant. It also withstands peeling, chipping, staining, cracking, bowing and warping. Easy to clean and care for, Polywood products will work in any area of the home, but particularly in areas of high moisture, such as a bathroom. Environmentally friendly, this product typically comes with a lifetime guarantee.

Thermalite™: A solid, non-toxic, synthetic material, Thermalite is a dense, polymer foam product that greatly resembles wood. Water-resistant, fire retardant, and stated to be more than two times greater at insulating than wood, no natural resources are destroyed in its manufacturing process.

Vinyl: Even the most expensive of vinyl shutters will still result in a product less costly than wood or metal. This is a good thing for those on a budget who can't

Shabby chic/reclaimed shutters offer an enchanting change of style.

The right shutter can instantly transform a room into an elegant, feminine retreat. And consider the difficulty of molding fine hardwood into specialty shapes, such as the sunburst arches above these shutters. The purchase of a shutter is considered an upgrade for the home and is frequently added to the value of a property. *www.kirtz.com*

resist the allure of this solid product. Dents and scratches will not show as readily as the color of the louver extends throughout the product. This product works well in wet environments. Limitations include the capability to choose from a wide color range and, vinyl does not look like wood. There is the possibility of warpage, which is lessened with the addition of metal reinforcement in the louvers.

Wood: Attractive and strong, this natural product offers both beauty and strength. Its wood grain is unmatched in appearance; no two pieces of wood are ever alike, so if you are looking for one-of-a-kind, natural beauty, wood is your option. Superior construction techniques allow wood panels to accommodate areas much longer and wider than ever. However, if your area is prone to moisture or if you prefer to clean with a water/chemical solution, wood may not be your best choice. As always, wood is recyclable. Typically made from poplar (least expensive), basswood (moderate), or alder (most expensive).

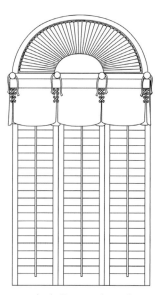

Three-panel shutters under valance with treated arch. *DreamDraper® design software, www.dreamdraper.com © 2009 Evan Marsh Designs, Inc.*

Good to Know: Types of Shutters

Improperly installed shutters are far too frequent a mistake. Above all else, when installing shutters, make sure the louvers angle up when the shutter is open. This is because (most especially when installed outside), driving rain will slough away and run down toward the ground rather than into an upward reaching louver — and then into your home. Also, remember that there are truly no standard window sizes. Each shutter should be made to custom fit your window. Here are some of the most popular styles:

Accordion: A shutter with a unique, vertical, folding blade system. Designed to cover a large expanse of glass quickly.

Bahamas (Bermuda): An exterior shutter. It can be crafted from metal, wood, or vinyl. While beautiful, its primary function is security and protection from severe storms. The difference is that this shutter is hinged at the top and opens out from the window like an awning.

Café: A smaller-style shutter used to cover only the bottom half of a window, for a combination of privacy and sunshine.

Eyebrow: A sunburst shutter that is wider than it is high.

Panel: A shutter panel on a track system, or a folding shutter, often used to cover a sliding glass door. It can sometimes have fabric, woven wood, or glass inserts.

Plantation: The name evoking mansions of the South, Plantation shutters have louvers over two inches wide and can even be over four inches wide. Panels are typically installed into the casement of a window.

Roller: Typically installed over a window, it can fit into that area in several ways, including to the wall surrounding the window, into the eave above a window, or in the window reveal. For security and protection from storms, this shutter operates on a mechanism that rolls it into place. It can be operated from inside a building. Protection from storms, this shutter operates on a mechanism that rolls it into place. It can be operated from inside the home.

Shutter blinds: Combines the larger louvers of the shutter with the ease of blind operation. Resemble wood blinds.

Storm/Hurricane: For southern U.S. properties and homes extending into the Caribbean, storm shutters are crucial to secure and protect dwellings during inclement weather. Although climate events have shown us that sometimes we are powerless to protect our homes from the magnitude of a violent storm, storm shutters go a long way to deflect torrential wind and water. While the home may stand after a hurricane, a poorly protected window may allow too much water to enter. Note that most highly protective shutter systems need time to be fitted and installed effectively. This is the type of window covering that requires planning and a reasonable timeframe for installation. Storm shutters are available in many kinds of materials, although metal is recommended for dire weather conditions.

Sunburst: Constructed in the shape of an arch, the sunburst pattern is so named due to its design in the form of "rays," all emanating from a central point usually on the bottom edge of the piece. Specialty sizes are considered an important and necessary part of shutter configurations. Quarter circle, half-circles, tunnels, octagons, ovals, hexagons, and more are available and waiting for your uniquely shaped windows.

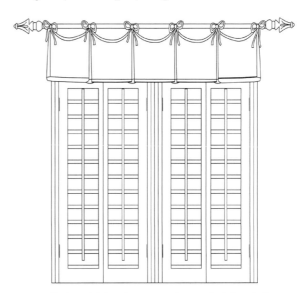

Designer tab top drapery panels over plantation shutters.
DreamDraper® design software, www. dreamdraper.com
© 2009 Evan Marsh Designs, Inc.

Custom valance and drapery panels over plantation shutters. *Decorating Den Interiors, Lesley Young, Ft. Mill, SC. www.decoratingden.com Photography: Olga Kenner*

Above: Real wood arched shutters with solid bottom panels. What makes this configuration so great is not only the custom arched design, but the privacy the solid bottom panels provide. *www.kirtz.com*

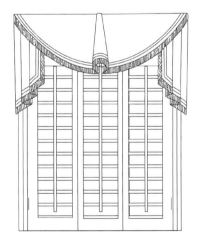

Three paneled shutters with soft valance, swags, and center jabot. *DreamDraper® design software, www.dreamdraper.com © 2009 Evan Marsh Designs, Inc.*

Double panel shutters under a pole-mounted Austrian shade. *DreamDraper® design software, www.dreamdraper.com © 2009 Evan Marsh Designs, Inc.*

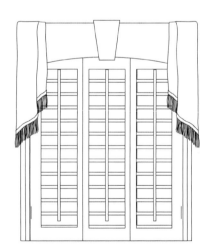

Three paneled shutters with soft valance, center jabot, and pleated cascades. *DreamDraper® design software, www.dreamdraper.com © 2009 Evan Marsh Designs, Inc.*

SunburstShutters.com

Sometimes matching the stain on nearby architectural elements is the best design option for shutters. Note how perfectly these walnut stained Plantation shutters match the kitchen cabinets. Sunburst Shutters offers Ovation solid wood shutters in dozens of stain colors to complement any home's color pallet. *Sunburst Shutters, www.sunburstshutters.com*

CharlesRandall.com

The author's personal residence. Our dogs, Tallulah (right), Dolce (foreground), and Lucia (looking out the pillows) are famous. My wife, Patricia, penned a story about them while we lived in Puerta Vallarta, Mexico called: *The Adventures of Tallulah, Lucia, and Dolce: Big Jungle Adventure*. Available in English and Spanish from *Amazon.com* 4 ½ inch real wood plantation shutters with tilt rods flank the Rogelio Diaz artwork

Three above: Don't forget that painted shutters can add the spark to make a room light up in a wonderful splash of color. *The Shutter Store, www.theshutterstore.com*

Above: Art glass inserts in these solid wood shutter panels let natural light in from the outside, while louvers situated below the glass continue to provide privacy.

Good to Know: Shutter Components

Shutters are typically comprised of the following parts:

1. Rails (including top, divider and bottom): These pieces are structural and range in height from approximately two inches to about 4½" high depending upon the height of the panel and size of the louver.

2. Louvers: Rotating on a pin and connected together by a tilt rod, these individual pieces can vary in size from a typical standard 1¼" up to over four inches, depending upon the material used and type of shutter product.

3. Tilt Rod: Connected to each of the individual louvers in the center, the tilt rod controls the light, privacy and ventilation associated with the shutter. Usually moves only up and down.

4. Stiles: The right and left structural pieces, which aid in holding the shutter together. Usually about two inches wide and holds the pins in place that connect to the louver.

Smocked pencil pleated draperies over a flat Roman shade and real wood shutters. Note how nicely the wood shutters match the wood molding on the above window. The wrought-iron grille adds another interesting design element. *Decorating Den Interiors, Nola Shivers and Linda Tully, Nixa, MO., www. decoratingden.com, Photographer: Jeremy McGraw.*

The value of shutters lies in their extreme durability and classic beauty. Fabric treatments, as well as most shades and blinds, will succumb to normal wear and tear. Shutters can remain in their original high-quality state for decades, if not centuries. Light and privacy control can vary from fully opening them away from the window for a full view, to closing the louvers for an almost black-out effect.

HunterDouglas.com

This fantastic design combines inside-mounted real wood arched shutters with beautiful coordinating silk striped fabric panels puddling onto the matching wood floor. *Hunter Douglas, www.hunterdouglas.com*

Modern black painted shutters without tilt rods work perfectly in this contemporary kitchen. *Blinds.com, www.blinds.com*

Solid panel real wood barn door shutters by Sunburst give the perfect finishing touch to this modern kitchen. *Sunburst Shutters, www.sunburstshutters.com*

DecoratingDen.com

DecoratingDen.com

DecoratingDen.com

Opposite page top: With a subtle archtop, shutters mirror the architecture and are perfect in areas where other window treatments might impede the ability to sit and enjoy the window seat. *Decorating Den Interiors, Angela Palmer, www. decoratingden.com, photo by Jeff Sanders*

Opposite page bottom: Café shutters with shaped flip top flat-panel valance with contrasting fabric. *Decorating Den Interiors, Lynne Lawson, www.decorating-den.com, photo by Randy Foulds*

This page: Softened with stationary fabric panels, these shutters are all about privacy. *Decorating Den Interiors, Nancy Barrett, www.decoratingden.com*

Bifold/Accordion shutters are also a good choice for sliding or view windows. *www.hunterdouglas.com*

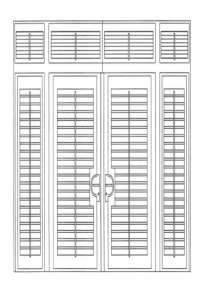

A large bank of shutters over French door and adjoining windows. *Custom rendering by DreamDraper® design software, www.dreamdraper.com © 2009 Evan Marsh Designs, Inc.*

Puddled, blouson tab tops over three panel shutters. *Custom rendering by DreamDraper® design software, www.dreamdraper.com © 2009 Evan Marsh Designs, Inc.*

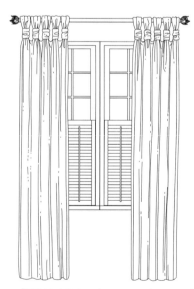

Designer tab top drapery panels over cafe shutters. *DreamDraper® design software, www.dreamdraper.com © 2009 Evan Marsh Designs, Inc.*

Arched shutters are always eye catching. The beauty of these shutters lies in the ability to close the bottom two-thirds of the louvers for privacy. While the top portion allows light in if desired. *www.hunterdouglas.com*

Bypass Shutters are a good option for Sliding glass doors. *www.hunterdouglas.com*

These stunning barn door shutters are composed of re-purposed wood and unique wrought iron rail and wheels. Sunburst Shutters, *www.sunburstshutters.com*

Leaded glass over wide blade shutters.

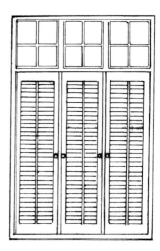

Traditional shutters under transom windows.

Traditional shutters under sunburst shutter.

SunburstShutters.com

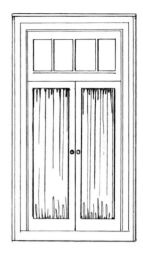

Fabric insert shutters under transom windows.

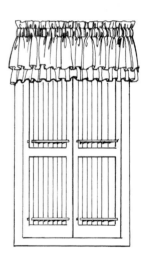

Gathered valance over louvered shutters.

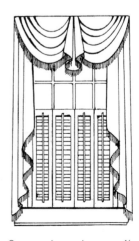

Swags and cascades over café shutter.

DECORATIVE HARDWARE & TRIMS

It is with decorative hardware and trims that the customization and individuality of a window treatment begins. A wonderful emphasis for the shape and form of a treatment, trim is at its most effective when placed along the edge or hem of a drapery or curtain, as well as used as a beautiful punctuation to the bottom of a roller shade, or as a decorative tape to soften the hard edges of a wood blind. Decorative hardware is another means to add emphasis. With many choices in materials — wrought-iron, steel, glass, carved wood, and more — to rings, tieback holders, rods, scarf brackets… your choices are many.

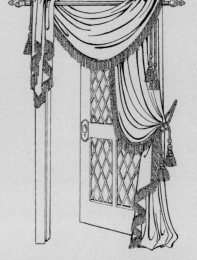

Left: Butterfly pleated draperies with decorative banding slightly offset from leading edge of panel. Silver decrative rod and rings with crystal finial. I love it! *Decorating Den Interiors, Barbara Elliott and Jennifer Ward Woods, Stone Mountain, GA., State., www.decoratingden.com*

Bullion trimmed swag and cascade is divine.

BrimarInc.com

History in the Making

As soon as there was a need, decorative hardware made its appearance. From the most rustic of wooden rods used to suspend a flimsy burlap panel centuries ago to the heavy wrought-iron beauties of today, hardware has evolved from a mere necessity into eye-catching focal points.

As for passementerie — or, decorative trimmings — it has long been a sign of wealth and social status to embellish a drapery treatment, piece of furniture, the rim of a lampshade or even the bottom of a picture frame, with braid, bullion, beads and especially, tassels of every shape and size. Ornate tassels can range from the extremely expensive and available only through an interior design professional, to simple adornments that can be made at home in five or ten minutes with just a skein of yarn and a piece of heavy cardboard.

Luscious bullion fringe, tassels, and cornice make this treatment stand out.

Decorative tassels are a luxurious means to turn an ordinary window treatment into something extraordinary. *Brimar®, www.brimarinc.com*

Today's Decorative Hardware & Trims

Today, the choices are endless. Delicate edging marries beads, feathers, tassels, and tiebacks to form beautiful works of window art. Use a contrasting color for a dramatic look, a tone-on-tone trim for a subtle accent. Place tiebacks according to the "one-third" rule — either one-third from the bottom of the treatment or one-third from the top — but never halfway.

But it is in the application, too, that many a treatment fails. Too much trim will cheapen a treatment; too little will look like an effort wasted. If you are in doubt, be sure to talk to your interior design professional. Other than that, enjoy the unique qualities that decorative hardware and trims can bring to your home.

This elaborate cornice plays host to a variety of trimmings from large and small decorative tassels to intricate small banding. *Decorating Den Interiors, www.decoratingden.com*

Abundant bullion fringe plays hide and seek with deep pleats, held in place with beautiful metallic rod and rings. *Decorating Den Interiors.* *www.decoratingden.com*

The Facts: **Decorative Hardware & Trims**

Advantages: Adds unique custom elements of individuality to any treatment and enhances the visual, as well as the aesthetic appeal of a room. The perceived and actual value of a window treatment increases with the addition of decorative hardware and trimmings and, if needed, can provide a focal point.

Disadvantages: Too much trim can overwhelm a window treatment. Heavy trims can potentially cause the adorned treatment to sag or stretch. The wrong style of hardware can overwhelm a delicate treatment, and a too delicate set of hardware can be lost within a heavy, formal treatment.

Cost: Can vary depending upon the type and material. Simple rods can be acquired for around $20 but can increase considerably for more ornate detailing and materials; as for trimmings, a simple key tassel starts at about five dollars, but a large, bead encrusted tassel is upwards of $100 or more.

Lifespan: 10 to 20 Years

Most Appropriate Locations: Decorative hardware and trim are appropriate for any treatment; it is the placement and style of the trim that makes the difference. In areas of high moisture, consider a glass bead versus a fringe or fabric-style trim

Care & Cleaning: Check the edges of your window treatment (where it may be handled most frequently) for wear and soiling. Re-sew beads that have come loose, spot clean according to manufacturer's directions. Many dry-cleaning services will not guarantee that beads and other embellishments will not come loose with cleaning (such as with a wedding dress)—especially when those trims have been attached with hot glue rather than sewn down.

This fabulous flip topper drapery panel is a bold statement in the dining room area, with its luscious bullion fringe grazing the floor and eye-catching contrast lining accenting with complementary tassel. A visual delight, this panel treatment enhances the space without blocking the doorframe. *Decorating Den Interiors. Design by Sharon Binkerd, ww.decoratingden.com*

Stroheim.com

Good to Know: Passementerie

Passementerie, also known as trimming, is available in many colors and styles. Here are a few.

Ball fringe: Small balls (such as a pom-pom or even beaded balls) are attached to a flat, raw edge that will be inserted into a seam before it is closed. A more casual look.

Braid: Like gimp (see definition next page), a braid is used primarily to conceal raw edges and seams.

Brush fringe: A more casual look than bullion, the brush fringe looks very similar to its moniker: like a soft, downy brush. When purchased, the brush fringe will have a long strand of protective chain stitches holding the fringe in place. This thread is removed after its installation onto the treatment is complete.

Bullion: Long, twisted lengths of rope form a dense fringe. Usually, five inches or longer, it is a lush edging for heavier fabric, such as velvet draperies, although it can be lighter and more casual. It has replaced ruffles as a more popular way to edge treatment.

Button: A decorative accent, typically covered with fabric or woven cord, used to provide a small indentation in an upholstered piece such as a cornice or, more often, a pillow or arm of an upholstered chair.

Cord: Created by twisting or braiding, a cord can be made of a variety of colors and fibers. Typically employed as an edging for upholstery but can also be used to edge a very heavy drapery panel. Has a "lip" to allow ease of attachment in between seams.

Edging: A decorative piece that has one raw edge and one embellished edge.

Eyelash fringe: Named because the short, tiny fringe resembles eyelashes.

Tone-on-tone trimming is sophisticated and elegant against these silk drapery panels.
Stroheim & Romann, www.stroheim.com

Fringe: Available in sizes from about one inch in length to about eighteen inches, fringe is a lighter style of bullion: whereas the bullion is more like twisted rope, fringe is more like multiple threads. It can also be a length of delicate tassels, a row of balls, or even beads.

Gimp: A thin, woven braid typically used to cover seams or to mask upholstery tacks or staples. Usually silk or metallic, it is finished on both edges and can be sewn on or glued.

Key tassel: A small, decorative tassel used for accentuating.

Lip cord: A decorative cord to which a narrow piece of fabric (the lip) has been attached. That fabric is slid into an open area (to be seamed) during the construction of a drapery. When the seam is stitched, the cord covers the seamed area, concealing it.

Loop fringe: Like brush fringe, only the fringe loops back into the finial or lip cord rather than being cut at the bottom.

Piping: A thin cord covered in a fabric that is used primarily to cover seams or finish edges of furniture or finish cornice boxes.

Rickrack: Rickrack is a flat piece of braided trim, shaped like a zigzag. It is used as a decorative element in clothes or curtains.

Rosette: A detailing piece of fabric sewn to look like a rose or other design. It resembles a flower and can be quite large when used at the top of drapery, or quite small, such as when used to dot the side of an upholstered chair. See photo examples in this chapter and on-page?

Tassel: Consisting of three main parts: the cord (used to suspend the tassel), the top (holds the fringe in place, can also be called a finial) and the skirt (the fringe that hangs from inside the top of the piece), a tassel can range from very simple. See photo examples in this chapter.

Evoking spring, pink and green will always be fresh and in style. This lively combination is at once gloriously distinctive and openly welcoming.
Houles et Cie, www.houles.com

Houles.com

A French pleated drapery panel hangs on a real wood decorative rod. The rod and rings are in a delightful gold finish that matches perfectly with the grey wall and straight cornice box with silver nailhead trim. *Decorating Den Interiors, Jan Bromberek, Oswego, IL., www.decoratingden.com*

This seashore-style window treatment celebrates the water stylishly with seashell holdbacks as well as grommets tied with jaunty rope. From the blue and white fabric, reminiscent of water and waves, to the nautical hardware, this treatment does everything right. *Donna Elle, Donna Elle Interior Design, www.donnaelle.com; photograph by Jeff Allen*

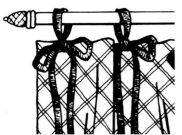

Tie top.

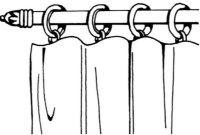

Traditional ring and rod header with stitched in rings.

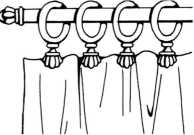

Shower curtain-style ring and rod.

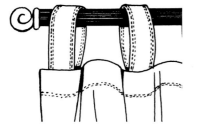

Tab top.

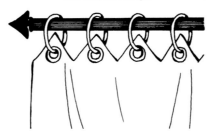

Grommet top with rings.

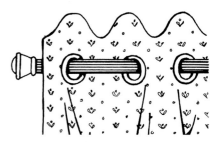

In-and-out grommet drapery header.

JamieGibbsAssociates.com

Tab top stationary panels in a golden toile pattern flank this French door, hanging from elegantly short metallic rods. *Jamie Gibbs & Associates, www.jamiegibbsassociates.com*

Gimp and beaded fringe are exceptionally lovely. What an exquisite treat to have in a home! *Conso® Products Company*

Could there be anything prettier at the window? Delicate passementerie is accented by the tassel tieback. The hard edges of this golden metal holdback are a terrific contrast to the soft sheer panel. *Decorating Den Interiors, www.decoratingden.com; photo by Ken Vaughn*

Decorative Hardware

While hardware falls into two categories: the visual and the non-visual, you can't have a traversing window treatment without it. Beautiful hardware makes your window treatment unique and eye-catching. See many photo examples in this chapter and in the Draperies and Curtains chapter.

Baton: A long wand made of wood, metal or acrylic, that attaches to the top edge of a drapery. Its main function is to offer an easy way to traverse draperies back and forth without having to touch (and thus, possibly soil) the fabric. Usually, it is hidden in the folds of the draperies when opened and hangs behind the drapery, rather than in front. Exception: Hotels usually place the baton on the outside of the drapery master-carrier to make sure the quest sees the wand.

Bracket: An indiscrete piece of hardware. Many newer brackets are meant to be seen. Brackets hold the drapery rods in place. If decorative, they are visible, such as at the end of poles, as a point of emphasis, but most often, brackets are hardware best left hidden.

Finial: Decorative hardware attached to the very ends of decorative rods, adding beauty and keeping the drapery from sliding off the end. Many photo examples are shown in this chapter, and the Draperies & Curtains chapter.

Holdback: A piece of hardware placed about one third to midway between the top and bottom of a window, used to hold draperies back to either side. Typically used in conjunction with a tieback.

Ring: There are different uses for the ring, a circular hardware piece available in many different sizes and materials. When small, it is used in conjunction with a rod and helps the drapery traverse. Used in combination with a drapery hook, which is hidden inside of a pinch pleat at the top of the drapery, for example. When used in a larger format, it can become a bracket used to sling a scarf treatment

This stunning piece of drapery hardware is used as a holdback. In essence, the fabric panel is tucked behind it. It would also be useful as a scarf bracket, one in which the scarf could drape across it if mounted at the top of a window frame. The detailing on this piece of hardware is beautiful and would add a unique beauty to any décor. *K-Blair Finials*

through or offer some type of containment for holding a part of the drapery. The larger format ring is stationary.

Rod: A straight piece of drapery hardware usually made of wood, polymer, or a metal such as wrought iron or steel that is suspended between two points using brackets or rod end holders. Attached at the top of a window frame, or even further up at or on the ceiling, the drapery rod is the primary piece of hardware used to suspend a window treatment.

DecoratingDen.com

A square finial at the end of an acrylic rod; brass brackets and rings; and a beautiful print make a wonderful custom window treatment. *Decorating Den Interiors, Gretchen Curk, Cincinnati, OH., www.decoratingden.com*

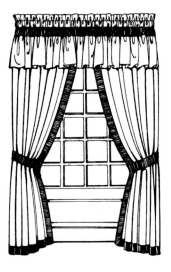

Rod pocket drapery with banding.

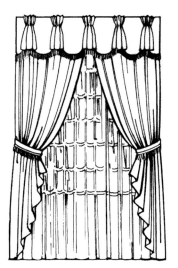

Space pleated Queen Ann valance with scalloped edge over tiebacks and sheers.

DecoratingDen.com

A good designer, like Gretchen Curk, will pull all the parts together and make a cohesive work of art. That's how I feel about this elegant window treatment. I especially like the tassel trim that matches perfectly with the drapery pattern. *Decorating Den Interiors, Gretchen Curk, Cincinnati, OH., www. decoratingden.com*

Rope tassels are always an excellent addition, where appropriate, to interior decors such as draperies, valances, furniture, bed coverings, and more.

Above: Decorative finials make a subtle but elegant statement.

Trims & Tassels

- Too much passementerie: too many beads, too many rows of fringe, too many tiebacks, gimp, braids, and more, can make a mess of a beautiful treatment. Choose your trims sparingly, and you will not be disappointed.

- Not all passementerie is formal. The wide variety of trims makes it possible to accentuate in countless ways: masculine, exotic, regal, fanciful, pretty, modern. The type of trim you select can set or enhance a mood and tie together disparate elements.

- Plan your trims carefully. A good rule is to choose a trim color that complements the main fabric and is also consistent with its style and treatment shape. Tone-on-tone coloration, however, is also very beautiful in its subtlety.

A short decorative rod with finials enhances a simple tied back panel. *Custom rendering by DreamDraper® design software, www.dreamdraper.com © 2009 Evan Marsh Designs, Inc*

DecoratingDen.com

This treatment is an excellent example of perfectly matched fabric and drapery hardware. A decorative rod can work as a less expensive top treatment and still look fantastic! *Decorating Den Interiors, Sharon Falcher and Sherica Maynard, Atlanta, GA., www.decoratingden.com.*

Wow! What a beautiful example of perfectly harmonized drapery hardware and trim: medallion holdbacks used to hang draperies, gimp trim, tassel trim, coordinating banding, and even a faux wrought iron window grille. *Decorating Den Interiors, Jeanne Sallee and Linda Tully, Lexington, KY., www.decoratingden.com.*

DecoratingDen.com

Gathered stationary sheers accented with beaded tassels bring Moroccan flair to this sitting area. It is the beautiful details, such as the shaped points of the sheers, that make this treatment so successful. *Sandy Powell, Signature Draperies & Design: Photograph by Michael Paiva*

Left: Unique and intricate finial designs will elevate a drapery rod to the upper end of the style. Notice the beautifully carved details on the round, middle finial, for example, or the regal flair of the lower finial. The drapery finial is an extension of the treatment's style and should be given as much thought as any other part of the design.
Paris Texas Hardware, www.paristexashardware.com

Exceptional stationary drapery panels are swagged from individual scarf brackets. Dripping with bullion fringe, each panel offers a unique solution. Notice how the center treatment spans the corner — a particularly difficult area to treat. *Decorating Den Interiors, www.decoratingden.com*

Above: Crimson velvet drapery panels on decorative rods; note the broad coordinating golden banding and luscious tassels. Private residence, Bel Air, California, *Jeanne Candler Design, www.jcandlerdesign.com, Photo: Charles Randall*

Right: Austrian shades inspired these crimson silk taffeta drapery panels with gathered draped headings. The decorative panels hang on gold leaf rosette holdbacks. Notice how the designer wrapped the rosettes around the outside of the bay window, to keep the smaller side windows in proportion. *Willow Drapery & Upholstery. Designer: Leigh Anderson, Glenview, IL., www.willowglenview.com Photographer: Barry Rustin Photography, Wilmette, IL., www.barryrustinphotography.com*

Delicate beads follow a graceful line along the edge of the treatment.

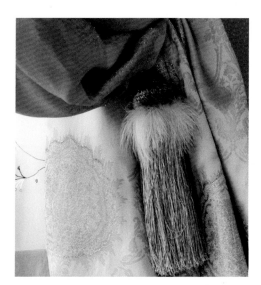

Upper: On the same window treatment as the one across the page, feathered tassels pull the drapery panel back from the window.

Middle: Larger cloth trim with matching tassel is a formal look. *Decorating Den Interiors, www.decoratingden.com; photo by Randy Foulds*

Lower left: Brown and blue beads with gimp edge the drapery and provide a grounding weight. *Decorating Den Interiors, www.decoratingden.com; photo by Randy Foulds*

Below: Intricate tassel with ribbons matches well with the beautifully patterned drapery panel.

DecoratingDen.com

Thinking outside of the box is always a good option when it comes to interior design. I love the way this designer used simple decorative rods to make a stunning drapery treatment. Since the blinds provide light and privacy control, why not get creative with the drapery hardware. *Decorating Den Interiors, Jan Bromberek, Oswego, IL, www.decoratingden.com.*

Pretty, delicate gimp and beading add a unique touch. *Decorating Den Interiors, Barbara Elliott/Jennifer Ward Woods, www.decoratingden.com: photo by Jeff Sanders*

Tassels are used in many ways — as accents, pulls and edging, etc. *Houles et Cie, www.houles.com*

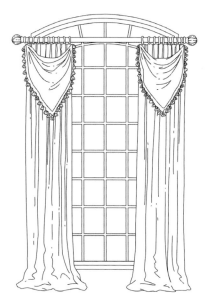

Elaborately pleated cascades tumble down the sides of the stationary drapery panels, enhanced by the three swags above.

Decorative rod over pleated draperies with attached swag flags. *Custom rendering by DreamDraper® design software, www.dreamdraper.com © 2009 Evan Marsh Designs*

A carefully wrapped tassel lies beautifully against the silk drapery panel.

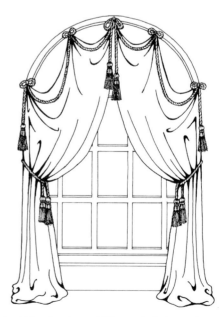

Simple yet elegant, the wine-tone tassel harmonizes well with the patterned fabric.

Instead of hiding the shape of this grand window, a drapery treatment was chosen to accent its graceful arch. Tassel detailing is an inspired choice.

DecoratingDen.com

These crisscrossed drapery panels over a decorative wooden rod are fit for a princess! There is something magical about this décor. This treatment reminds me of being mesmerized the first time I walked through Sleeping Beauty's Castle, at Disneyland®, as a young boy. *Decorating Den Interiors, Lindy and Pam Walker, Jonesborough, TN., www.decoratingden.com.*

This room displays a great example of less is more. Just a small amount of pompom trim makes this design pop—great use of combining drapery hardware with a soft cornice and canopy. *Decorating Den Interiors, Rebecca Lane, and Jamie Gage, www.decoratingden.com.*

This top treatment employs a clever use of drapery hardware to create a feminine awning. Adding the crown over the bed was a stroke of design excellence; what a lucky little princess! *Decorating Den Interiors, Jan Bromberek, Oswego, IL., www.decoratingden.com.*

Top: Color blocked ring top drapery panels over relaxed Roman shade. Fantastic display of coordinating colors. *Decorating Den Interiors, Terri Ervin, Dacula, GA., www.decoratingden.com*

Right: Over-the-top decorative flowers become a focal point in this girl's bedroom, offering both fun style along with the means to swag the drapery panels away from the window. *Casa Fiora, www.casafiora.com, photo courtesy of Casa*

DRAPERY & BED COVERINGS

For some, the bedroom is merely a place to sleep. For others, it is a playroom, a reading room, or a quiet place to catch up on work. Yet, no matter how much time one spends in the bedroom, the look and feel of the space are of utmost importance. And thankfully, it is space with options that extend well beyond the decision between draperies, blinds, shutters, or other window coverings. When beginning to design in the bedroom, there is an infinite number of starting points. But whether choosing the window, the floor, or the walls, eventually you will come to the bedding. A well-chosen bedspread can quietly blend with a sophisticated color scheme or can quickly become the rooms focal point.

Custom pleated cornice box over draperies and sheers. The extended headboard is a creative touch.
Decorating Den Interiors, Kathie Golson & Evelyng Jimenez, Orlando, Fl., www.decoratingden.com

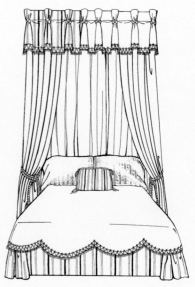

Goblet pleated valance with a trimmed edge; lush draperies and matching bed skirt and pillow.

FabriCut.com

History in the Making

Around 3000 years before Christ was born, well-to-do Egyptians had had their beds moved off the ground and slept on raised surfaces. Bed linens then evolved, soon becoming symbols of prosperity. As time moved on, the trend moved northward to the Roman Empire, where Romans began stuffing mattresses with wool, feathers, reeds, and hay. Starting with the Renaissance, Europeans began stuffing their mattresses with straw and feathers and then covered them with silks, velvets, or satin materials. Bedding support systems eventually became fantastical objects of decoration. The first frames utilized cast iron or wood, some with elaborate designs and carvings. Cotton became the preferred stuffing material.

It was not until the 19th century that Heinrich Westphal, a German inventor, gave the world the innerspring mattress. Eventually, the innerspring mattress became what we know today as merely the "box spring mattress."

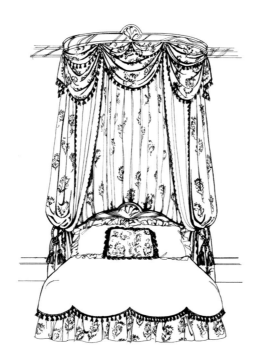

A beautiful combination of wallpaper and matching fabric evokes and old-world period-style. A custom corona finishes the design.

Today's Draperies & Bed Coverings

Today the choices have evolved once more into memory foam, gel, pillow tops, individually wrapped Innerspring, waterbed, air bed, latex mattresses, and finally, my favorite: the adjustable bed.

Since the cost has dropped dramatically over the years, today's bedroom décor often includes coordinating top treatments such as swags, cornices, and an array of bed accents, such as shams, skirts, and headboards. Motifs are often in sophisticated floral prints or light, airy colors that complement the room decor. Or even a more augmented involvement: a pink and gray gingham bedspread may find its place in a room with a perfectly matched Queen Ann valance, surrounded by simple walls and pale pink pillows.

And when a bedspread is ready to become the centerpiece of a bedroom, the fabric can become as vivacious as reality will allow. Still, bed coverings should always complement window treatments and other furnishings.

This beautiful bedroom consists of French pleated draperies with leading-edge coordinating banding hanging on metal rods and rings. The print covered bedspread is a delight. *Decorating Den Interiors, Barbara Elliott & Jennifer Ward Woods, Stone Mountain, GA., www.decoratingden.com*

Double asymmetrical cornice boxes with coordinating banding, nailhead trim, and pleated cascades. *Decorating Den Interiors, Jeanne Sallee & Linda Tully, Lexington, KY., www.decoratingden.com*

DraperyAvenue.com

A perfect example of transitional style. Tone on tone draperies hanging on custom stainless-steel rods and rings. I love the oversized headboard. An excellent example of thinking outside the box. *Designed and made by Custom Drapery Workroom Inc., www.draperyavenue.com*

A gathered valance showcases an elaborate custom wood cornice and bedposts.

Soft scalloped cornice with brush fringe; lush drapery panels and gathered dust ruffle. Matching fabric on the bolsters.

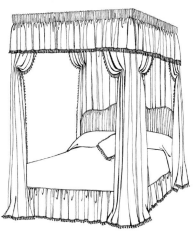

Pencil pleated top treatment with matching side panels and dust ruffle trimmed in tassel fringe.

Straight cornice boxes with trim. Rope ties and tassels. Blinds add needed privacy. *Decorating Den Interiors, Jeanne Sallee & Linda Tully, Lexington, KY., www.decoratingden.com*

Three layers of fabric: sheers, silk panels, and a stationary tied-back drapery panel are enhanced by a fourth and fifth layer: a luscious seven-fold board-mounted swag with accompanying tail top treatment. Notice, too, how the treatment also works beautifully as a corona over the bed frame — a sweeping focal point. *Photo: Charles Randall*

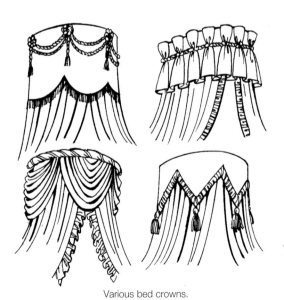

Various bed crowns.

Half-round ruffled valance with fabric draped over holdbacks with upholstered headboard and throw spread.

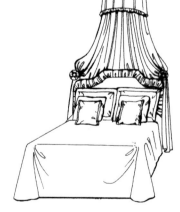

Half-round box pleated valance with draped fabric held by rosettes and upholstered headboard with throw spread.

GailaniDesigns.com

The top and bottom of this custom cornice box have different shapes yet still match perfectly. The rounded returns make a truly unique design. Add some drapery jewelry for added details, and you have a cornice box masterpiece. *Gailani Designs Inc., ASID Affiliated, Naperville, IL., www.gailanidesigns.com*

Dainty wall fabric is a great foil for the larger-scale pattern on the bed. *Stroheim, www.fabricut.com/stroheim*

Fabricut.com

An award-winning design. One can enjoy delicate see-through sheers when one has sheer shading shades for privacy when needed. *Decorating Den Interiors, Kimberly Paulus, Montgomery, TX., www.decoratingden.com*

Floral drapery panels on white decorative rods and rings anchor this peaceful feminine sanctuary. *Decorating Den Interiors, Valerie Ruddy, Montclair, NJ.,www.decoratingden.com*

WillowGlenview.com

Shirred backdrop panels tied back with tassels under an antique corona. *Willow Drapery & Upholstery. Designer: Lynn Favero, Glenview, IL.,* *www.willowglenview.com*

I have always loved the regal effect of bed crowns. Add some silky draperies and a coordinating white bedspread and say goodnight.

Decorating Den Interiors, Barbara Elliott & Jennifer Ward Woods, Stone Mountain, GA., www.decoratingden.com

Bed coverings

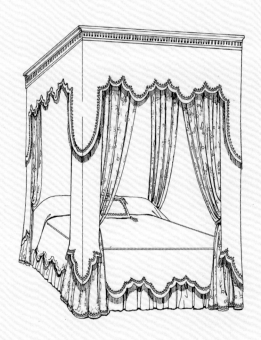

Drapery panels for privacy flank each side of the bed. Upholstered cornice, wood canopy, and matching coverlet.

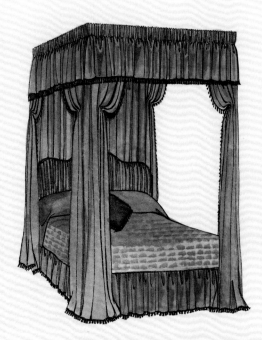

Smocked pencil pleated top treatment with matching side panels and dust ruffle trimmed in tassel fringe; upholstered headboard.

Bed coverings

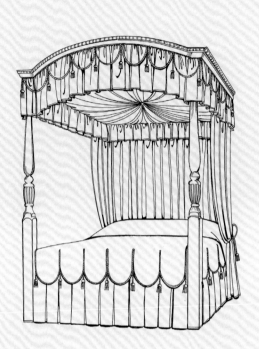

Gathered arched valance with shirred fabric covering the ceiling.
Scalloped coverlet over box pleated bed skirt.

Swags, double cascades, and drapery panels are the ultimate in custom bedding.

Bed coverings

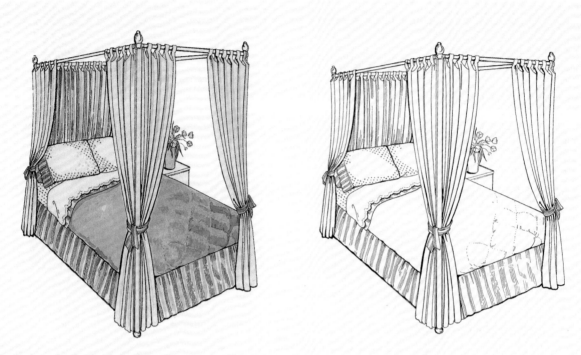

Tab top draperies gathered smartly into hourglass shapes with matching fabric tiebacks.

Elaborately trimmed fabric is installed just slightly above the bedposts and then wrapped whimsically. Coordinating pillows and long tassels work nicely with this design.

Bed coverings

Fabric scarves cascade down each side of the bed; scalloped coverlet with brush fringe; gathered dust ruffle; matching headboard and pillows.

Scarf swags with small knotted cascades; matching upholstered headboard and shirred dust ruffle.

Bed coverings

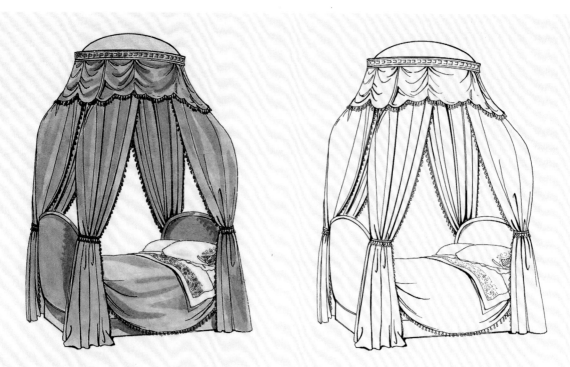

Custom made round corona with lush drapery panels; tassel and fringe decorated coverlet.

Crown corona with double Bishop-sleeve panels, oversized tassel accents and
matching coverlet.

Crown corona with cascade and bow accents, gathered upholstered headboard and scalloped gathered dust ruffle.

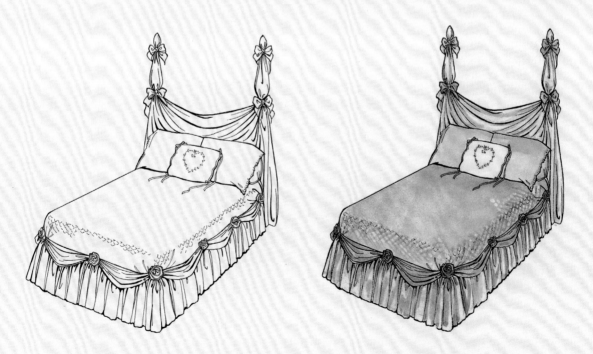

Gathered dust ruffle with swag and rosette accent; fabric draped headboard with bow accents.

Bed coverings

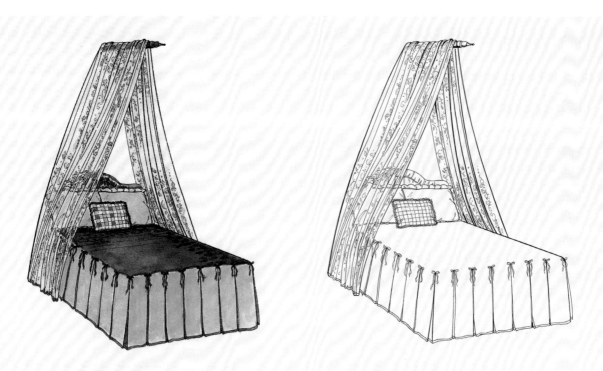

Fabric draped over a decorative pole, box-pleated bedspread with tassel accents.

Gathered fabric is used on the headboard, corona, and dust ruffle. Pleated drapery panels are held in place with decorative hardware.

Bed coverings

Banner-style canopy is hung from decorative hardware. Matching upholstered head and footboard with scalloped brush fringe-trimmed bed skirt.

Scalloped inverted box-pleated valance with sheer drapery panels. Quilted bedspread with gathered sides.

Bed coverings

A half-round corona with swags and jabots; decorative holdbacks extend from the wall to hold draperies in place; swagged coverlet over gathered dust ruffle with coordinating bolster.

Fabric draped over a decorative pole and secured with large tassel tiebacks; scalloped bed skirt; bolster and pillows.

Box pleated bed skirt under braid-trimmed coverlet; floral drapery panels with matching tiebacks and goblet pleated top treatments.

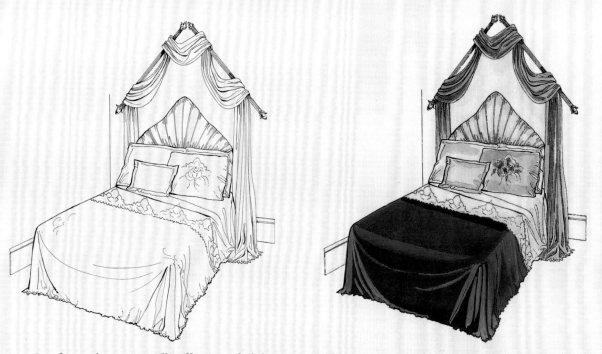

Scarf swag hangs casually off two angled decorative rods over a standard bedspread. Note how the headboard mirrors the angles of the rods.

Bed coverings

A wood cornice holds a gathered fabric valance and drapery panels; matching dust ruffle; and a scalloped coverlet.

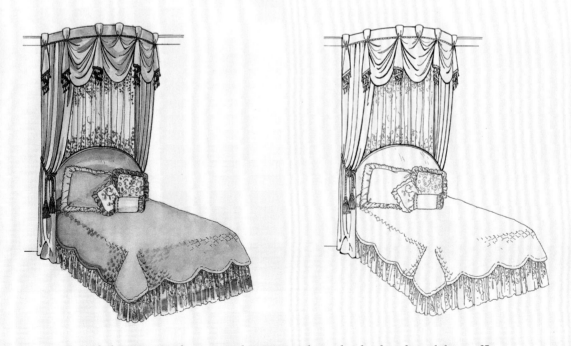

Rounded Kingston valance over draperies and tassel tiebacks; pleated dust ruffle with pillows to match.

Bed coverings

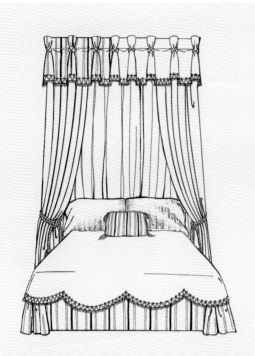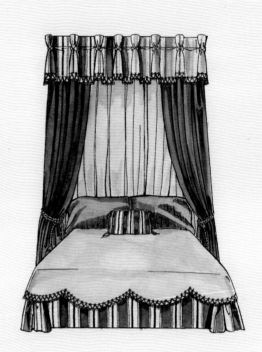

Goblet pleated valance with a trimmed edge; draperies over sheers as a backdrop, and matching dust ruffle and pillow.

Goblet pleated drapery panels are attached via rings on decorative rods that extend from the wall. Gathered dust ruffle with double braid and tassels.

Bed coverings

Bishop sleeve drapery panels are set off by an elaborately swagged cornice, matching dust ruffle and coordinating pillows.

Goblet pleated arched valances; jabot and braided tassel accents and dust ruffle with coordinating pillows.

Bed coverings

A real wood cornice box with shell motif holds a pretty swag and jabots top treatment as well as full, pleated drapery panels with braided tassel tiebacks. Coordinated coverlet; upholstered headboard.

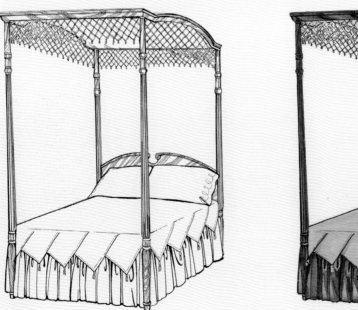

Criss-crossing fabric latticework passementerie on the canopy, overlapping triangles on the coverlet, and a gathered dust ruffle make for a one-of-a-kind custom bed covering.

Bed coverings

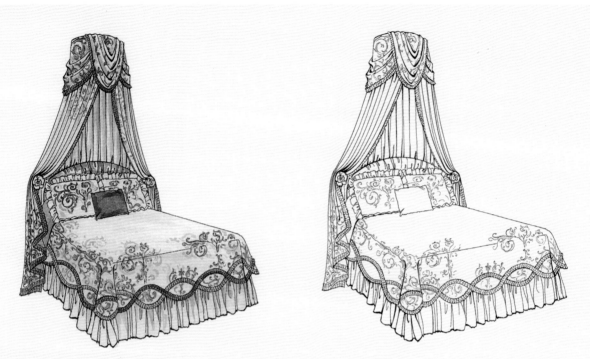

Swag draped corona with lushly edged pleated draperies contained by decorative rosettes; pleated dust ruffle; matching coverlet.

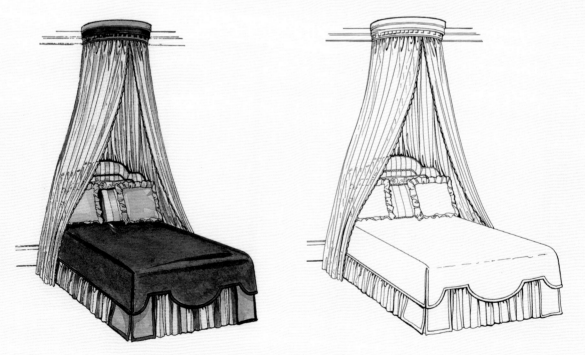

The simple circular corona holds sheer fabric panels. Upholstered headboard, scalloped coverlet, and gathered dust ruffle.

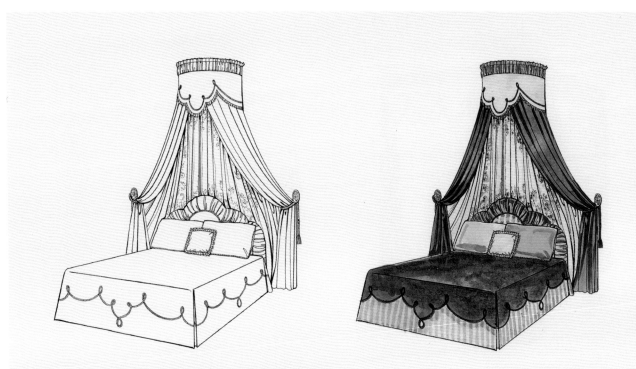

Soft cornice lined in welt houses wide drapery panels; scalloped comforter touts the same welt. Gathered fabric custom headboard.

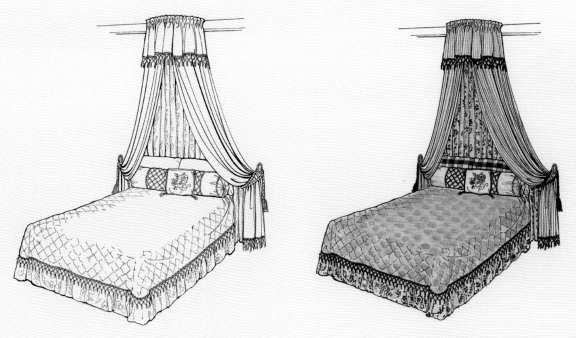

Elaborately fabric gathered circular corona with trim, drapery panels with contrast fabric, and dust ruffle in a coordinating fabric.

Bed coverings

Elaborately carved bedposts are a focal point; fabric valance with matching brush fringe holds attention as well.

Fabric from the back of bedspread to the ceiling and then to the front of the bedspread, finally reaching the pretty swag. Matching dust ruffle, pillows, and headboard.

Bed coverings

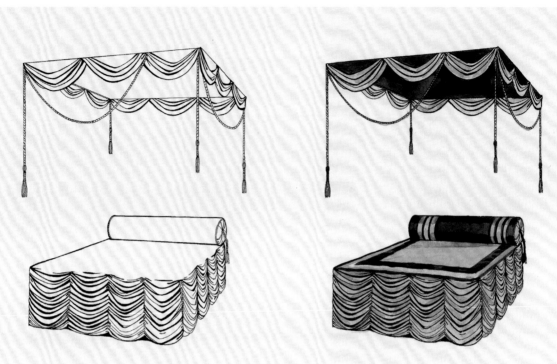

Fabric is swagged off all four sides of the canopy, punctuated with braid and tassels.
Elaborate Austrian-style bedspread adds drama.

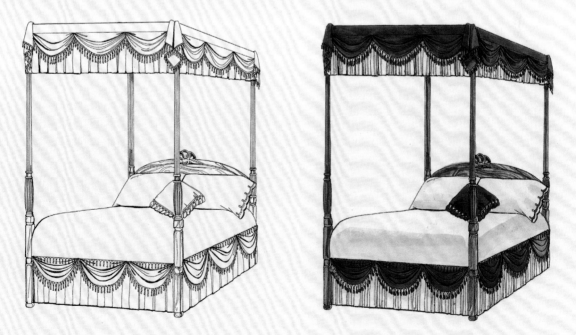

Swags and jabots with tassel trim decorate both the top and bottom of this bed ensemble;
a box pleated valance and dust ruffle complete it.

Bed coverings

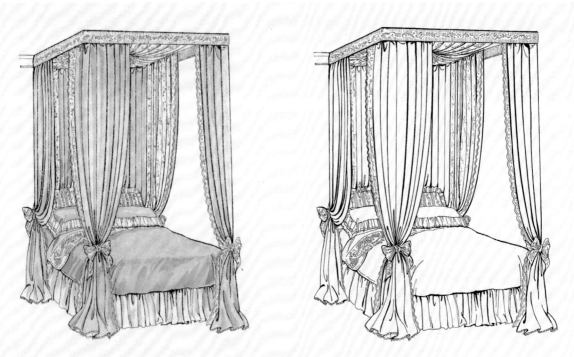

Drapery panels with lace banding and matching dust ruffle. Note the centered gathered fabric ceiling: very feminine, and expensive.

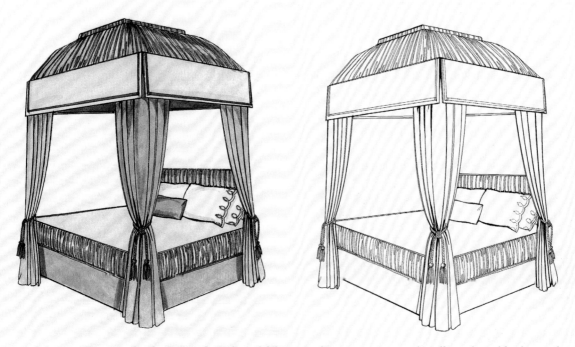

Crisp flat-panel tailored valances with gathered fabric on the upper canopy, headboard, and bedspread. Don't try this one yourself. Professional drapery & bedspread workrooms only!

Bed coverings

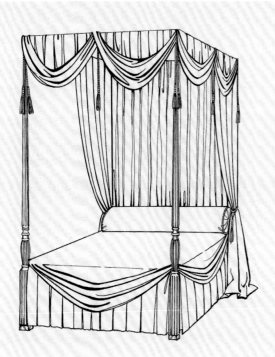

Tailored bed ensemble displays an inverted box pleated dust ruffle; a soft scarf swag adorns the pleated box ceiling-mounted valance. Decorative tassels add a designer touch.

An arched canopy bed with thick tassel fringe; matching coverlet, and pretty drapery panels are a designer delight.

Bed coverings

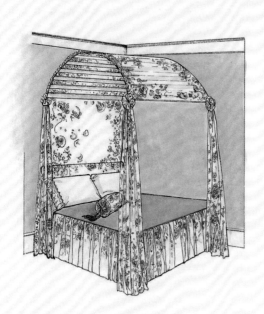
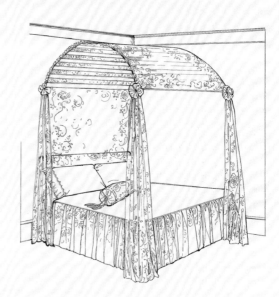

Bedspread with full length gathered sides: coordinating headboard, drapery panels, and canopy.

Tent style canopy with matching dust ruffle, bedding, and pillows.

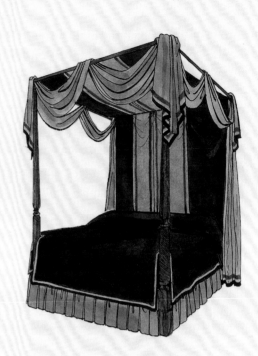

Swags and jabots with contrast banding are used in conjunction with a simple coverlet and pleated dust ruffle.

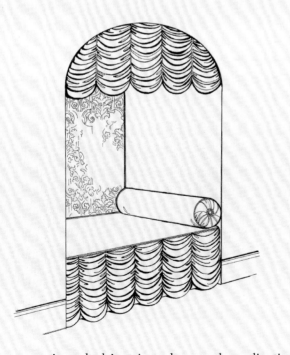

An arched Austrian valance and coordinating bed skirt work perfectly in this alcove.

Bed coverings

Accent panels cozy-up this alcove. Scalloped coverlet adds interest and flair.

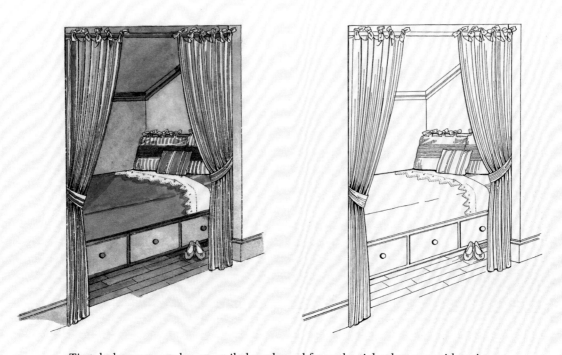

Tie tab drapery panels can easily be released from the tiebacks to provide privacy.

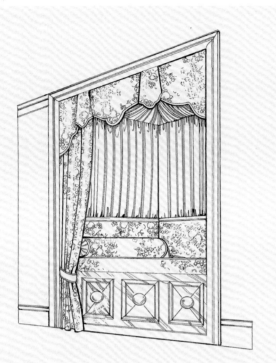

A small daybed area with draped walls and ceiling; pleated panel and soft cornice with jabot accents.

Arched goblet pleated valance with matching draperies accent a sleigh bed.

Bed coverings

A sheer scarf swag loops around the metal bed hardware in graceful style.

A romantic country floral print with ruffles accent covers this small area beautifully.

A scarf swag with a large center jabot echoes the wall angles. A second swag with cascades hangs across the window. Coordinating dust ruffle and fabric covered bed bench complete the design.

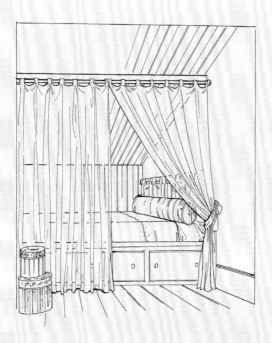
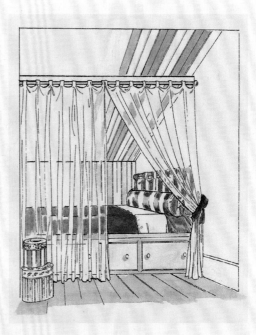

Tab top draperies hang on a decorative rod and cover the sleeping area completely when released from the tieback. Note the tab detailing on the headboard, too.

Bed coverings

 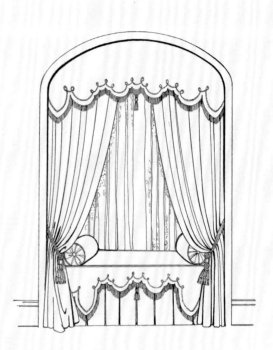

Soft embellished cornice with coordinating bed coverlet; fabric panel inserted between the bed and wall to soften.

Gathered valance and dust ruffle with upholstered headboard and drapery panel make great use of this tucked in space.

Pleated swags with rosette accents at the top and bottom; Bishop sleeve panels and
upholstered sideboard.

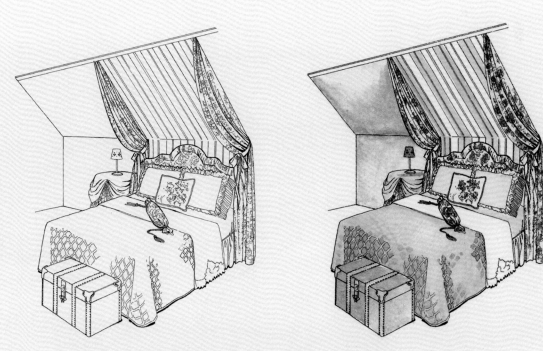

Drapery panels are hung into the sloped ceiling and held back with casual fabric bows.
Headboard and pillows have matching fabric.

Bedspread styles

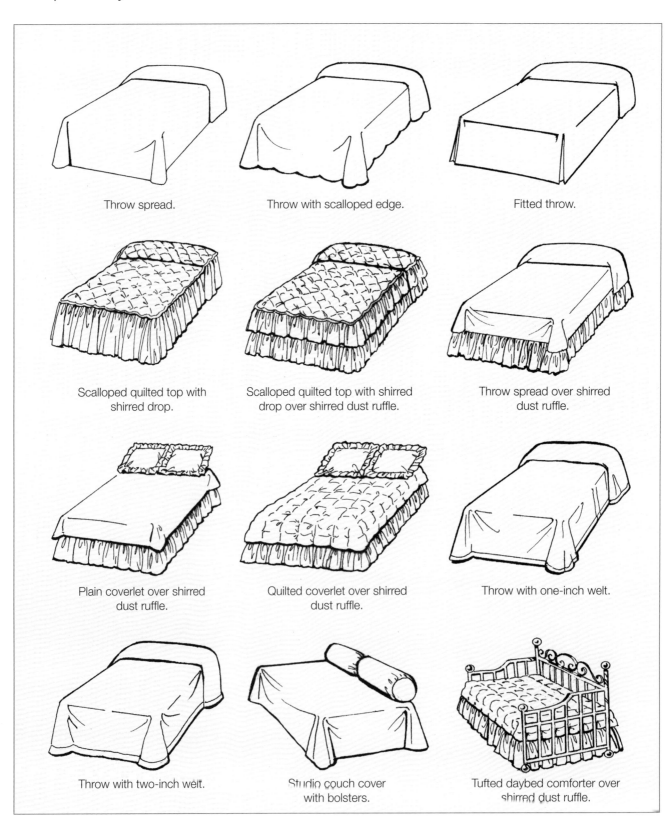

Throw spread.

Throw with scalloped edge.

Fitted throw.

Scalloped quilted top with shirred drop.

Scalloped quilted top with shirred drop over shirred dust ruffle.

Throw spread over shirred dust ruffle.

Plain coverlet over shirred dust ruffle.

Quilted coverlet over shirred dust ruffle.

Throw with one-inch welt.

Throw with two-inch welt.

Studio couch cover with bolsters.

Tufted daybed comforter over shirred dust ruffle.

Upholstered benches, bolsters & shams

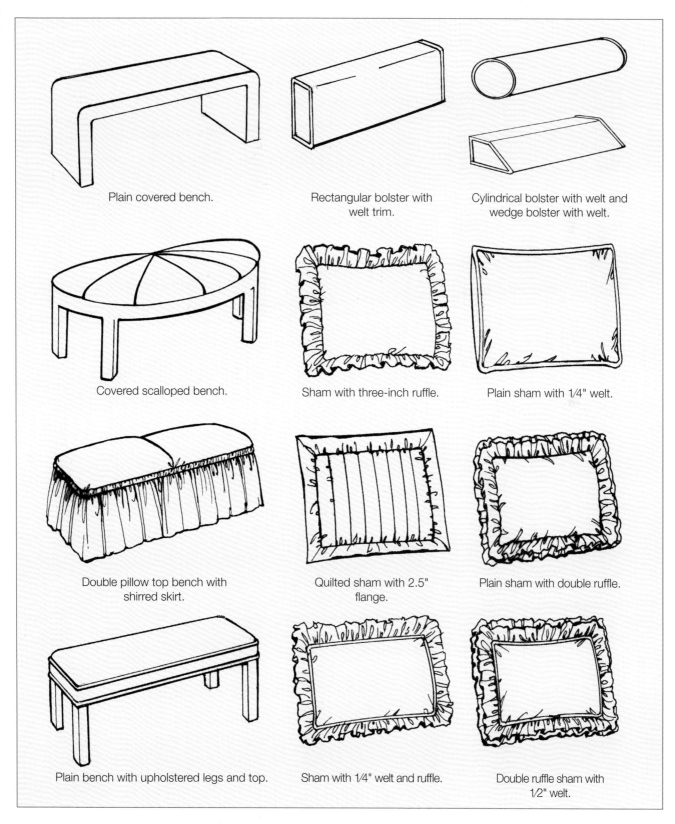

Plain covered bench.

Rectangular bolster with welt trim.

Cylindrical bolster with welt and wedge bolster with welt.

Covered scalloped bench.

Sham with three-inch ruffle.

Plain sham with 1/4" welt.

Double pillow top bench with shirred skirt.

Quilted sham with 2.5" flange.

Plain sham with double ruffle.

Plain bench with upholstered legs and top.

Sham with 1/4" welt and ruffle.

Double ruffle sham with 1/2" welt.

Upholstered headboards

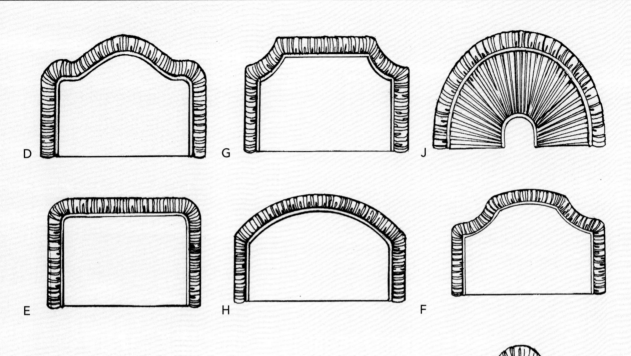

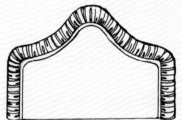

Upholstered headboards

Sumptuous and luxurious, the upholstered headboard is not only stylish but also offers comfort for those individuals who like to read in bed yet loathe leaning against a wood or iron headboard. Plus, the shape of the headboard and the colors and fabric patterns make headboards perfect for those who want to exhibit individual style in their most private home area.

Dimensions

Style D, I, F, G –
 Twin = 41" wide x 51" high
 Full = 56" wide x 53" high
 Queen = 62" w x 55" high
 King = 81" wide x 56" high

Style J –

 Twin = 41" wide x 53" high
 Full = 56" wide x 55" high
 Queen = 62" w x 57" high
 King = 81" wide x 57" high

Style E & H –

 Twin = 41" wide x 49" high
 Full = 56" wide x 49" high
 Queen = 62" w x 51" high
 King = 81" wide x 53" high

Dust ruffles

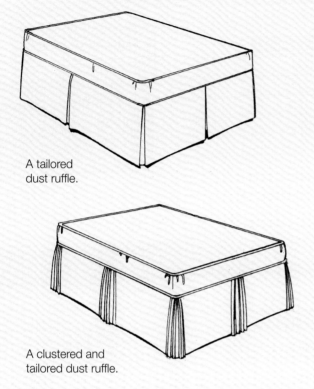

A tailored
dust ruffle.

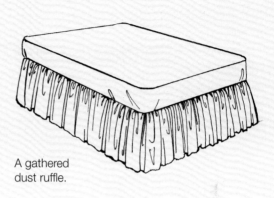

A gathered
dust ruffle.

A clustered and
tailored dust ruffle.

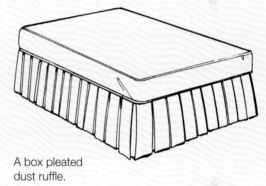

A box pleated
dust ruffle.

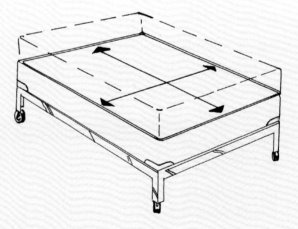

Dust ruffles/bed skirts/dusters

A dust ruffle (also called bed skirts and dusters), which fits in between the mattress and the box spring, is a clever way to not only provide your bed with a finished appearance, effectively hiding the more unsightly but necessary box spring but also covers the distance between the box spring and the floor. There are four popular styles: tailored, box pleated, gathered, and cluster gathered.

How to measure

Exact measurements are necessary.
 A. Measure the length of the boxspring
 B. Measure the width of the boxspring
 C. Measure the drop from the top of the boxspring to the floor

Spreads & upholstered benches

Spreads

	36"	48"	54"
Twin	12 yards	8 yards	8 yards
Full	12 yards	12 yards	12 yards
Queen	15 yards	12 yards	12 yards
King	15 yards	12 yards	12 yards

Additional yardage requirements:
For prints: add 1 yard

Additional yardage optional features:
For reverse sham: add 3 yards;
For jumbo cord: add 2 yards

Bolsters

	36"	45"	54"
36"	1.5 yards	1.5 yards	1 yard
39"	2 yards	1.5 yards	1 yards
60"	2 yards	2 yards	2 yards
72"	2.5 yards	2 yards	2 yards

Additional yardage requirements:
Add one repeat of pattern for prints

Dust ruffles

	36" fabric		45" or wider fabric	
	Tailored	Shirred or 4" box pleat	Tailored	Shirred or 4" box pleat
Twin	3.75 yards	8.5 yards	2.75 yards	6.5 yards
Full	3.75 yards	8.5 yards	2.75 yards	7 yards
Queen	4.5 yards	10 yards	3 yards	7.5 yards
King	4.5 yards	10 yards	3 yards	7.5 yards

Comforter yardage
Twin, Full, Queen = 7 yards/side;
King = 11 yards/side

Pillow shams
1.5 yards; Ruffles, add 1.5 yards

General information
Bedspreads are made to fit the following standard bed sizes: Twin: 39 x 75; Full: 54 x 75; Queen: 60 x 80; King: 72 x 84. Standard drops: Bedspread: 21"; Coverlet: 12"; Dust ruffles: 14"; Pillow tuck: 15"

Throw pillows & cushions

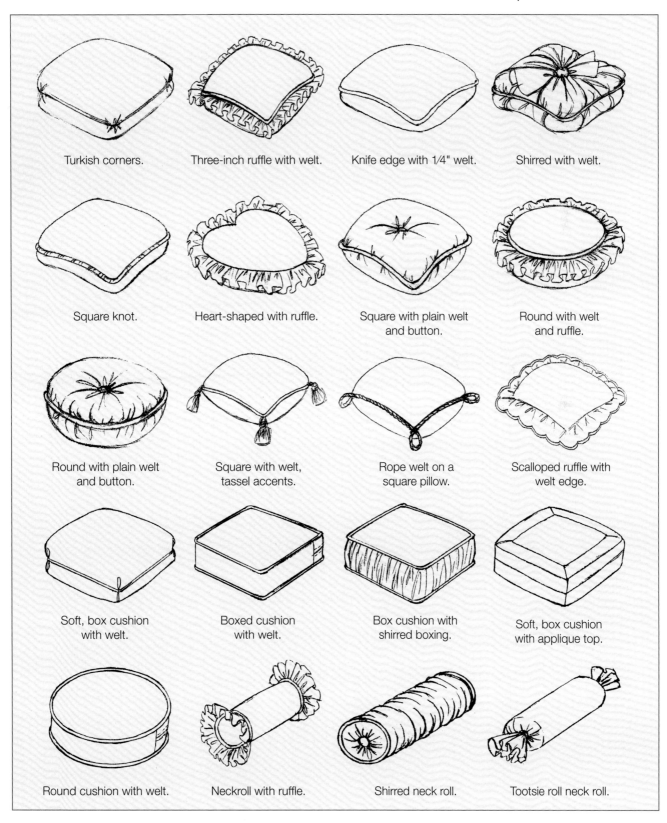

Turkish corners.

Three-inch ruffle with welt.

Knife edge with 1⁄4" welt.

Shirred with welt.

Square knot.

Heart-shaped with ruffle.

Square with plain welt
and button.

Round with welt
and ruffle.

Round with plain welt
and button.

Square with welt,
tassel accents.

Rope welt on a
square pillow.

Scalloped ruffle with
welt edge.

Soft, box cushion
with welt.

Boxed cushion
with welt.

Box cushion with
shirred boxing.

Soft, box cushion
with applique top.

Round cushion with welt.

Neckroll with ruffle.

Shirred neck roll.

Tootsie roll neck roll.

Glossary

A

Accordion: A shade with a unique, vertical, folding blade system. Designed to cover a large expanse of glass easily. *See also* Pleated

Acoustical properties: How a window treatment reacts to various sound waves by absorbing, reflecting, or transmitting.

Arch-top: A curtain or drapery for the specialty shaped arch top window. A special frame is sometimes constructed with small hooks or pegs to shadow the curved area of the window. Loops are attached to this simple curved top treatment, and it is hooked into place. It is a stationary treatment, although the sides can be pulled out of the way.

Austrian: A formal treatment that offers shirred, vertical panels (versus the horizontal panels of the Roman shade). Note that this treatment, when installed and/or created improperly, will tend to pull in on the sides.

B

Bahamas (Bermuda): An exterior shutter that can be crafted from metal, wood, or vinyl. While beautiful, its primary function is security and protection from severe storms. The difference is that this shutter is hinged at the top and opens out from the window like an awning.

Ball fringe: Small balls (such as a pom-pom or even beaded balls) are attached to a flat, raw edge that will be inserted into a seam before it is closed. A more casual look.

Balloon shade or Valance: A fabric shade made with vertical rows that can be gathered and raised horizontally to the top of the window. Soft and puffy, the treatment is pretty when raised and offers a full, gathered look with inverted pleats. It resembles its cousin, the balloon valance, a stationary treatment.

Baton: A long wand that attaches to the top edge of a drapery. Its main function is to offer an easy way to traverse draperies back and forth without having to touch (and thus, possibly soil) the fabric. Usually, it is hidden in the folds of the draperies when opened and hangs behind the drapery, rather than in front. Hotels prefer the baton in front of the drapery for easy access.

Bishop sleeve: Tieback draperies that have been bloused vertically once or twice and most resemble the puffy sleeve of a fancy garment.

Box pleat: A flat, symmetrical fold of cloth sewn in place to create fullness, spaced evenly across the top of a drapery. The fabric is sometimes folded back on either side of the pleat to show, for example, a contrasting fabric.

Bracket: An indiscrete piece of hardware, the bracket holds the drapery rod in place. Sometimes it is visible, such as at the end of a pole where it is a point of emphasis, but most often, the bracket is a piece of hardware best left hidden.

Braid: Like gimp (*see definition*), the braid is used primarily to conceal raw edges and seams.

Brocade: Rich and heavy, this multi-colored jacquard (*see definition*) fabric is typically used in upholstery but sometimes in draperies. Occasionally incorporates metallic threads as part of its all-over raised patterns or floral designs. Traditionally created from a background of cotton with rayon/silk patterns.

Brush fringe: A more casual look than bullion, the brush fringe looks very similar to its moniker: like a soft, downy brush. When purchased, the brush fringe will have a long strand of protective chain stitch holding the fringe in place. This thread is only removed after its installation onto the treatment.

Bullion fringe: Long, twisted lengths of rope form a dense fringe. Typically, three to five inches or longer, it is a lush edging for heavier fabric (such as velvet) draperies, although it can be lighter and more casual. It has replaced ruffles as a popular way to enhance treatments.

Burlap: Loosely constructed, this plain weave jute fabric is most often seen as housing for sacks of coffee beans or as backing on some types of flooring products. However, in recent years, this rough, coarse fabric has made its way into trendy interiors, reinvented as casual draperies.

Burnout: A technique used on many kinds of fabric but in general is a chemical solution applied to destroy a portion of the fabric while leaving other areas intact. An example would be burning a floral pattern out of the pile in a velvet piece while leaving the backing fabric intact. Burnout sheers are also popular, as they allow light to filter through at various intensities.

Button: A decorative accent, typically covered with fabric or woven cord, used to provide a small indentation in an upholstered piece such as a cornice, or on furniture.

C

Café curtain: Designed as a two-tier treatment, café curtains are set at a variety of heights for maximum privacy and light control. They are usually kept closed, though they can traverse if necessary.

Café shutter: A smaller-style shutter used to cover only the bottom half of a window, for a combination of privacy and sunshine. See Shutter chapter.

Calico: Used primarily for simple curtains, this cotton fabric boasts small floral patterns (typically) on a contrasting background. An inexpensive fabric, calico is thin and not particularly colorfast, but crisp and pretty when ironed.

Canvas: A sturdy, plain weave cloth, this cotton or cotton/polyester cloth offers a stiff and tailored, yet casual look. Best used for stationary drapery panels. Consider duck or sailcloth (lighter weight canvas) if you require a little bit of draping.

Cascade: A zigzag-shaped piece of fabric falling gracefully from the top of a drapery or top treatment. It can also be called a jabot, depending upon the shape.

Cellular: see Honeycomb

Chintz: This cotton cloth offers bright colors, patterns, and floral motifs. Consider having it lined if used in a window that receives direct sunlight. Sometimes chintz is finished with a slight glaze to offer a polished look, although it will wash or wear off with repeated handling. It was very popular in the 18th century, though it is still used frequently today due to its lower cost and bright patterns. For curtains or draperies.

Cloud shade: This fabric shade/valance has a gathered heading that cascades into soft poufs when opened. Like the balloon shade, it can be finished with or without a decorative skirt at the bottom edge. A cloud valance is also an option.

Colorfastness: A material's capacity to resist color change when exposed to sunlight and various liquids.

Cord: Created by twisting or braiding, a cord can be made of a variety of colors and fibers. Typically used as an edging for upholstery but can also be employed on a very heavy drapery panel. Has a "lip" to allow ease of attachment in between seams.

Cornice: A rigid treatment that sometimes serves as a mask for holding attached draperies or for hiding various window treatment hardware or even masking architectural flaws. The cornice is typically constructed of a chipboard-style wood or lightweight material over which padding is placed, then covered with fabric, and finished with trim or cording to cover any seams. A good focal point; usually mounted on the outside of a window frame.

Curtain: A simple treatment, usually unlined and stationary or possibly hand-drawn.

D

Damask: A finer, thinner fabric than brocade, it mixes shiny and dull threads to create beautiful patterns of high luster. It can be crafted of silk, cotton, rayon, or linen. Its patterns are usually reversible, an example being two-color damask in

which the colors reverse depending upon which side is shown. For draperies.

Dotted Swiss: A pretty, delicate, lightweight cotton fabric best suited for curtains. Small raised dots printed on either side of the fabric are the identifying detail. Most often, they are woven into the fabric; they can now be found applied to the surface.

Drapery: A heavier treatment, lined, and able to open and close in several different ways. It can also be stationary, which typically means it flanks either side of a window, rather than hanging in front of it.

E

Embossing: Deliberate texturing (high and low areas) in fabrics (in particular) but also seen in vinyl and faux products. Embossing accomplishes functional and aesthetic goals.

Eyebrow: A sunburst shutter (*see definition*), but it is wider than it is high.

Eyelash fringe: Named because the short, tiny fringe resembles eyelashes. See Fringe for a deeper explanation of this type of passementerie.

F

Fabric/Vane combinations: Fabric/vane combinations are vanes (like blind slats) between which fabric has been suspended. Closed, these products look like a regular shade. With the treatment still in a closed position but with the vanes rotated open, they filter the light, thus allowing more control than a regular shade.

Finial: A decorative hardware piece attached to the end of a pole or rod, which keeps the drapery from falling off the end.

Fire resistance: The ability of a window treatment to withstand fire or to provide protection from it.

Fire retardant: A chemical used on a window treatment to retard the spread of fire over that surface.

Flip topper: Typically, a flat, contrast lined fabric panel that flips over a rod. The flipped portion will frequently be decorated to draw attention, such as using beads or other trim and may also be cinched or triangulated in some way for added emphasis.

Focal point: The major point of interest in a room, such as a fireplace or large window treatment.

French pleat: A three-fold pleat found at the top of a drapery. Also known as a pinch pleat.

Fringe: Available in sizes from about one inch in length to about eighteen inches, fringe is a lighter style of bullion: whereas the bullion is more like twisted rope, fringe is more like multiple threads. It can also be a length of delicate tassels, a row of balls, or even beads.

G

Gimp: A thin, woven braid typically used to cover seams or to mask upholstery tacks or staples. Usually silk or metallic, it is finished on both edges. It can be sewn on or glued.

Gingham: Usually seen in a plaid or checked pattern, gingham is a plain weave cotton fabric used most often for café curtains and very light draperies, such as seen in a child's room. Typically, white with one color accent.

Goblet pleat: Like a pinch pleat, only the top of the pleat resembles the shape of a goblet. Sometimes the goblet is filled with batting to provide bulk or contrasting fabric for emphasis.

Grommet: Used for a modern look on flat-paneled draperies, the grommet is installed onto the header of the drapery panel, and then, depending upon the size of the grommet, the rod is slipped through the grommets or the treatment is hung by stringing cording through the grommets for a more unusual look.

H

Hand: How a fabric feels when a hand is run over its surface.

Holdback: A piece of hardware placed about one-third to midway between the top and bottom of a window, used to hold draperies back to either side.

Honeycomb: Named after the cellular shape of the comb of the honeybee, honeycomb shades are a flexible, forgiving material that will accommodate any shape window. With the option of single, double, or triple honeycombs, these cells trap air, making them perfect for homes requiring sound and thermal insulation. Best, they can be installed either horizontally or vertically, and are available in a variety of material weights, from sheer to complete light blockage. Also known as Cellular shades. Honeycombs are available in a variety of sizes from 3/8" to 3".

Hourglass: A permanently installed treatment that is attached at the top and bottom of two small rods.

I

Interfacing: Fabrics used to offer support and give shape to the primary fabric. Some are designed to be stitched to the primary fabric; others can be fused through heat.

Interlining: An insulation of sorts to pad, stiffen, and protect the decorative fabric, as well as provide added insulation between the outside and inside of the home. Interlining is sewn to the backside of the decorative fabric and then covered with the lining, which typically faces the street side of the window. Interlining is not seen but provides a great deal of protection and oomph to a drapery panel.

Inverted pleat: Basically, a reverse box pleat, which conceals the extra fabric in the back. The pleat meets in the middle, rather than is folded back at the sides.

Italian stringing: A historical way of drawing fabric in which diagonally strung cords are attached to the back of the drape about one-third of the way down. These cords are manipulated to draw the drapery open and closed. For this to work, the top of the drapery must be stationary.

J

Jabot: A decorative stationary side panel used in tandem with a swag. Also known as a cascade or tail.

Jacquard: Refers to a type of weave more so than a fabric. The Jacquard loom was invented in France, 1804 by Joseph Jacquard. Brocade, damask, and tapestry are some of the fabrics manufactured with a jacquard attachment, which permits separate control of each of the yarns being processed.

K

Key tassel: A small, decorative tassel (see definition) used for accentuating.

Knife pleat: Evenly spaced, tight, crisp, narrow pleats that run vertically across the length of the top of a drapery.

L

Lace: A light, openwork cotton fabric typically used for sheers or curtains, its delicate mesh background consists of openwork designs.

Linen: Stronger and glossier than cotton, linen fibers are obtained from the interior of the woody stem of the flax plant. It is strong but not pliable and will wrinkle easily. Its tough, textured beauty makes it an interesting look at the window in curtain or drapery form. It has excellent sun resistance.

Lining: A layer attached to the backside of decorative fabric or interlining to protect drapery fabric from sun rays and potential water damage from leaky windows. Adds bulk to a drapery.

Lip cord: A decorative cord to which a narrow piece of fabric (the lip) has been attached. That fabric is slid into an open area (to be seamed) during the construction of a drapery. When the seam is stitched, the cord covers the seamed area, concealing it.

Loop fringe: Like brush fringe, only the fringe loops back into the finial or lip cord rather than it being cut at the bottom.

Louvers: Rotating on a pin and connected by a tilt rod, these individual shutter pieces can vary in size from 1 inch to over four inches, depending upon the material used and type of shutter product.

M

Matchstick shade: A shade like woven wood and grass shades. Horizontally placed sticks of toothpick-thin bamboo are woven together and then will fold up in pleats like a Roman shade or operate as a standard shade. Better used in a sun porch area where the issue of sun filtering is most important.

Matelassé: Meaning "padded" or "quilted" (French), this medium to heavy double cloth fabric is usually made from silk, cotton, rayon, or wool. For draperies.

Mesh: Synthetic materials of various densities of weave and color options offer a high-tech look. Typically, a rollup, these shades can be motorized to add to their futuristic appeal.

Moiré: Meaning "watered" (French) this silk, rayon, cotton or acetate fabric has a distinctive wavy pattern on the surface that reflects light in the same way that light reflects off the water.

Muslin: For casual curtains and draperies, cotton muslin can be fine to coarsely woven. Typically used as liner fabric but has been the primary material. Coloration is neutral.

O

Organza (Organdy): This lightweight, crisp, sheer cotton fabric is finished with starch that will wash out. Will wrinkle quickly if crumpled or not finished with a wrinkle-resistant finish. It can take a variety of finishes and embellishments, including bleaching, dyeing, frosting, flocking, and more. For curtains and draperies.

P

Pinch Pleat: see French Pleat

Piping: A thin cord covered in a fabric that is used primarily to cover seams.

Plaid: Designs consisting of crossed stripes, many of them originating in Scottish tartans.

Plantation shutter: Plantation shutters have louvers over two inches wide and can be over four inches wide. Panels are typically installed into the casement of a window. The larger louver allows for a clearer viewing area when open.

Pleated shade: A single layer of sturdy fabric with crisp pleats that fold up like an accordion when raised. Fabrics can range from very sheer to totally private, and the pleats are usually about one inch in size.

Portiere: A drapery treatment that hangs in either a doorway or room entrance. Usually stationary, its main function is to soften and beautify an area. When operational, it can serve as a sound barrier between two rooms and alleviate drafts.

R

Rails (including top, divider, and bottom): These shutter pieces are structural and range in height from approximately two inches to about 4 1/2" inches high depending upon the height of the panel and size of the louver.

Repeat: The distance from the center of one motif of a pattern to the center of the next.

Rickrack: Typically, a serpentine-shaped, thin flat braid used for edging, such as on dotted Swiss curtains.

Rod: A straight piece of drapery hardware usually made of wood, polymer, or a metal such as wrought iron or steel that is suspended between two points with brackets or rod end holders. Attached at the top of a window frame, or even further up yet at ceiling level, the drapery rod is the foremost piece of hardware used to suspend a window treatment.

Rod pocket: A hollow tube-like sleeve located at the top of a drapery (and sometimes top/bottom of a curtain) that will accommodate a rod. The rod is attached to the wall or ceiling and the drapery, suspending from it, can traverse back and forth, with some difficulty.

Roller: Vinyl or fabric, this shade is operated with a spring or clutch system that rolls up into a tube when open. Roller shades are available in sheer, semi-sheer, and opaque fabrics. There have been improvements made throughout the years, and the clumsy mechanisms of the past have been replaced with the capability for precise positioning, zero snapback, and decorative valances to hide the top of the roller.

Roman: This corded shade sometimes has rods set horizontally on the backside of the fabric, which, when raised, form a series of sideways pleats, usually about four to six inches deep. The beauty of a Roman shade is that it implies the look and feel of drapery, but it raises and lowers horizontally. It can be made with either flat folds or overlapping (hobbled) folds. Not recommended for window applications wider or longer than 84".

Rosette: A fabric piece used primarily for accentuating. It resembles a flower or other design and can be quite large when used at the top of drapery, or quite small, such as when used to dot the arm of an upholstered chair. It can also showcase a tassel hanging from the middle.

S

Satin: With a matte back and a lustrous front, satin is available in many colors, weights, and degrees of stiffness. Traditionally for evening and wedding garments, as well as high-end bedding, it is sometimes used at the window. Expensive and slippery but used occasionally for drapery.

Satin finish: A fabric finish with a soft sheen.

Scarf: A single, lengthy piece of lightweight fabric. It either wraps loosely around a stationary rod, or loops through decorative brackets placed on either side of a window frame.

Sheer: A light, typically see-through fabric, never lined. It is only used for beauty and some sun control. Usually used in conjunction with draperies, shades, or blinds.

Austrian shade: A traditional shade taken one step further to offer romantic shirring on each of the pleats. An elegant look. For the best effect, soft fabrics with good drapeability are suggested.

Shutter blinds: Combines the larger louvers of the shutter with the ease of blind operation. Resemble wood blinds.

Shutter panel: A shutter panel on a track system, or a folding shutter, often used to cover a sliding glass door. It can sometimes have fabric or glass inserts.

Silk: One of the first materials used for draperies, silk is a natural filament, a product the silkworm creates when constructing its cocoon. There are many kinds of silk: tussah (wild silk, which is shorter and wider), shantung (raw and irregular), and dupioni (uneven and irregular threads), to name a few. Shiny and luxurious, it is a beautiful choice for drapery panels but will be affected by sun and water. It is best to line and interline this fabric when used at the window to protect it and lengthen its life.

Solar shade: A spectacular tool to control the harmful rays of the sun, solar shades filter and diffuse bright sunlight without sacrificing the view. A downside is that most solar shades are not meant to offer privacy, so they are best used in conjunction with another treatment, such as a drapery.

Stain-resistant: The degree to which a window treatment can resist permanent discoloration and soiling.

Stationary drape: Usually hangs to either side of the window and acts as a decoration. It is not meant to provide protection from the sun or offer privacy.

Stiles: The right and left structural pieces, which aid in holding the shutter together. Usually about two inches wide and holds the pins in place that connects to the louver.

Sunburst: Typically constructed in the shape of an arch, the sunburst pattern is so named due to its design in the form of "rays" all emanating from a central point usually on the bottom edge of the piece.

Swag & Tail: A section of draped fabric at the top of the window that resembles a sideways "C" shape (swag) coupled with a vertical "tail," which hangs on either side of the swag. Usually, it has at least three or more folds.

T

Tab/tie: A series of tabs at the top of the drapery, either a closed loop or a tie, which a rod either slides through or the treatment is tied to.

Taffeta: A crisp fabric known best for its wonderful "rustle" sound, taffeta is a lustrous plain weave fabric usually made from synthetic fibers but sometimes made from silk. Best used for draperies, it has a crisp hand and some bulk.

Tapestry: Heavy and deliciously dense, the tapestry is often handwoven and features elaborate motifs such as pictorials, floral, and historical scenes. While it is never used for curtains, tapestries are frequently used as wall hangings and occasionally fitted with rod pockets to hang in front of a window.

Tassel: Consisting of three main parts: the cord (used to suspend the tassel), the top (holds the fringe in place, can also be called a finial) and the skirt (the fringe that hangs from inside the top of the piece), a tassel can range from very simple (such as a key tassel) to extremely heavy and ornate. Can either have a "cut" skirt (the yarn is trimmed at the bottom) or a looped skirt, in which the yarn loops down from the finial and then back up inside.

Tent fold: A drapery that is constructed to resemble an old-fashioned pup tent opening, in that the middle edge of the treatment is pulled back and secured simply, overlapping the rest of the drapery, rather than pulling it back as well. Will conceal much of the window, even when open.

Tieback: A shaped piece of fabric or cording used to hold a drapery panel away from a window.

Tilt rod: Connected to each of the individual louvers in the center, the tilt rod controls the light, privacy, and ventilation associated with the shutter. Usually, it moves only up and down.

Tint: A color produced when a pigment is mixed with white.

Toile: French for fabric or cloth, toile is best known as *Toile de Jouy*, a finely printed design resembling a pen and ink drawing. Found primarily on cotton fabric, toile de Jouy depicts romantic, idyllic scenes of pastoral countrysides, florals, and historical motifs. For curtains and draperies.

Tone-on-tone: A pattern using two or more variations of the same hue to create depth and interest.

V

Valance: A simple to elaborate treatment, the valance is a piece of decorative fabric usually hung from a rod, a piece of decorative hardware, or a wooden board. Valances can take on many shapes: poufed, scalloped, pointed, arched, and rectangular and can also be pleated or gathered.

Velvet: Plain and figured velvets are beautiful and soft, and best employed as drapery fabric. A medium weight cut-pile fabric typically constructed of silk, rayon, cotton or synthetics, its high luster, and smooth hand drape beautifully. Crease-resistant and inexpensive, velvet wears well.

Voile: A lightweight sheer fabric usually made of cotton or polyester. Voile is plain and loosely woven. Perfect for curtains or draperies, it gathers and drapes well.

W

Wood: This natural product offers both beauty and strength. Its grain is unmatched in appearance; no two pieces are ever alike. Used for cornices and decorative hardware. As always, wood is recyclable.

Wool: A natural animal fiber that captures dye well and is soft and versatile.

Woven grass/wood: Beautiful blends of wood, bamboo, reeds, and grasses make woven shades a natural, warm choice, but they require more stacking space than the thinner honeycomb and pleated shades. Banding options add a beautiful finishing touch. Request a privacy backing if you want them to do more than filter light. *See also* Matchstick blinds.

Resources

Books

Bugg, Carol Donayre, *Smart & Simple Decorating*, TIME-LIFE BOOKS, Alexandria, VA, 1999

Coleman, Brian D., *Scalamandré: Luxurious Home Interiors*, Gibbs Smith, Salt Lake City, UT, 2004

Demir, M., *Home Fashions Fourth Edition*, Charles Randall, Inc., Orange, CA, 2005

Evelegh, Tessa, *House Beautiful Window Workshop*, Hearst Books, a division of Sterling Publishing Co., Inc., NY, NY, 2004

Gibbs, Jenny, *Curtains and Draperies: History, Design, Inspiration*, The Overlook Press, Woodstock, NY, 1994

Home, Traditional, *Traditional Home® Window Style*, Meredith Corporation, Des Moines, IA, 2002

Homeowner, Creative, *The New Smart Approach to Home Decorating*, Creative Homeowner® A Division of Federal Marketing Corp., Upper Saddle River, NJ, 2003

Hoppen, Stephanie, *The New Curtain Book*, A Bulfinch Press Book, Boston • New York • London, 2003 Jones, Chester, *Colefax and Fowler The Best in English Interior Decoration*, A Bulfinch Press Book, Boston • New York • Toronto • London, 1989

Linton, Mary Fox, *Window Style*, A Bulfinch Press Book, Boston • New York • London, 2000

Miller, Judith, *Influential Styles*, Watson-Guptill Publications, New York, NY, 2003

Miller, Judith, *Judith Miller's Guide to Period-Style Curtains and Soft Furnishings*, The Overlook Press, Woodstock, NY, 1996

Parks, Carol, *Complete Book of Window Treatments & Curtains*, Sterling Publishing Co., Inc., New York, NY, 1995

Randall, Charles T., *The Encyclopedia of Window Fashions Sixth Edition*, Charles Randall, Inc., Orange, CA, 2006

Whitemore, Maureen, *Home Furnishings Workbook*, Charles Randall, Inc., Orange, CA, 1999